The Millennium Dev
and Beyond

G000153016

The Millennium Development Goals (MDGs) have contributed to reductions in poverty and improvements in the human condition in many parts of the world since their "invention" in 2000 and 2001. It nonetheless remains the case that today, as on all the previous days of the twenty-first century, almost 1 billion people will go hungry.

Debates about whether the MDGs have made a positive contribution to poverty eradication and/or whether they have achieved as much as they should have done are becoming more frequent as 2015 and the "end of the MDGs" approaches. This book highlights that active debate about what the MDGs have achieved and what that means for the crafting of a post-2015 international framework for action must become a priority. The book begins by examining the global context of the goals from a variety of perspectives, and moves on to focus on the region that continues to be the most impoverished and which looks likely to fall short of meeting many of the MDGs: Africa.

Presenting both a broad overview of the issues and drawing together prestigious scholars and practitioners from a variety of fields, this work offers a significant contribution to debates surrounding both global poverty and the success and future of the MDGs.

Rorden Wilkinson is Professor of International Political Economy in the School of Social Sciences and Research Director of the Brooks World Poverty Institute (BWPI), at the University of Manchester.

David Hulme is Professor of Development Studies, Director of the Brooks World Poverty Institute (BWPI) and Head of the Institute for Development Policy and Management (IDPM) at the University of Manchester.

Routledge Global Institutions Series

Edited by Thomas G. Weiss
The CUNY Graduate Center, New York, USA
and Rorden Wilkinson
University of Manchester, UK

About the series

The Global Institutions Series has two "streams." Those with blue covers offer comprehensive, accessible, and informative guides to the history, structure, and activities of key international organizations, and introductions to topics of key importance in contemporary global governance. Recognized experts use a similar structure to address the general purpose and rationale for organizations, historical developments, membership, structure, decision-making procedures, key functions, and an annotated bibliography and guide to electronic sources. Those with red covers consist of research monographs and edited collections that advance knowledge about one aspect of global governance; they reflect a wide variety of intellectual orientations, theoretical persuasions, and methodological approaches. Together the two streams provide a coherent and complementary portrait of the problems, prospects, and possibilities confronting global institutions today.

Related titles in the series include:

Global Health Governance (2012)
by Sophie Harman

The United Nations Development Programme and System (2011)
by Stephen Browne

Global Poverty (2010)
by David Hulme

Global Governance, Poverty, and Inequality (2010)
edited by Jennifer Clapp and Rorden Wilkinson

Global Food and Agricultural Institutions (2009)
by John Shaw

The World Health Organization (2009)
by Kelley Lee

The Millennium Development Goals and Beyond

Global development after 2015

Edited by Rorden Wilkinson and David Hulme

Routledge
Taylor & Francis Group

LONDON AND NEW YORK

First published 2012
by Routledge
2 Park Square, Milton Park, Abingdon, Oxon, OX14 4RN

Simultaneously published in the USA and Canada
by Routledge
711 Third Avenue, New York, NY 10017

Routledge is an imprint of the Taylor & Francis Group, an informa business

British Library Cataloguing in Publication Data
A catalogue record for this book is available from the British Library

Library of Congress Cataloging in Publication Data
The Millennium Development Goals and Beyond : development after
2015 / edited by Rorden Wilkinson and David Hulme.
  p. cm. – (Routledge global institutions series ; 65)
  Includes bibliographical references and index.
  1. Economic assistance–Developing countries. 2. Economic
development–Developing countries. 3. Developing countries–Economic
conditions–21st century. 4. Developing countries–Social conditions–21st
century. I. Wilkinson, Rorden, 1970- II. Hulme, David.
  HC60.M51957 2012
  338.9109172'4–dc23
                    2012004167

ISBN: 978-0-415-62163-2 (hbk)
ISBN: 978-0-415-62164-9 (pbk)
ISBN: 978-0-203-10479-8 (ebk)

Typeset in Times New Roman
by Taylor & Francis Books

Contents

Illustrations

Figures

Tables

Contributors

Margaret Joan Anstee served the United Nations for over four decades. In 1987 she became the first woman Under-Secretary-General and, in 1991, the first woman to head a military peacekeeping operation as Special Representative of the Secretary-General in Angola. She lived and worked on economic and social programs in all developing regions of the world. Her varied experience also included directing several major humanitarian and disaster relief operations, leading several UN reform efforts, coordinating all UN programs in the field of narcotic drugs and heading a major peacekeeping mission. She has written several books on her experiences, notably *Orphan of the Cold War: The Inside Story of the Collapse of the Angolan Peace Process 1992–3* (Macmillan, 1996); *Never Learn to Type: A Woman at the United Nations* (John Wiley and Sons Ltd, 2003); and *The House on the Sacred Lake and other Bolivian Dreams— and Nightmares* (Book Guild, 2009), as well as many articles on UN-related matters. She also lectures widely, especially on UN reform, peacekeeping and peacebuilding.

Yusuf Bangura is a Research Coordinator at the United Nations Research Institute for Social Development (UNRISD). He is the lead author of the institute's recently published flagship report (2010), *Combating Poverty and Inequality: Structural Change, Social Policy and Politics.* His publications include (as editor) *Democracy and Social Policy* (Palgrave Macmillan, 2007); (as co-editor) *Public Sector Reform in Developing Countries* (Palgrave Macmillan, 2006); and "Ethnic Inequalities in the Public Sector: A Comparative Analysis," *Development and Change* 37, no. 2 (2006).

Walden Bello is a member of the House of Representatives of the Republic of the Philippines, where he is chairman of the Committee on Overseas Workers Affairs. Before his election to public office he was

Professor of Sociology at the University of the Philippines from 1994 to 2009. He is the author of 15 books, including *Food Wars* (Verso, 2009); *Dilemmas of Domination: The Unmaking of the American Empire* (Henry Holt, 2005); and *Deglobalization: Ideas for a New World Economy* (Zed, 2002). He was named Outstanding Public Intellectual by the International Studies Association in 2008 and was the recipient of the Right Livelihood Award (also known as the Alternative Nobel Prize) in 2003.

H. Russel Botman holds a doctorate in theology from the University of the Western Cape, where he would later serve as professor and Dean in the Faculty of Theology. He was appointed Vice-Rector (Teaching) of Stellenbosch University in 2002, and became Rector and Vice-Chancellor in 2007. At the national level he serves as a Director of Higher Education South Africa. At continental level, he is a Vice-President of the Association for African Universities. On the international stage he has received recognition from the United Nations of South Africa for his contribution to the advancement of the Millennium Development Goals. He believes that science should drive Africa's development, and has been the prime mover in the HOPE Project as a vehicle for Stellenbosch University's transformation and positioning in the twenty-first century.

Admos Chimhowu is a Lecturer in the Institute for Development Policy and Management in the School of Environment and Development at the University of Manchester. He is also an Associate Director of the Brooks World Poverty Institute. His research interests include agrarian change and social transformation; land reforms, poverty and livelihoods; migration, remittances and poverty; and spatial inequality and regional development.

Sakiko Fukuda-Parr is Professor of International Affairs at the New School University in New York. She is a development economist specializing in capabilities and human development, and currently works on human rights measurement, MDGs, development paradigms, and the role of ideas. She has taught at Columbia University and was a Research Fellow at the Kennedy School of Government, Harvard University. From 1995 to 2004 she was lead author and director of the UNDP *Human Development Reports.* Her other recent publications include *The Gene Revolution: GM Crops and Unequal Development* (Earthscan, 2006), *Readings in Human Development* (Oxford University Press, 2004), *Capacity for Development: Old Problems, New Solutions* (Earthscan/UNDP, 2002), and numerous papers and book chapters. She founded and was co-editor of the *Journal of Human Development*. She was appointed to the UN ECOSOC Committee on Development Policy in 2009, and serves on the boards of policy advocacy nongovernmental organizations (NGOs), including the Center for Economic and Social Rights, and Knowledge Ecology International. She is a graduate of the University of Cambridge (UK), the Fletcher School of Law and Diplomacy (USA), and the University of Sussex (UK).

Sophie Harman is a Senior Lecturer in International Politics at City University London. Her research interests are the politics of global health, international political economy, and global governance with a specific focus on the World Bank and HIV/AIDS. Sophie has previously published three books: *Governance of HIV/AIDS: Making Participation and Accountability Count* (Routledge, 2009), *The World Bank and HIV/AIDS: Setting a Global Agenda* (Routledge, 2010), and *Global Health Governance* (Routledge, 2012). She is the founding trustee of Trans Tanz, an NGO that provides free transport to Tanzanian health centers for people living with HIV.

David Hulme is Professor of Development Studies and Head of the Institute for Development Policy and Management (IDPM) at the University of Manchester. He is also Director of the Brooks World Poverty Institute and Chief Executive Officer of the Effective States and Inclusive Development (ESID) Research Centre at Manchester. He has worked on rural development, poverty and poverty reduction, microfinance, the role of NGOs in development, environmental management, social protection and the political economy of global poverty for more than 30 years. His main focus has been on Bangladesh but he has worked extensively across South Asia, East Africa and the Pacific. His most recent books include *Global Poverty* (Routledge, 2010), *Just Give Money to the Poor* (Kumarian Press, 2010), and *What Works for the Poorest?* (Practical Action, 2010).

Katherine Marshall is a Visiting Professor at Georgetown University's School of Foreign Service and Senior Fellow at the Berkley Center for Religion, Peace, and World Affairs. She leads the World Faiths Development Dialogue (WFDD). She has worked for four decades on international development, primarily with the World Bank, where she held leadership positions including Country Director for west and southern African countries. Her current teaching and research focus is on the intersections of development and faith. She publishes and speaks widely, including as a blogger for the *Huffington Post* and the *Washington Post*. She sits on several non-profit boards, including the Opus Prize Foundation, the International Selection Committee for the Niwano Peace Prize, the Washington National Cathedral Foundation board, the World Bank Community Connections Fund, and AVINA Americas. Her advanced degrees are from Wellesley College and Princeton University.

Craig N. Murphy is M. Margaret Ball Professor of International Relations at Wellesley College and co-director of the Center on Governance and Sustainability at the University of Massachusetts Boston. He is past president of the International Studies Association and past chair of the Academic Council on the UN System as well as founding co-editor of its journal, *Global Governance*. His books include *International Organization and Industrial Change: Global Governance since 1850* (Polity Press, 1994), *The UN Development Programme: A Better Way?* (Cambridge University Press, 2006), and, with JoAnne Yates, *The International Organization for Standardization: Global Governance through Voluntary Consensus* (Routledge, 2009).

Ilaria Regondi is a researcher at South Africa's Health Economics and HIV/AIDS Research Division (HEARD) of the University of Kwa-Zulu-Natal. Her academic interest lies in exploring the socio-economic impact of the HIV epidemic, particularly in urban settings. As an Overseas Development Institute (ODI) Fellow, her latest research investigates the HIV-sensitive nature of South Africa's social protection system and the presence of behavioral disinhibition following medical male circumcision. Before joining HEARD, she was a member of the World Bank's Health, Nutrition and Population team in the East Asia and Pacific region. She holds a Master's degree in International Economics and Global Health from Johns Hopkins University's School of Advanced International Studies.

Frances Stewart is Emeritus Professor of Development Economics at the University of Oxford. In 2010 she received the Mahbub ul Haq award, from the United Nations, for lifetime services to Human Development. She has an honorary doctorate from the University of Sussex. She is chair of the United Nations Committee for Development Policy. Her books include *Technology and Underdevelopment* (Macmillan, 1976), and *Planning to Meet Basic Needs* (Macmillan, 1985). She is also co-author of UNICEF's influential study *Adjustment with a Human Face* (Oxford University Press, 1987), and of *War and Underdevelopment* (Oxford University Press, 2001) and *Horizontal Inequalities and Conflict: Understanding Group Violence in Multiethnic Societies* (Palgrave, 2008).

Ramesh Thakur is Director of the Centre for Nuclear Nonproliferation and Disarmament, Australian National University (ANU), Professor of International Relations in the ANU's Asia-Pacific College of Diplomacy, and Adjunct Professor in the Institute of Ethics, Governance and Law at Griffith University. He was formerly Senior Vice-Rector of the UN University (and UN Assistant Secretary-General), Distinguished Fellow of the Centre for International Governance Innovation, and Foundation Director of the Balsillie School of International Affairs in Waterloo, Canada. His recent books include *The United Nations, Peace and Security: From Collective Security to the Responsibility to Protect* (Cambridge University Press, 2006), *Global Governance and the UN: An Unfinished Journey* (Indiana University Press, 2010), *The Responsibility to Protect: Norms, Laws and the Use of Force in International Politics* (Routledge, 2011), and *People vs. the State: Reflections on UN Authority, US Power and the Responsibility to Protect* (UN University Press, 2011). His next major project is *The Oxford Handbook of Modern Diplomacy*.

Thomas G. Weiss is Presidential Professor of Political Science at The CUNY Graduate Center and Director of the Ralph Bunche Institute for International Studies. Past President of the International Studies Association (2009–10) and Past Chair of the Academic Council on the UN System (2006–09), he has written or edited some 45 books and 185 articles and book chapters about multilateral approaches to international peace and security, humanitarian action, and sustainable development. He is also co-editor (with Rorden Wilkinson) of the *Global Institutions* series in which this book appears. His essay in this volume draws on the second edition of *What's Wrong with the United Nations and How to Fix It* (Polity Press, 2012) and *Thinking about Global Governance: Why People and Ideas Matter* (Routledge, 2011).

Alan Whiteside is the founder and Executive Director of the Health Economics and HIV/AIDS Research Division (HEARD). HEARD has, since 1998, been situated at the University of KwaZulu-Natal and conducts applied research and development interventions to mobilize evidence for impact in health and HIV in the Southern Africa Development Community (SADC) and east Africa region. Professor Whiteside is the author of *HIV/AIDS: A Very Short Introduction* (Oxford University Press, 2008). He started and edited the newsletter *AIDS Analysis Africa*, was appointed by Secretary-General Kofi Annan as one of the Commissioners on the Commission for HIV/AIDS and Governance in Africa, and was an elected

Member of the Governing Council of the International AIDS Society. His main research interest at present is the economic and development impact of HIV/AIDS. He has published widely.

Rorden Wilkinson is Professor of International Political Economy in the School of Social Sciences and Research Director of the Brooks World Poverty Institute, both at the University of Manchester. He is author of, among other things, *The WTO: Crisis and the Governance of Global Trade* (Routledge, 2006), and *Multilateralism and the World Trade Organisation* (Routledge, 2000); co-editor of (with Thomas G. Weiss) *International Organization and Global Governance* (Routledge, forthcoming), (with Jennifer Clapp) *Global Governance, Poverty and Inequality* (Routledge, 2010), (with Donna Lee) *The WTO after Hong Kong* (Routledge, 2007), and (with Steve Hughes) *Global Governance: Critical Perspectives* (Routledge, 2002); and editor of *The Global Governance Reader* (Routledge, 2005). He co-edits (with Thomas G. Weiss) the *Global Institutions* series in which this book appears.

Foreword by the series editors

Rorden Wilkinson and David Hulme's edited book is the fifth in what we anticipate will be a growing number of research volumes in our "global institutions" series that examines crucial global problems and possible global policies and solutions. *The Millennium Development Goals and Beyond: Global development after 2015* grew out of a high level summit organized in South Africa in January 2011, immediately following the second evaluation of the MDGs at the United Nations in fall 2010 (the first was in 2005).

In addition to these longer research volumes, the series strives to provide readers with user-friendly and short (usually 50,000 words) but definitive guides to the most visible aspects of what we know as "global governance," as well as authoritative accounts of the issues and debates in which they are embroiled. We now have over 60 books that act as key reference points to the most significant global institutions and the evolution of the issues that they face. Our intention has always been to provide one-stop guides for all readers—students (both undergraduate and postgraduate), interested negotiators, diplomats, practitioners from nongovernmental and intergovernmental organizations, and interested parties alike—seeking information about most prominent institutional aspects of global governance.

The new research stream incorporates lengthier works by key authors as well as edited compilations, the collective wisdom from which helps push the envelope on important topics linked to global institutions. In this case, Wilkinson and Hulme have assembled essays by a group of world-class scholars and practitioners who provide the reader with a critical snapshot of the past and a baseline from which to look towards the evaluation of the time-bound quantitative targets that expire in 2015. The book encourages us to look to the next phase—indeed, its title and subtitle reflect the book's conclusion that the experiment has been worthwhile and that a subsequent set of targets is in order.

Ideally, these volumes will be used as complementary readings in courses in which other specific titles in this series are pertinent—in this case, we point readers to a host of books on poverty and development, as well as relevant regional and universal organizations.[1] Our aim is to enable topics of importance to be dealt with exhaustively by specialists as well as enabling collected works to address issues in ways that bring more than the sum of the individual parts, while at the same time maintaining the quality of the series.

As always, we look forward to comments from our readers.

Thomas G. Weiss, The CUNY Graduate Center, New York, USA
December 2011

Notes

1 Kwame Akonor, *African Economic Institutions* (2010); Jacqueline Braveboy-Wagner, *Institutions of the Global South* (London: Routledge, 2009); Stephen Browne, *The United Nations Development Programme and System* (2011); Jennifer Clapp and Rorden Wilkinson, eds., *Global Governance, Poverty, and Inequality* (2010); Sophie Harman, *Global Health Governance* (2012); David Hulme, *Global Poverty* (2010); Kelley Lee, *The World Health Organization* (2009); Franklyn Lisk, *Global Institutions and the HIV/AIDS Epidemic* (2010); Samuel M. Makinda and F. Wafula Okumu, *The African Union* (2008); Lawrence Sáez, *The South Asian Association for Regional Cooperation* (2011); and John Shaw, *Global Food and Agricultural Institutions* (2009).

Foreword by Walden Bello

The current global economic crisis threatens to reverse the gains in reducing global poverty that were made in the boom years of the 1990s and the first decade of this century. With long-term stagnation descending on the US and Europe and austerity programs becoming the favored social policy in these traditional centers of the global economy, millions more may be added to the estimated one billion people globally that currently live under the poverty line.

Efforts to reduce poverty in the global South have not been unimpressive. The decline in the numbers of poor people triggered by rapid economic growth in China, Korea, and other East Asian countries were complemented by the positive results of conditional cash transfer programs in countries like Brazil and Mexico. Efforts to replicate these successes are now underway in more than 20 other countries.

Yet the challenges remain huge, and even as the social and economic barriers to people emerging from poverty remain formidable, the population problem has reemerged as a major concern as the globe's population hits 7 billion in early 2012. In some parts of the developing world, population growth and fertility rates have dropped, but they have not dropped fast enough. In other cases, the decline in fertility rates has been from "very high" to "high." This is the case in Sub-Saharan Africa. As the New York Times points out, of the 20 countries where women average over five children, almost all are in this region. Now accounting for 12 percent of the world's population, Sub-Saharan Africa will account for more than a third by the end of this century should current trends continue.

Yet it is crises like the one that the world is now in that often call up the reserves of courage, determination, and innovation that allow nations to surmount challenges. In the North, the main response to the specter of the return of mass poverty is expansionary fiscal and monetary policies that allow crippled economies to grow again. In the so-called emerging economies, like China, Korea, and Brazil, the main line of attack on poverty is an attack on the structures of inequality that have made these fast-growing economies some of the most unequal in the world. In Latin America, the Middle East, and South Asia, new ecologically friendly development strategies must be put in place of failed neoliberal or statist economic regimes. In Africa as well in places like the Philippines and Timor Leste, rational population management must be a central part of the policy mix.

The essays in this volume—contributed by some of the most knowledgeable and committed scholars and activists in the field—take stock of the progress so far in the global war against poverty. Their aim is to come up with policy prescriptions that can take that campaign forward. Their conclusions make for sobering reading. As we approach 2015—the date by which countries should have halved the proportion of their populations living in poverty—those few states that are well on the way to reaching this target, and the other Millennium Development Goals, must be congratulated. But they cannot afford to sit on their laurels, especially as a stagnant global economy threatens their gains. More than ever, the cooperation of those who have attained the MDGs, those that are approaching them, and those that still have some distance to go is vital since no part of our world is really economically and socially secure unless the rest of the world is too.

Walden Bello
Manila, Philippines
April 2011

Acknowledgments

This book—and its sister volume[1]—is a work of advocacy. It emerges from our collective motivation, and scholarly and professional endeavors, to make a small difference to improving the world that we know. As concerned academics and practitioners our efforts are designed to make an intervention into increasingly stagnant debates about the Millennium Development Goals (MDGs) in a way that opens up a space for thinking about how we address the most pressing development concerns of today and tomorrow in a manner that builds upon, but nonetheless significantly betters, the sum of global efforts manifest in the MDGs. In pursuit of this goal, we have also set out to offer a forensic examination of the MDGs: their successes and failures, the record of "progress" towards their achievement, and the changing global context in which they exist. Our efforts leave us deeply concerned about the lack of progress in securing basic development gains for large sections of the world's population as well as about the rising inequalities in income, health, wealth and wellbeing that confront humanity.

This book emerges from the inaugural Global Poverty Summit, which was held in Johannesburg, South Africa between 17 and 19 January 2011. A thoroughly stimulating event, the Summit brought together more than 50 of the world's foremost authorities on poverty, trade and development to: press for substantive action in, and innovative ways to move forward on, the MDGs and the World Trade Organization's Doha Development Agenda (DDA); and to share knowledge with, and learn from, those interested and engaged in poverty issues but who do not normally have access to global policymaking.

The Johannesburg Global Poverty Summit, the website that accompanies it (www.povertydialogue.org), and our ongoing efforts to affect change in global public policy would not have been possible without the kind and generous support of Rory and Elizabeth Brooks and their foundation. Rory and Elizabeth are rare among those people who can make a difference. They act on word, lead in deed, engage with passion. They also provided invaluable advice and assistance throughout the process. We are also grateful to the University of Manchester for its part in funding this initiative, as well as for the resources and support of the Ralph Bunche Institute at The City University of New York's Graduate Center and CUTS International, as well as their respective executive heads—Thomas G. Weiss and Pradeep Mehta.

We are also grateful to Bridget Fury for her tireless work in overseeing the logistics of the Summit, for helping shape the event, and for sharing the burden in crafting the process by which we were able to bring together such a stellar array of right thinking individuals to push for global change. Without the ceaseless energy and hard work of Emma Leach in managing the Summit we would also not have been able to manage to produce such a successful event and two books of such high quality—our sincerest thanks. We would also like to extend our gratitude to Ereshnee Naidu, Fredrick Njehu, Nomvuyo Nolutshungu, James Scott, Di Sutherland and Abednigo Twala, who provided valuable help and assistance in the run-up to, and during, the Summit.

The Summit, the Statements on the MDGs and the DDA that we worked so hard to produce, the books that have come out of our collective endeavors, and the events to come, would not have been possible without the industry, enthusiasm, intellect and energy of the gathered participants. We are indebted to, among others, Yonov Frederick Agah, Charles Abugre Akelyira, Miriam Altman, Samuel Amehou, Margaret Joan Anstee, Yusuf Bangura, Walden Bello, Ujal Singh Bhatia, Debapriya Bhattacharya, Tendai Biti, H. Russel Botman, Rashad Cassim, Bipul Chatterjee, Admos Chimhowu, Jennifer Clapp, Peter Draper, Sakiko Fukuda-Parr, Aida Girma, Sophie Harman, Bernard Hoekman, Faizel Ismail, Rosebud Violet Kurwijila, Donna Lee, Liepollo Lebohang Pheko, Katherine Marshall, Pradeep Mehta, Ricardo Melendez-Ortiz, Richard E. Mshomba, Craig N. Murphy, Supachai Panitchpakdi, Ilaria Regondi, Nigel Richards, Jomo Kwame Sanadaram, Frances Stewart, Joseph E. Stiglitz, Melanie Stravens, Sun Zhenyu, Ramesh Thakur, Brendan Vickers, Thomas G. Weiss, Alan Whiteside, Agostinho Zacarias and Fikre Zewdie. Thanks are also due to Rudi Dicks, Alan Hirsch, Uma Kothari, Neva Makgetla and Herbert Mkhize, who offered their kind assistance in helping shape aspects of the Global Poverty Summit. We also owe a debt of thanks to Denise Redston and all those at Brooks World Poverty Institute who supported our efforts, to Oliver Turner for his first-rate editorial assistance, and to our families for their help and support throughout this and other endeavors.

Rorden Wilkinson and David Hulme
Manchester, UK
December 2011

Note

1 James Scott and Rorden Wilkinson, *Trade, Poverty, Development: Getting Beyond the WTO's Doha Deadlock* (London: Routledge, 2012).

Abbreviations

3G	Global Governance Group
AAU	Association of African Universities
ADB	African Development Bank
AMR	Annual Ministerial Review
ARV	anti-retroviral
ASNAPP	Agribusiness in Sustainable Natural African Plant Products
AU	African Union
BIMARU	Bihar, Madhya Pradesh, Rajasthan and Uttar Pradesh
BRIC(S)	Brazil, Russia, India, China (and South Africa)
CAADP	Comprehensive Africa Agriculture Development Programme
CCC	Copenhagen Consensus Center
CEDAW	Convention on the Elimination of all forms of Discrimination against Women
CMEPSP	Commission on the Measurement of Economic Performance and Social Progress
DAC	Development Assistance Committee (OECD)
DBS	Direct Budget Support
DCF	Development Cooperation Forum
DDA	Doha Development Agenda (WTO)
DFID	UK Department for International Development
ECA	Economic Commission for Africa (UN)
ECOSOC	Economic and Social Council (UN)
EITI	Extractive Industries Transparency Initiative
EPTA	Expanded Programme of Technical Assistance
FDI	foreign direct investment
G-7/8	Group of 7/8 leading industrial states
G-20	Group of 20 leading finance ministers
GDGs	Global Development Goals

GDP	gross domestic product
GNI	gross national income
GNP	gross national product
GPS	Global Poverty Summit
HD	human development
HDI	Human Development Index
HDR	human development report
HI	horizontal inequality
HIV/AIDS	Human Immunodeficiency Virus/Acquired Immune Deficiency Syndrome
HPI	Human Poverty Index
ICC	International Criminal Court
IDG	International Development Goal
IFI	international financial institution
ILO	International Labour Organization
IMF	International Monetary Fund
IPE	International Political Economy
LDC	least developed country
MAP	Multi-Country AIDS Program (World Bank)
MD	UN Millennium Declaration
MDGs	Millennium Development Goals
MTEF	Medium-Term Expenditure Framework
NEPAD	New Partnership for Africa's Development
NGO	non-governmental organization
NIEO	New International Economic Order
ODA	overseas development assistance
ODI	Overseas Development Institute
OECD	Organisation for Economic Co-operation and Development
OHCHR	Office of the High Commissioner for Human Rights
PANGeA	Partnership for Africa's Next Generation of Academics
PBC	Peacebuilding Commission
PMTCT	prevention of mother-to-child transmission
PPP	purchasing power parity
PRGF	Poverty Reduction and Growth Facility
PRS	Poverty Reduction Strategy
PRSP	Poverty Reduction Strategy Paper
R2P	Responsibility to Protect
SADC	Southern Africa Development Community
SPF	Social Protection Floor
SU	Stellenbosch University

TRECCAfrica	Transdisciplinary Training for Resource Efficiency and Climate Change Adaptation in Africa
UDHR	Universal Declaration of Human Rights
UN	United Nations
UNAIDS	Joint UN Programme on HIV/AIDS
UNCTAD	UN Conference on Trade and Development
UNDESA	UN Department of Economic and Social Affairs
UNDP	UN Development Programme
UNESCO	UN Educational, Scientific and Cultural Organization
UNFPA	UN Population Fund
UNICEF	UN Children's Fund
UNIFEM	UN Fund for Women (now UN Women)
WFDD	World Faiths Development Dialogue
WTO	World Trade Organization

Introduction: moving from MDGs to GDGs

Development imperatives beyond 2015

David Hulme and Rorden Wilkinson

The Millennium Development Goals (MDGs) have contributed to reductions in poverty and improvements in the human condition in many parts of the world since their "invention" in 2000 and 2001. It nonetheless remains the case that today, as on all the previous days of the twenty-first century, almost 1 billion people will go hungry, 20,000 children will die from easily preventable health problems, 1,400 women will die from causes associated with maternity that are easy to diagnose and treat, and more than 100 million primary-age children will not attend school. Every day, in this affluent world, hundreds of millions of people experience extreme forms of deprivation that inflict suffering and reduce or terminate their future prospects of having a good life and being productive (let alone having the capacity to determine for themselves what that productivity might be). The lack of access to a dollar's worth of medicine can mean a child dies. An increase in the price of rice by a few cents per kilogram means that the women and children in a family have to go to bed hungry.

Our grandparents could perhaps claim that mass poverty was an inevitable feature of their world—there were simply not enough resources, nor the technology to transform resources, to meet the needs of all of the world's people. They may or may not have been correct, but this is not a claim that we can make. Today the world has enough food for everyone to be fed, and the resources and technology to provide basic services—primary education, health services and even social assistance—are available. The problem is that our world is organized in such a way that around 1.5 to 2.5 billion people (depending on how you define poverty) have little or no access to the most basic of human needs.

In recent times the rich and powerful have made big promises about "ending poverty." At the Millennium Summit in September 2000, 189 nations, and no fewer than 149 national leaders, met in New York and committed themselves to " ... freeing the entire human race from want." They signed the Millennium Declaration (MD—the basis for the MDGs), identifying a set of goals that promised to halve extreme poverty across the world by 2015. That year, 2015, is to be a sort of "half way house" on the road to totally eradicating poverty. Freeing humanity from poverty is no longer an aspiration for moral philosophers or the odd visionary leader—it is to be a mega-project to which all the nations and peoples of the world are committed. After decades of half-hearted public statements about "international development" things appeared to have changed at the Millennium Summit and "poverty eradication" moved, seemingly, center stage.

Back in 2000, as world leaders smiled for group photographs, patted backs and congratulated each other, there was a strong case that such an endeavor was long overdue. In a world of unprecedented affluence, why had it taken so long for leaders to agree to meet the most basic needs of so many fellow human beings living in extreme poverty? Why were so many people in rich countries struggling with obesity and suffering from "affluenza" while 31 percent of the world's children were moderately or severely stunted and a woman in Mali was 155 times more likely to die during pregnancy than a woman in the United Kingdom?

The MD was not the first time that people have talked about eradicating poverty. Indeed, in 1947 the Universal Declaration of Human Rights envisioned a world in which:

> Everyone has the right to a standard of living adequate for the health and well-being of his family, including food, clothing, housing and medical care ... Everyone is entitled to a social and international order in which the rights and freedoms set forth in this Declaration can be fully realised.
>
> (UDHR, Articles 25 and 28)

What was unique in 2000 was the focused global consensus for poverty eradication: quantitative targets were agreed and commitments were made by heads of government that all countries would contribute to this task through a mixture of extra finance, domestic and international policy reforms and practical action. This commitment was confirmed in the Monterrey Consensus of March 2002, when the rich countries of the world promised to significantly increase their financial support for the achievement of the MDGs while the poorer countries promised to improve their governance and reduce corruption. The stage seemed set for an unprecedented assault on global poverty ... and then things began to falter as the new millennium lost its novelty, commitments faded, promises were neglected or forgotten, and other international issues based on "rich world" concerns (national security, terrorism, energy security, trade liberalization) were given a higher priority.

The graduation of global poverty onto the international agenda might be seen as evidence of progressive social change on the grandest scale. Alternatively, it could be seen as the world's most successful confidence trick—with rich nations, powerful organizations and global elites (in rich *and* poor countries) retaining the existing structures of power and resource access whilst maintaining their legitimacy—and at next to no cost for themselves. The reasons why different countries, organizations and people supported the processes leading up to the MDGs are complex—a mixture of compassion for poor people and self-interest, altruism and selfishness, wanting to do good and wanting to appear to be doing good.

While the MDGs spell out "what is to be achieved," they do not explain "why" so many people are poor, "what should be done" and what policies ought to be pursued to eradicate poverty. These are highly contested issues around which no global consensus was possible in 2000. This remains the case today. The political economy of the late twentieth and early twenty-first centuries has permitted the issue of global poverty to become part of the international agenda through the efforts of aid donors, United Nations (UN) agencies and the General Assembly, and civil society (particularly in rich countries). However, the power of different actors, reflecting their material capabilities, has allowed them to frame the ways in which global poverty is understood and determine the processes (MDGs, Heavily Indebted Poor Countries Initiative, Poverty Reduction Strategy Papers (PRSPs), trade negotiations, aid contracts, access to concessional finance) by which it is to be tackled. While the neoliberal explanatory frameworks and policies of the 1980s have been weakened, orthodox economic analysis still privileges economic growth over human development and key institutions, such as the International Monetary Fund (IMF) and World Bank, remain suspicious of heterodox economic strategies that open up more of a role for state action. The policy statements of UN agencies, the World Bank and IMF, national governments and many non-governmental organizations (NGOs) may make it sound as though there is a consensus on global poverty reduction but "how" to do this is fiercely contested. There is a technical side to these contests but also a political side—who gains most and who might lose if specific poverty eradication strategies are selected?

While polemicists can identify a single overriding cause for extreme poverty (this may be a lack of growth because of state intervention, the structural nature of capitalism and unequal social relations, or a simple lack of compassion), rigorous and less aggressively ideological analysts of mass poverty demonstrate the causal complexities. A set of economic, social and political factors, varying from country to country, often within countries and over time, have to be understood. These factors interact in complex ways so that prediction, and hence prescription, is not straightforward. Policies and actions in support of poverty eradication require both *a priori* technical analysis (thinking through) and ongoing social learning that changes values and behaviors (acting out). Interventions are not only about getting the economic and social policies right but also about changing international social norms, raising the likelihood of institutions becoming more effective and improving national and global governance over time.

Debates about whether the MDGs have made a positive contribution to poverty eradication and/or whether they have achieved as much as they should have done are becoming more frequent as 2015 and the "end of the MDGs" approaches. The framing of many of these discussions often depends on whether or not the analyst argues that "the glass is half full" or "the glass is half empty." On the positive side one can point to the raised awareness of mass poverty that the MDGs have achieved, particularly in the media in the rich world, and the clear evidence that the MDGs have not contributed to the ongoing decrease in aid levels that has been in evidence since the end of the Cold War. Conceptually, the MDGs have been associated with the reshaping of "what" poverty is seen as—in earlier eras it was seen simply as a lack of economic growth, but nowadays a human development or multi-dimensional concept is much more likely to underpin datasets and analysis and media reporting. In many poorer countries the MDGs (and associated PRSPs and Poverty Reduction Strategies) have led to much improved data on poverty and deprivation and a greater focus on the budgets for education and health.

There is, however, a downside. The content of the MDGs can be argued to have abrogated any focus on macroeconomic development and, despite the addition of "decent work" to the MDG targets in 2005, to have neglected the role of employment in national and international strategies. The failure to place quantifiable and time-specific measures for Goal eight (the goal where the rich world promises to behave differently in international processes and strategies) has meant that the Organisation for Economic Co-operation and Development (OECD) membership, and other emerging powers, have been able to wriggle out of changing the way they operate. This could mean that it becomes a norm in some parts of the world *not* to be accountable for commitments to global poverty reduction—leaders can make international promises but national electorates will not demand accountability on them in the way they would do for promises made about national policies and outcomes. Finally, there is the problem that the evolution of the MDGs was strongly guided by OECD actors. This led to an over-emphasis on the role of foreign aid in strategies and processes for poverty reduction and the sidelining of "national ownership"—the key players in global poverty reduction are the national governments of the countries in which very poor people live, not aid donors or international agencies.

As argued throughout this book, an active debate about what the MDGs have achieved and what that means for the crafting of a post-2015 international framework for action must become a priority. Our contribution to what a post-2015 framework ought to look like, The Johannesburg Statement on the Millennium Development Goals, is appended to this book directly following the original MDGs. In it we bring together the fundamentals of what we think a new and more robust program of action should be founded on. However, our modest endeavor is to *contribute* to a debate, not to capture and dominate that debate in an overly righteous fashion. Nonetheless, what is clear is that the absolute number of people living in extreme poverty and/or experiencing the deprivation of one or more basic needs is staggering and concerted action is required, now. The progress made in reducing poverty since 2000 has been too slow and, with the food, financial and fuel crises (but, especially food prices), some of the progress that had been made is already being reversed. Despite the growing affluence of the world, human insecurity appears to be increasing. Climate change is already having a negative impact on the lives of the poor (climate skeptics can challenge this from their comfortable armchairs but they should talk with poor people in Bangladesh, or many of the small tropical island states threatened by sea-level rises, about their lived experiences, as we have). As we send this manuscript to press, the possibility of global financial contagion seems more likely than at any previous time. We must recall that while the MDGs were being agreed at the UN General Assembly in 2000 and 2001, a mile down the road, in Wall Street, casino capitalists were creating sub-prime mortgage derivatives that would drive tens of millions into poverty.

So, the time is right to think about how we move from the MDGs to a set of Global Development Goals (GDGs) that accelerate the reduction of extreme poverty across the world *and* build the foundations of a more comprehensive global development program. These goals and their attendant program need to raise awareness and make poverty eradication more central to the international agenda, as did the MDGs; however, they also need to go beyond this in terms of both their scope (taking on macroeconomic policy issues, employment and inequality) and in their implementation (setting up accountability processes that make it more likely that what governments say they will do for the poorest people in the world is what they *actually* do). The run-up to the MDGs was a time of heated and energized debates at UN conferences and summits and a vast range of other forums. The setting of the MDGs seems to have been associated with the technicalization of international debates and, with a focus on measurement and elite discussions about precisely "what is happening." These technical debates are essential but we also need to reignite some of the energy and passion of the pre-2000 debates that drove forward thinking about eradicating poverty. If this book can reactivate a little of this energy and the passion, and move towards the formulation of the post-2015 Global Development Goals, we shall have succeeded in our modest ambitions.

Our collective endeavor

As with any edited volume, this book is the product of our collective industry. It is also a record of why we think a new set of GDGs must be adopted and put in place by the time the MDGs come to an end in 2015. Inevitably, we differ on points of emphasis, though for such an array of scholars and practitioners working across a variety of traditions these differences are remarkably few. What is clear is that for the most part we agree wholeheartedly on what needs to be done.

The volume is organized so that it allows each of us to offer our view of what is right and wrong with the MDGs, why we should do something about it, and how we should do it, so that we are able to pursue aspects of a broader analysis that we believe warrants special attention or reflects the experiences and/or knowledge that we have. We begin by looking at the "global context" of the MDGs. Here we offer chapters that locate the MDGs within a longer historical endeavor by the UN to tackle underdevelopment (Anstee); flesh out the consequences of embedding a particularly narrow development narrative around the MDGs (Fukuda-Parr); underline the need to continue the good that has been done and revise it to meet new challenges (Thakur); worry about whether we are being inclusive and egalitarian in our approach to development and not gendered and exclusionary (Harman); consider whether we are harnessing the capacity of previously excluded and unengaged faith actors in pressing forward change (Marshall); and challenging the institution that ought to be at the heart of a global push for better development—the UN Economic and Social Council (ECOSOC)—to embark on much-needed reform (Weiss). We then move on to focus specifically on that region of the world that continues to be the most impoverished and which looks likely to fall short of meeting many of the MDGs: Africa. This section begins with three chapters that explore the differing challenges to, as well as thrown up by, MDG achievement (Murphy, Chimhowu and Hulme, and Stewart). The section then focuses on the intractability of HIV/AIDS (Regondi and Whiteside), before considering how to move beyond Africa's underdevelopment (Bangura), and building the intellectual resources for equitable growth and social enrichment (Botman). Our aim is to be comprehensive in our coverage. Inevitably, there are areas that we have missed. Nonetheless, our omissions do not detract from our collective endeavor or the necessity of pressing for change.

Global context

In chapter 1, Margaret Anstee begins the analysis proper with an historical and institutional *tour de force* of the background to the formulation of the MDGs. Here she situates the MDGs within long-running attempts by the UN to deal with underdevelopment. In so doing, she is able to identify clear areas wherein urgent action is required, highlighting the necessity of increasing development resources, reforming key UN institutions and ways of operating, as well as promoting the right kind of ownership of development programs. Anstee's claim is that the MDGs are just, and should be seen as, the latest manifestation of UN efforts to improve the lives of much of the world's population. Yet, they are also uniquely "turn of the millennium" in their formulation as quantifiable targets to be met and progress to be measured. Moreover, the MDGs mark a departure from four decades of efforts to promote a particular kind of development and are the product of a change in focus away from economic growth as the key development imperative, to one focused more on social and human development.

Yet, although the MDGs were the product of attempts to correct the problems of previous UN efforts they are not in themselves unproblematic. As all of the contributions to this volume show, rates of achievement among the world's developing countries will vary dramatically. Moreover, while the MDGs attempted to offer a way of measuring progress, the way they set out to measure progress all too quickly turned out to be problematic. That said, the MDGs, like previous UN development efforts, are themselves a stage in an ongoing process to bring about meaningful development. Thus, their positive aspects should not be discarded in any revisionist process.

It is this need to maintain forward momentum and a desire to build upon positive developments that led us to gather in Johannesburg and to formulate our vision of how to proceed as set out in the Johannes-burg Statement on the Millennium Development Goals appended to this book. Anstee highlights with great clarity these imperatives and details how the clarion call for a new set of GDGs can be taken for-ward. In so doing, she dedicates the remainder of her chapter to the triple challenges of resource mobilization, institutional reform, and the importance of national ownership of and involvement in the develop-ment process before highlighting the necessity of any set of GDGs to tackle growing global inequalities.

Sakiko Fukuda-Parr's chapter builds further momentum in the case for a new set of GDGs beyond 2015. In developing her argument, Fukuda-Parr offers a powerful critique of the impact of the MDGs on development as a meaningful endeavor to help promote health and economic and social wellbeing. She argues that while there is much to be celebrated in the MDGs, their impact has also been to distill devel-opment imperatives down to eight prerogatives achievable "only" by meeting certain (largely) quantifiable targets. While there is inevitably a tradeoff in confecting any narrative that attempts to quickly and acces-sibly convey the urgency of a situation and specify what needs to be done, Fukuda-Parr argues that the MDG narrative actually took global development away from the hard-fought concerns set out in the Millennium Declaration to a narrow and overly stylized understanding of the problem and its solutions. In the reformulation of a new set of GDGs, then, attention must be diverted to recrafting the development narrative so that it more closely resembles the "sustainable, equitable and human rights-based development" articulated in the MD. Her task is to reveal how such a redesign might come about as well as to high-light the 10 most pressing issues that should be front and center in this endeavor.

Thakur picks up the baton from Anstee and Fukuda-Parr with an analysis of the necessary elements for rebalancing global power, wealth and wellbeing required in a set of GDGs. Here Thakur illustrates how the MDGs built on the foundations provided by critiques of previous ways of "doing" development, establishing, as they did, a secure base for improving, as a set of interconnected goals, more than just the mone-tary aspects of human life; and he shows how the MDGs express some of the best, as well as reflect a little of the worst, developments in the recent global political economy. Thakur also shows how the MDGs powerfully illustrated the utility of having goals formulating global development commitments even if the quantitative measures attached to some of these goals are problematic. As he puts it, to "consolidate and build on their [the MDGs] undoubted successes and address pressing new global concerns, a new set of GDGs should be articulated, comprising measurable targets and indicators, while confronting the shortfalls and gaps in MDG achievements." Thakur's contribution is refreshing. In his uniquely democratic way, he explores the major challenges facing developing (particularly least developed) countries, building a compelling case for a specific set of GDGs that are flexible, targeted, appropriate and aspirational.

Sophie Harman begins the shift away from more general discussions of the MDGs towards pointed analyses of key issues. The purpose here, as in all of the other chapters that follow, is to piece together a more appropriate set of GDGs that builds upon, but also corrects omissions in the MDGs. As Harman rightly points out, until relatively recently MDGs three (gender equality) and five (maternal health) have received scant attention, and examining the relationship between men and women more generally (and the differential impacts of poverty and inequality upon each) has been very much at the margins of debate on the MDGs. As she puts it, the mechanisms that have been put in place to achieve the MDGs for women have "been too little and too late and have undermined efforts to help women living in poverty." The formulation of a new set of GDGs thus represents a timely moment to address these anomalies.

Through a meticulous examination of the manner of women's inclusion in the MDGs, the problems with responses and targets dealing specifically with (as well as inherently affecting) women, and the gendered nature of the targets set, Harman is able to come up with a set of recommendations that are much more appropriate for *all* of the world's population and which do not merely "add women and stir."[1] These recommendations behoove us to fully recognize and appropriately value women's role in social reproduction and in the development process. Crucially, they avoid the embedding of gender roles that is evident in the programs and policies set out to deliver the MDGs, which have tended to highlight the precarity of women only in relation to their roles as mothers and carers or as more reliable recipients of cash transfers and other forms of social protection.

Katherine Marshall's aim is a little different from Harman's. Rather than focus on a marginalized majority as a way into exploring the problems with and solutions for the MDGs, Marshall sets out to review the linkages between, and the roles of, faith actors in the realization of the goals and aspirations embodied in the MDGs. Here, Marshall's aim is to reflect on the capacity of faith actors to make a difference in delivering human development beyond 2015. She constructs an insightful and compelling argument.

Marshall begins by exploring a key tension between the MDGs and the outlook of many of the world's religions. She notes that the basic premise of the MDGs is to eradicate poverty, whereas for many religions, while mobilization of charitable giving in support of the poor and vulnerable is a near universal moral good, poverty is understood as an enduring feature of the human condition. As a consequence, "the idea of ending poverty as a central and achievable goal has taken root rather slowly." This underlying tension, Marshall argues, explains initial lukewarm support for the MDGs among faith actors and sits alongside the "rather off-putting" business/measurement discourse in which the MDGs are couched. Twelve years after their formulation, faith actors have begun to take the MDGs on board as a basis for advocacy and action, yet the disconnect remains. It is the capacity of faith actors to mobilize resources and do good, and the need to harness this capacity, that Marshall then explores.

Thomas Weiss's chapter takes us on a stage further to reflect upon the institutional architecture for monitoring and implementing the MDGs. Here, Weiss takes up the call of Anstee and Thakur among many others in this volume, to explore the prospects and possibilities for reform of ECOSOC. In so doing, he argues that four areas of change need addressing to make what Weiss believes may be the "UN's most unwieldy and least powerful deliberative body" fit for the task of dealing with its vast "everything but security" agenda. These areas are: putting an end to the "theater" of North/South tensions; consolidating the UN portfolio so that it works more for people and less against itself; recognizing and pursuing its own comparative advantage; and realizing that ideas matter and that investing in their production for the good of the globe is essential. Weiss's argument is both pithy and sobering. Clearly he has his finger on the pulse of UN reform, and clearly ECOSOC needs to be front and center in any effort to accelerate and better efforts at global development beyond the MDGs.

Focus on Africa

We move away from the global performance, prospects, silences and actors of the MDGs of section one to focus specifically on Africa in section two. Our decision to focus on Africa is deliberate. Paragraph 27 of the Millennium Declaration committed the development of the world organization to support, among other things, "lasting peace, poverty eradication and sustainable development" in Africa. As we highlighted above, Africa remains the source of much concern and a continent in which overall progress towards the MDGs is at best poor. We focus on

Africa now as the continent with the greatest need, as a place where proclamations of general "poor progress" hide great variations (geographically as well as across issues and within and between groups) that are both hopeful and worrisome. Our efforts, then, are focused on highlighting the needs of Africa with a view to concerted effort being a key focus of a set of GDGs beyond 2015.

Craig Murphy begins the section with a sharp and insightful chapter exploring the principal lessons to be learnt from the challenges to achieving the MDGs in Africa. He begins this task with an account of why his skepticism about the usefulness of the MDG system as a mechanism for reducing poverty has waned over the past decade. Murphy's insight here is an important frame for the whole of the MDG project and underlines the need to carry momentum forward with a new set of GDGs: the forms of measurement and the manner of striving towards MDG achievement might be problematic but the idea that poverty can and should be solved on a global scale has become a "super norm" that has become embedded, and has generated a momentum that should not be allowed to falter. Murphy then contextualizes this realization with a sobering look at the MDG performance of the continent and an account of what these continent-wide figures say and obscure. Importantly, Murphy reminds us that just because Africa will miss the MDG targets does not mean that it has "failed." Concerted action is nevertheless required to overcome those obstacles to Africa doing much better.

Admos Chimhowu and David Hulme press the argument further in Chapter 8. Here they probe national and international responsibilities in doing development better, and they use this analysis as a foundation for building a case for what comes after the MDGs' expiry date. Like Murphy, Chimhowu and Hulme consider the "behind the headline" progress of Africa's record on the MDGs; also like Murphy, they underline the importance of the MDGs as a global norm on the unacceptability of extreme poverty on a mass scale (the existence of which is thrown into sharper relief by the extent of affluence that is also characteristic of the early twenty-first century). In so doing, they reaffirm the necessity of national ownership of poverty-reduction strategies as a means of avoiding the imposition of incongruous "one size fits all" development programs; they emphasize that this must go hand in hand with better and more accountable national governance, serious attempts at long-term resolutions to the most intractable conflicts, better education and greater incentives for skilled workers to remain and fully participate in the domestic economy, more efficient and accountable uses of aid, and guarding against the dangers of brushing over the innovation and entrepreneurial endeavors in which Africans engage. For these strategies to work, however, they need to sit alongside serious international commitment to matching word and deed in areas such as the World Trade Organization's (WTO) Doha round, the transfer of technology from the industrial to the developing world, the global environment, international aid, and the reform of key global institutions (of which the IMF, World Bank and UN Security Council are perhaps the most pressing). There is no doubt that Chimhowu and Hulme's analysis requires a demanding program of action; there is also no doubt of its importance.

Frances Stewart continues the forensic examination of the causes of Africa's underdevelopment in Chapter 9. Here she notes that while the MDGs have significant advocacy potential as well as sizable symbolic power as the product of a unique global moment, the way in which they were formulated and the targets pursued tend to flatten out country performance and thereby obscure significant progress in some areas (even if the targets are still unlikely to be met), while celebrating less remarkable cases and achievers. What the MDGs really obscure, however, are instances of rising inequalities and criminality as well as other social ills. Her conclusion, thus, is that a reformulated set of GDGs beyond 2015 must promote a particular kind of development that is consistent with a broader set of social objectives designed to promote and lock in place economic development and to share the fruits of that development more equitably throughout society.

For Stewart, a major hurdle to overcome, and one that a new set of GDGs must seek to engender, is a failure to secure sustained growth. As she points out, a lack of growth starves economies of the capacity to harvest tax revenue to fund social services, enhance employment opportunities, and put in place safety nets to prevent a fall back into poverty. Three factors have, for Stewart, been at the root of Africa's growth failure—violent conflict, gross mismanagement of the economy and hugely adverse terms of trade—and each has its unique set of causes, each of which Stewart marks out while underlining the importance of addressing horizontal inequalities (that is, inequalities between groups) in promoting the conditions for sustained growth, peace and development. Stewart also warns that a post-2015 set of GDGs additionally needs a prescient and reactive element, putting in place sufficient planning for threats to wellbeing on, or just over, the horizon. She names the two most pressing as climate change and food shortages, but her long-term message is clear.

The power of Stewart's argument lies in her meticulous examination of the MDG "performance" data and her conviction that horizontal inequalities represent among the biggest challenges to meaningful development. Ilaria Regondi and Alan Whiteside pick up on one of the many growing global inequalities—in this instance on lived health experiences and HIV/AIDS—and explore how this dreadful epidemic, and the responses to it, play out in the context of a new set of GDGs. Regondi and Whiteside's account is compelling. They argue that the funding and confidence crises currently afflicting the global HIV/AIDS response, coupled with rates of infection that continue to outpace treatment, necessitate that a new set of GDGs must treat HIV/AIDS as an urgent priority. For them, this GDG response ought to comprise three elements: (i) a reformed version of the current MDG framework expanded to emphasize the necessity of longer-run societal transformation; (ii) a greater emphasis on interventions and policies rather than on indicators; and (iii) the integration of a "life-cycle" approach that targets health and wellbeing from birth through to death. However, these additions would not, for Regondi and Whiteside, be sufficient in themselves. A new set of GDGs would also have to address the most compelling criticisms leveled at the MDGs as well as build upon their strength. It is difficult to see how Regondi and Whiteside's argument is anything other than "on the money."

Our analysis continues to gather steam in Chapter 11. Here Yusuf Bangura explores what is required to make significant inroads into eliminating poverty in Africa. His analysis focuses on four areas, bringing together themes that others in the book also highlight: the importance of growth strategies that generate sustained and sustainable production, employment and income; the necessity of building human capital; setting in motion drivers for beneficial and harmonious economic and social transformations; and the implementation of effective measures designed to promote productive employment and equitable distribution as well as domestic resource mobilization and beneficial social policy and good governance. However, as Bangura rightly points out, while the MDGs currently formulated are wanting in key areas, and adjustments need to be made in a new set of GDGs, global development goals cannot hope to, and should not be, the sum of our efforts to transform poverty-stricken societies. GDGs serve a useful purpose in highlighting problems and in directing action but without integrated and comprehensive, not to mention complementary, strategies, meaningful poverty reduction and development will not come about. That said, perhaps the most important missing element in discussions of the MDGs and what will replace them after 2015 is the role of, and the need for, education. It is to this crucial area that we now turn in what has to be part of a wide and secure foundation for combating African, as well as global, underdevelopment.

Russel Botman's challenge is to find ways to lock in the limited causes for optimism that exist in Africa's development through nurturing more and better quality higher education across the continent, as well as to find ways to ensure that the knowledge generated contributes to Africa's growth. As he rightly points out, higher education ought to get much more attention than it does "because it generates, transfers and applies the knowledge required for development to take place." Unfortunately, given their focus on the poorest, higher education does not feature in the MDGs. However, if Africa is to be able to achieve the kind of development necessary to lift the continent's population out of poverty and to keep them there, a new set of GDGs need to advocate a much more integrated and holistic approach to development.

In support of his argument, Botman explores the positive input that university research can have by looking at two examples: the first example looks at the impact of research on agricultural production; the second example examines the benefits of improvements in Africa's intellectual resources for the continent's development. In so doing, he provides a powerful argument for reconnecting higher education with a more meaningful and appropriate development strategy that, guided by a new set of GDGs, will help promote the right kind of national ownership of the development process that Africa needs, and which all of the authors in this volume have highlighted.

Where to now?

Appended to this book are the MDGs and the Statement we crafted in Johannesburg in response to their content, purpose and progress towards their achievement more than a decade after they were formulated. Our Statement stands as both a collation of our heartfelt contributions, a declaration of what we should do now, and an advocacy tool for pressing, with the greatest urgency, for a UN Summit to be convened to adopt a new set of GDGs. We share a conviction that these new GDGs must:

- Promote *national ownership* of the development process by: (i) adapting the goals to national circumstances and priorities; (ii) creating mechanisms whereby external aid conforms to priority needs identified in national development plans prepared by the countries themselves; and (iii) putting in place financial aid and technical assistance to strengthen the analytical, policy development and program delivery capacity of target countries.
- Ensure *equitable economic growth*.

- *Reset the balance* between the productive sectors of the economy and the social sectors of the nation.
- Incorporate *climate change* and the need for mitigation and adaptation.
- Pay special attention to *food availability and affordability.*
- Include the need to *reduce inequalities* between individuals and groups within and among countries.
- Reformulate specific goals to *reflect progress,* such as a shift in priority from primary education to the attainment of universal literacy through completed secondary education qualifications.
- Ensure that the *rights* of all vulnerable and minority groups are enacted in legislation and enforced.
- Establish conditions to enable women to lead lives *free from the threat of violence* and with equal opportunities for realizing their wellbeing.
- Adopt a more rigorous set of *reporting, monitoring and accountability* mechanisms for developing country efforts and results, donor pledges and the performance of international institutions.

While it is the case, as we show throughout the book, that the MDGs are in many ways problematic, they have consolidated and helped embed a global norm of poverty reduction. Without a replacement set of goals to correct anomalies and address problems as well as to take forward positive aspects of the MDGs and build upon them, great damage will be done to the gains already made and a large proportion of the world's population will continue to live in forms of poverty and destitution that we as a global community have the capacity to eradicate. This is our challenge, and it is one at which we must work hard.

Note

1 Sandra Harding, *Whose Science? Whose Knowledge? Thinking from Women's Lives* (Cornell: Cornell University Press, 1991), 194.

Part I
Global context

1   Millennium Development Goals
Milestones on a long road

Margaret Joan Anstee

This chapter traces the successive attempts undertaken since 1945, under the aegis of the United Nations (UN), to bring about worldwide economic and social development and the improvement of living standards everywhere, through the establishment of international goals, the latest example being the Millennium Development Goals (MDGs), adopted by consensus in 2000 and planned to reach their term in 2015. Drawing on the experience of the last 65 years, I analyze the major steps that have to be taken in order to make the far more rapid progress in reducing poverty and inequality, both within and between nations, that is now ever more urgently required in the light of the deteriorating international situation. These steps encompass resources, operational practices and institutions, including major reform of the UN and measures to ensure genuine (and long overdue) national ownership of development programs which should enshrine national priorities and plans rather than priorities by donor countries and aid organizations. I argue that these wide-ranging changes are in the interests of both developed and developing countries. Much greater international commitment is required, as is universal recognition that development and security are interdependent. The road so long trodden is now reaching a critical crossroads.

Overview

Goals and targets have become a central feature of today's world. They are used in industry and commerce, in advertising and virtually all walks of life but they are the particularly favorite instruments of governments and politicians, whether in power, to demonstrate achievement, or, in opposition, to substantiate the reverse. Targets can be a useful tool: they set a goal to be reached, against which progress can be measured. However, they can also prove a double-edged sword: for example, if they are not properly formulated, are artificial, unrealistic, or ill-adapted to the circumstances. On their own they are meaningless unless supported by adequate resources, appropriate institutions and effective monitoring mechanisms. They can become an end in themselves and introduce an element of inflexibility that is inimical to progress unless they are regularly reviewed and adapted to changing circumstances. Usually they are couched in quantitative rather than qualitative terms, which means that they rely on figures and statistics that can all too easily be subjectively misinterpreted or, much worse, manipulated for political purposes. We are all familiar with the progression "lies, damned lies and statistics" that Mark Twain probably apocryphally attributed to Benjamin Disraeli but which was certainly a common political dictum in the latter part of the nineteenth century. While it was coined in a national context it flourishes in the international environment of today.

The setting of goals and targets for development is not a new phenomenon. You could say that it has been the hallmark of the global involvement of the UN in development since it embarked on this field of activity more than half a century ago. The road to worldwide economic advancement has proved longer and rockier than was anticipated, punctuated at times by encouraging progress and at others by disappointing setbacks. Over the past 66 years various approaches have been adopted in order to overcome the obstacles and achieve the desired end. Hence, the MDGs are not an innovation but a continuation of what has gone before, albeit in a different guise. They mark a new direction in the emphasis on social development targets of direct relevance to people, reflecting the increased importance being given to human development. This, in turn, derives from the new concept of security defined not merely in terms of defense and military criteria but embracing wider aspects of human welfare.

Earlier milestones: the evolution of UN goals for economic and social development

Among the general public the UN is usually perceived as a mainly political organization, despite the fact that around 80 percent of its regular budget is dedicated to economic and social work. Granted, the Preamble of the UN Charter gives the maintenance of international peace and security as the Organization's primary aim: "to save succeeding generations from the scourge of war." However, it also singles out the need "to promote social progress and better standards of life in larger freedom." Nonetheless, work in the economic and social fields was fairly timid in the early years. The 1940s and 1950s saw the issue of a number of seminal reports on development, particularly with regard to the special case of less-developed, newly independent countries as the process of decolonization progressed, and the General Assembly adopted many pertinent resolutions during those years.

One of these resolutions (General Assembly Resolution 304 (IV) of 16 November 1949) gave a new dimension and increased momentum to this work by creating the first operational program of technical cooperation, the Expanded Programme of Technical Assistance (EPTA). This was followed a few years later by the UN Special Fund (1959) to undertake pre-investment studies. In 1966 they were merged to form what we now know as the UN Development Programme (UNDP). Parallel to the initiatives of the main body of the UN, its Specialized Agencies, including the World Bank, were also embarking on increasingly ambitious programs of development cooperation in their respective fields.

In those early days there was a certain optimism, almost euphoria, about the possibilities of achieving a reasonable level of development worldwide within a generation or two. It was not long, however, before disillusion and discontent set in, especially among the developing countries, many of which were feeling their oats in their new state of independence and considered the UN to be excessively Western-oriented. In 1964, at the first meeting of the UN Conference on Trade and Development (UNCTAD), the Group of 77 was formed as a bloc that could present developing countries' concerns in a more uniform and forceful manner. As their bargaining power increased they began to clamor for a realignment between the asymmetric power relationships of North and South. This became known officially as the New International Economic Order (NIEO), adopted by a General Assembly Resolution in 1974. The NIEO dominated all economic debate in the General Assembly during the rest of the 1970s. It was an ambitious attempt to change international power relations and bring about a redistribution of incomes and assets from industrial to developing countries that its proponents considered essential for attaining development and better living standards in those underprivileged regions. Their far-reaching proposals met with strong opposition from some Western member states, however, and in the end little came of the endless and often fractious discussions.

A decade earlier the mood had been more optimistic. On 25 September 1961 President John F. Kennedy, in an address to the General Assembly, launched a proposal for a Development Decade. Soon afterwards the General Assembly adopted an historic decision (Resolution 1710 (XVI) of 19 December 1961) which designated the 1960s as "the United Nations Development Decade" with the declared intent "to accelerate and progress towards self-sustaining growth of the economy of the individual nations and their social advancement." Such were the hopes at that time that it was thought possible to solve the problems of the developing countries within a decade. It was perhaps the earliest attempt to promote development through targeting. The General Assembly established a minimum annual growth rate of 5 percent in aggregate national income for the so-called less-developed countries by 1970. A significant number of low-income countries achieved that target and a few even exceeded it. Nonetheless, the results of the Development Decade were generally regarded with disappointment because there were few visible improvements in living standards, partly because of a faster rate of population growth than anticipated.

As a result, while that Development Decade had originally been envisaged as unique and complete in itself, it had to be followed by others and became known as the First Development Decade. The Second Development Decade, for the 1970s, envisaged a higher growth rate of 6 percent per annum but laid more emphasis on poverty reduction, reflecting the realization that economic progress did not automatically improve living conditions for the mass of the people. It included targets for education, employment and health, the flow of aid resources as well as special measures for the newly defined category of less-developed countries which were seen to be falling behind. Again, some countries exceeded the 6 percent target but the overall annual gross domestic product (GDP) growth of developing countries averaged only 5.6 percent in 1971–80.

Targets for the Third Development Decade (1981–90) increased aspirations for economic growth to 7 percent annually and went further in specifying detailed social goals in fields such as employment, hunger and malnutrition, life expectancy, literacy, primary healthcare, safe water and sanitation. By the 1980s, however, the world economic and financial situation had deteriorated drastically with increasing debt and recession. The Bretton Woods institutions, the International Monetary Fund (IMF) and the World Bank, became the prime movers in determining international economic and financial policies, advocating swingeing measures of stabilization and structural adjustment that became known as the Washington Consensus. Ideas such as the employment and basic needs strategies that had formed a central concern of the Third Development Decade were swept off the global agenda. The Bretton Woods institutions focused on a narrower set of economic objectives, determined by market forces, in contrast to the goals of human advance and poverty reduction which formed the major goals of the UN from the 1980s onwards. Only a handful of countries achieved the 7 percent GDP growth rate for that decade and overall growth in developing countries averaged only 4 percent annually. The Fourth Development Decade (1991–2000) maintained the target of 7 percent growth but only seven countries achieved it and the average growth for all developing countries during the decade was 4.7 percent.

Targeting was also extended to the provision of aid and the external resource flows needed in order to reach the established goals. In 1969 the Pearson report (so called because the mission that prepared it was headed by Lester B. Pearson) called for developed countries to devote 0.7 percent of their GDP to concessional development aid. That target has been reiterated many times since in innumerable reports and international gatherings but so far has been honored more in the breach than the observance, except by a handful of countries.

This brief canter across more than half a century (1945–2000) demonstrates that, while the economic growth imperative remained predominant, there were increasing efforts to give more weight to issues of social and human development. These were epitomized by such events as the annual publication, starting in 1990, of the UNDP Human Development Report, designed to provide a broader and more authentic measurement of human welfare and the World Summit on Social Development held in Copenhagen in 1995, the initial planning for which was begun, under my direction, at the UN Office at Vienna in the early 1990s.

As has been shown, the Development Decades were not an unqualified success and at the UN Millennium Summit, held in New York in 2000, a new approach was adopted with the promulgation of the MDGs. In a sense they replaced the Development Decades, a new set of milestones in the long search for a better life for all. During the previous 40 years the initial economic and quantitative emphasis had gradually become nuanced with more attention to the social aspects of development and "softer" issues, but it was still the former that was given greater importance. Now the pendulum swung dramatically in the opposite direction: of the eight goals adopted in 2000, seven are exclusively social in character, concentrating on the qualitative improvement of human welfare: poverty and hunger; primary education; gender equality; child mortality; maternal health; HIV/AIDS and malaria; and environmental sustainability. The concentration on these objectives is welcome. At the same time, care must be taken to prevent the pendulum from swinging too far in the opposite direction, as has happened so often in the past. It is essential to achieve a balance between the economic and social, for the two are interdependent. The attainment of those social targets depends on adequate economic growth in order to ensure the national funding without which it is impossible to guarantee their sustainability and continuous improvement over the longer term.

Whether the MDGs are achieved or not (in some cases they may well be, while in others the prospects look less hopeful), 2015 will clearly not mark the end of a road that still stretches far ahead. One of the main drafters of the MDGs, Mark Malloch-Brown, has written in his book, *The Unfinished Global Revolution*, that they "were written hurriedly in a UN office building, using the language of earlier global agreements." He goes on to describe them as "a poorly worded, incomplete stab at a global commitment among all of us in the global community. Their drafting is not the stuff of great history, but they are a start."

In 2015 new milestones will have to be established and they must be economic as well as social. This need is clearly stated in the January 2011 Johannesburg Statement on the Millennium Development Goals when it calls on the UN to convene a summit in 2015 to adopt a new set of Global Development Goals (GDGs) and cites among the requirements "Resetting the balance between the productive sectors of the economy and the social sectors of the nation."

Resources

No development targets can be reached without adequate and appropriate resources, both financial and technical. The essential core of these resources must come from developing countries themselves, otherwise there can be no national ownership. Nonetheless, substantial financial support will be needed from the outside world.

- *Predictable and sustained flows of external resources*
  Global recession and the general economic downturn inevitably have an effect on the provision of finance for development. It was therefore encouraging that, at the UN Summit held in 2010 to review the situation, developed countries pledged to provide US$40 billion over the next five years towards achieving the MDG goals. Past experience, however, not only in the context of MDGs but also of many similar appeals for development financing, does not bode well for the fulfillment of these commitments. The most egregious example is the scandalous failure of most developed countries to devote 0.7 percent of their GDP to development assistance, the target first enunciated as long ago as 1969 in the Pearson Commission, subsequently endorsed by the General Assembly and constantly reiterated as high on the international agenda on many occasions ever since. Similarly, the commitments undertaken at the G8 Summit held in Gleneagles in 2005 to provide US$25 billion in aid to Africa by 2010, as well as debt cancellation and relief, are far from being fully

honored (by 2010 only about US$11 billion had been delivered). Donor countries should make specific, multi-year pledges of aid to support international development commitments undertaken by the UN and there should be much stricter monitoring of fulfillment of pledges. Annual reports should "name and shame" countries and organizations that fail to meet their commitments.

- *Innovative new sources of funding*
  Given the present paucity of resources it is essential to seek innovative sources of funding. During the previous decade some useful new forms of doing so were developed. A good example is the International Finance Facility for Immunisation, which sells bonds on capital markets to raise funds for the GAVI Alliance, a public/private partnership that increases access to vaccination and has saved millions of lives. It was unfortunate that the similar, but somewhat broader, proposal made by the then UK Chancellor of the Exchequer, Gordon Brown, to the Gleneagles summit in 2005 for the creation of an International Finance Facility, a mechanism to provide aid and debt relief by floating government bonds for aid on international money markets, was rejected by the United States. The current international financial climate is even less propitious for the adoption of such a mechanism but it should be kept on the drawing board and revived whenever circumstances become more favorable. Simultaneously, increased efforts should be made to find other new and innovative sources of funding from both the public and the private sector. Recent renewed interest in the Tobin tax is an interesting step in the right direction.

- *Optimum use of available resources*
  While it is commendable that many different sources have been tapped to provide financing for the achievement of the MDGs, including both private and public sectors as well as the involvement of a very large number of non-governmental organizations (NGOs), this does mean that there is a plethora of actors, each with their own agenda and priorities which do not necessarily coincide with the most urgent needs of the country being assisted. Lack of coordination between them inevitably leads to duplication and less than optimum use of the scarce resources available. In order to avoid this unacceptable wastage, action is needed on a number of fronts and new modalities must be put in place by 2015 to avoid similar difficulties arising in the next stage.

In order to establish a logical framework for the provision of assistance and to ensure genuine national ownership, a new kind of country plan is required. This would supersede the various and often overlapping planning requirements imposed in the past by international organizations, together with built-in conditionality, such as the World Bank's Poverty Reduction Strategy Papers (PRSPs), UNDP's Development Assistance Framework (UNDAFs) and Common Country Assessments (CCAs), which have tended to adopt a "one size fits all" approach. Instead, each country would prepare a highly individualized development plan focusing on the internationally agreed targets for the period after 2015. This would define the total resources, both financial and human, required in order to achieve these goals; the amount of these resources available nationally; and, deriving from this, the additional financial and human resources required from outside in order to make up the difference between the two. External organizations and agencies and NGOs would be required to tailor their assistance to fill the gaps identified by this process, according to their capacities, rather than deciding their own priorities which may not necessarily coincide with the priority needs of the country concerned and which can all too easily result in duplication of areas in which the country has proven capacity or which are already being covered by another source of aid. The nationally owned plan, by defining the national resources that government would make available for its implementation, would constitute its own commitment to do so. This would provide a yardstick by which the honoring of the government's commitment could be regularly monitored, as well as the contribution made by external sources. Such a process would place more emphasis on country ownership in the definition of priorities and a greater obligation on external donors to respond to them. It would improve the relevance of external support to national needs and ensure the optimum use of scarce resources by placing more emphasis on genuine country plans. Donors, whether international, bilateral, or from private or NGO sources, would be required to tailor their response to fill the resource gaps identified by the country itself and not just arbitrarily provide aid that reflects their own priorities and/or capacities.

In connection with its proposal for a summit in 2015 to adopt a new set of goals, the Johannesburg Statement emphasizes that particular consideration should be given to "Promoting national ownership by (i) adapting the goals to national circumstances and priorities; (ii) creating mechanisms whereby external aid conforms to priority needs identified in national development plans presented by the countries themselves; and (iii) putting in place financial aid and technical assistance to strengthen the analytical, policy development and programme delivery capacity of target countries."

The institutional framework

Adequate resources will not be enough on their own, nor will they be delivered to maximum benefit unless effective institutional arrangements and policies exist for that purpose at both the international and national levels. Without them no successor program to the MDGs, however well formulated, will have any chance of reaching its goals and making a genuine impact on world poverty.

The United Nations system

As the forum in which international development goals are formulated, debated and promulgated, the UN is the major lead player and has a central responsibility in ensuring that optimum arrangements are in place for an effective response. That response requires coordinated action not only from the UN itself but also from the numerous agencies and organizations that make up the UN system. Its components encompass the whole gamut of economic and social sectors that form part of the complex process of development, both in terms of policy formulation and of operational activities to assist governments in translating theory into action. During the many decades over which I have been working on economic and social development I have seen a succession of ideas being plugged extolling particular approaches or sectors as the magic wand to accelerate the elusive process of development and poverty reduction. I called them "developments fads" and in turn they each faded away, only to be succeeded by others. The one great lesson of the 66 years since the UN became involved in these issues is that development efforts will not succeed unless they are integrated.

Much lip service has been given to the theory of integrated development, not least by the UN which first formulated it, but its performance in putting theory into practice has been sadly lacking. It has been widely recognized for a long time that the UN system is dysfunctional and that an immense wastage of resources occurs as a result of rivalry and duplication between the various organs and specialized agencies dealing with development cooperation. It is high time that the UN (and by this I mean the member states and not just the Secretariat, which cannot take action unless mandated to do so by the comity of nations of which it is composed) undertook long-overdue measures to put its own house in order.

The failure to act much earlier is not for the want of trying. The problem has been evident from the very early years of the organization. It stems from the ad hoc manner in which the various UN entities were set up in the euphoria that prevailed after the end of World War II. They were all given an ambiguous autonomous or semi-autonomous status which they became increasingly reluctant to relinquish. An early proposal for an International Development Authority, endowed with sufficient resources and authority to launch an integrated attack on the problem of development, did not prosper. Instead a collegiate structure was set up to underpin the first operational organizations, EPTA and the Special Fund, operating on a consensual basis. By the mid-1960s it was clear that this approach was far from producing optimum results. To redress this situation, Sir Robert Jackson was commissioned to carry out a Study of the Capacity of the United Nations Development System, a task in which I was privileged to serve as his Deputy. His seminal report was published in 1969 as a parallel to the Pearson report: the latter focused on what needed to be done in order to bring about world-wide development while the Jackson report, as it came to be known, made detailed proposals for the reform of the UN system to make it possible for that work to be done. The ultimate aim was vividly described in Sir Robert's letter to a fictitious head of state that prefaced the final report. It was to enable "governments and UN organizations" to "look forward with vision and determination toward the end of the century and map out a strategy for development that will seize people's imaginations and give hope to those who are in need and inspiration to those who have the power to make great changes."

The report's wide-ranging proposals envisaged a strong central role for UNDP, exercising "the power of the purse" as the sole central funding agency for all development cooperation channeled through the UN system. At the same time there would be maximum decentralization to the country level where there would be a single united presence under the leadership of the Resident Representative, in which all programs and agencies would be represented and would speak with the same voice. In this way an integrated approach, with optimum use of resources, would have been assured. The Capacity Study was widely acclaimed but became known as the "Bible" because, like the Bible, its precepts, although universally acknowledged as the way ahead, were never implemented, bedeviled by vested interests and petty rivals among member states and "barons" in the feudal bureaucracies of the Specialized Agencies. Sir Robert's vision for the rest of the century was never fulfilled.

Instead, the succeeding decades have seen many attempts to reform the UN that have still not succeeded in dealing with the centrifugal forces that tear the system apart. The tragedy is that there is no mystery as to what needs to be done. The principles first enunciated in the Capacity Study have echoed and re-echoed in the innumerable reports on reform—too many to summarize here—produced during the last 40 years. The latest manifestation was appropriately entitled "Delivering as One" and was produced by the UN High Level Panel on System-wide Coherence in 2006. In all cases, including this latest one, implementation and follow-up have been partial and disappointing for the same reasons as tolled the bell for the Capacity Study: shortsighted and narrow self-interest on the part of both member states and senior officials in the Secretariats.

The question therefore is not what to do but how to bring about the self-evident changes that are essential if the UN is ever to operate efficiently, avoid duplication and ensure optimum use of the resources entrusted to it. That would require a fundamental sea change in the attitudes of both member states and UN bureaucracies and it is hard to see how to bring that about when the present financial problems seem to be fomenting a climate of "every country for itself," to the detriment of international cooperation. Nonetheless, surely the seriousness of the situation, as the MDG deadline nears, constitutes a wakeup call for other attitudes to prevail? It is sadly no coincidence that the eighth MDG—to develop a global partnership for development—is the one on which least progress has been made. This must be rectified before the next phase is launched and it should be a major item on the agenda of the proposed 2015 conference.

There is a crying need for leadership and it is time for the UN Secretary-General and responsible member states of the UN to call for narrow national interests to be subordinated to a united effort to make the UN system fit for purpose. There is no need to set up yet another costly and time-consuming commission to prepare yet another report. The proposals are all there and all that is needed is an analysis of the common themes running through the innumerable past reports as a basis for immediate action. Effective implementation of the "Delivery as One" report of 2006 would be a positive move. At the proposed conference in 2015 all member states should be called upon to make a public commitment to settle their differences and make genuine reform possible.

Developed donor countries

Developed donor countries should put in place policies and structures that enable them to make and honor commitments in two key areas to:

- maintain and increase the development aid to developing countries, particularly through multilateral channels, with the aim of reaching the 0.7 percent of GDP as soon as possible; and

- ensure that any bilateral aid that they provide is tailored to meet the priority needs of the country as set out in that government's development plan and to refrain from imposing their own priorities.

Recipient countries

Efficient and effective government on the part of the receiving countries is essential if international development goals are to be achieved, the aid provided is to reach the right people and combined national and international resources are to make a tangible and sustainable impact on poverty. In many developing countries, especially among the poorest of them in Africa, the necessary institutional framework either does not exist or, if it does exist on paper, does not function effectively. It is not easy to change the situation in the short run.

Obviously the receiving government must demonstrate firm commitment to the Millennium Project or its successor after 2015, not only in its national strategy (the new kind of country plan envisaged above), but, even more importantly, in its implementation of that strategy. In some cases the national administration may not be fully equipped to undertake these vital tasks. Where progress towards democratic and effective government is hampered by internal conflict or for political, traditional or cultural reasons it may take several generations to overcome these hurdles. Where the underlying conditions are more favorable but inefficiencies occur through lack of administrative and technical experience, improvements can be achieved, and the disadvantages of a deficient political system at least partially overcome, by the provision of technical assistance. It is not enough to throw money at poverty-reduction programs in order to make them successful. Human resources to carry them out are just as important as financial contributions. In recent times technical assistance has become the Cinderella and poor relation of international development cooperation. This is a serious error that needs to be redressed. In assessing the external assistance required by the developing country in carrying out its country plan, more attention should be given to the adequacy of the human resources available on the spot and provision made to fill any gaps with training and technical assistance. The Johannesburg Statement addresses this issue with its recommendation that particular consideration should be given to "putting in place financial aid and technical assistance to strengthen the analytical, policy development and programme delivery capacity of target countries" (my emphasis). Assessing the fulfillment of the target country's commitment and the effectiveness of the national administration of the MDG program and its successor should be a standard feature of periodic evaluations.

Development and security

During the first half century of the life of the UN, economic and social development was a dominant theme. Latterly fears about security, both national and international, are at the forefront of people's minds worldwide and high on the priority agenda of governments. Concerns about military and defense security are, of course, as old as the hills but we are now facing a new situation that distracts attention from the problem of poverty. We have reached a point of standoff between "development first" and "security first." With recent terrorist attacks, the wars in Iraq and Afghanistan and global recession, the balance has come down very sharply on the side of security, increasing still further the perennial huge difference between military spending and resources for development. Recession and the concomitant drastic decline in the standard of living in donor countries foster popular opposition to taxpayers' money being spent to assist developing countries. Politicians having to make swingeing cuts in budget expenditures find themselves facing a difficult dilemma. The people opposing development aid are voters and in democracies there is always an election just around the corner. It is much easier to cut development expenditure than that on defense and military hardware.

Superficially such arguments contain a logic that is hard to refute, but a little reflection shows that they are based on shortsighted thinking and in the long run will do more harm than good. They are at variance with the growing realization that human security in its broadest sense is as important as the traditional concept defined in purely military and defense terms. A world in which a billion people struggle to survive on less than US$1 a day cannot be a peaceful one. The causes of most of the conflicts that the UN strives to resolve today are rooted in poverty, marginalization and exclusion from access to resources and to the levers of power and government. This is hardly a new phenomenon—it was, for example, lack of bread for the starving masses that sparked the French Revolution. The UN High Level Panel on Threats, Challenges and Change, reporting in 2004, said "Development and security are inextricably linked." Dealing with conflicts once they have erupted is much more expensive and difficult than investing in measures for improving living standards and so preventing them in the first place.

Severe economic hardship is also a major cause of modern massmigration from poor developing countries to developed countries. This brings in its wake political and social upheavals that could also have been avoided by timely measures to provide incentives for potential migrants to stay at home, where they would probably prefer to remain anyway if living conditions were not so intolerable.

The immense flow of immigration nowadays, the negative public reaction to it in the receiving country, combined with the need to observe international human rights, constitutes one of the most difficult dilemmas confronting politicians in the developed world.

There is therefore a need for much greater understanding on the part of governments of developed countries and the general public, on whose political support they rely, that there is no dichotomy between development and security. Expenditure on reducing poverty and misery in developing countries is not simply a humanitarian act but an investment in security everywhere and so in the interests of all concerned, including the developed donor countries themselves.

The vertiginous expansion of international communications allows the media to play an inordinately influential role in the formulation of government policies. On the one hand, it all too often exercises a negative impact on public perceptions and policies in developed countries by highlighting nightmare scenarios. On the other, these same incredibly rapid communications mean that everyone in developing countries, except in the very remotest corners of the world, can see "how the other half lives," and make comparisons that generate discontent with their lot and with their own government in particular.

There is a crying need through public relations campaigns and other appropriate means, to bring home to governments and to the public, especially in the developed countries, that assistance towards promoting international development, and reducing poverty worldwide, as envisaged in the MDGs, is not just a charitable act or an unwarranted burden on the taxpayer in difficult financial times, but an invaluable and ultimately self-interested investment in the security of people everywhere. Development and security go hand in hand.

Inequality

One of the greatest—perhaps the greatest—threat to world peace and security is the rapidly growing gap between the rich and the poor, both within countries, whether developed or developing, and between countries, the so-called North/South divide. This is also a brake on genuine development in its broadest sense and, unless it is addressed, neither poverty reduction nor the fundamental objectives of the MDGs or any successor program, can be achieved. Yet this problem of inequality and the maldistribution of income, once a major topic in development economics, has received scant attention in recent decades. The Millennium Declaration paid passing lip service to it, stating that "the persistence of income inequality is also troubling," but did not support this vague affirmation with any specific policies or targets. This is an omission that must be addressed by requiring that measures to reduce inequality are included in receiving countries' development strategies and national plans, and that progress towards narrowing the gap between rich and poor becomes a standard yardstick to be evaluated in regular monitoring exercises.

The Johannesburg Statement urges that consultations undertaken in the process of adopting a new set of GDGs should pay particular consideration to "the need to reduce inequalities between individuals and groups within and among countries." It is essential for the proposed summit in 2015 to give prominence to this key theme, not only in the discussions at the conference itself but even more importantly in the resulting program of action and in the monitoring mechanisms set up to ensure its effective implementation.

Conclusion

There have been many milestones along the road to worldwide economic and social development, the latest being the MDGs that member states adopted by consensus in 2000, and which are meant to achieve their aims in 2015. There has been progress on a number of fronts and this should not be ignored, but it is increasingly evident that there is still a very long and difficult road ahead before there can be any hope of achieving for everyone in the world the "better standards of life in larger freedom" so nobly envisaged in the Preamble to the UN Charter. Once again, the current goals foreseen in the MDGs, admittedly limited in their scope, will only be partially reached. There are many reasons for this but the main constant obstacle at every turn over the last 66 years has been the lack of genuine political will and commitment on the part of individual member states. At the present time the situation is almost worse, with national sovereignty, despite its declining practical relevance in an increasingly globalized world, and narrow national interests (often misperceived) taking precedence over the international solidarity that is now needed more than ever.

Regrettably, any new program projected to go on after 2015, however excellently elaborated, runs a severe risk of suffering the same fate as its predecessors unless the attitudes and policies of all member states are completely transformed. This is an extremely tall order. Yet the recent dramatic upsurge in mass uprisings, protesting against unacceptable living conditions and perceived social injustice in so many different regions of the world, both developed and developing, should give pause for thought. We can no longer go on complacently targeting milestones

that we never quite manage to reach. There should be a general realization by peoples and governments everywhere that the road we have
pursued so far no longer stretches straight ahead. We have reached a
crucial crossroads. The proposed summit in 2015 gives a unique opportunity to chart a new path. What is done or not done then and afterwards
will have far-reaching and portentous consequences for humanity.

2 Recapturing the narrative of international development

Sakiko Fukuda-Parr

Though it is difficult to assess whether the Millennium Development Goals (MDGs) have contributed to poverty trends across the world,[1] their impact on the discourse of international development has been powerful. By articulating the complex challenges of development in eight goals and concrete 2015 targets, the MDGs have had unprecedented success in drawing attention to poverty as an urgent global priority. The emphasis on poverty is a cause for celebration, yet this has not been without consequence for other important priorities, and has influenced how the problems of development and solutions to them are understood or communicated. The MDGs have created a new narrative of international development centered on global poverty as a compelling moral concern for the world at large. This narrative convincingly appeals to rich country "publics and parliaments" as well as new global philanthropists. However, the simplification of development into eight goals has reduced the development agenda to meeting basic needs, stripped of the Millennium Declaration's (MD) vision for development with social justice and human rights. It has left out any mention of equity, empowerment of people, and building sustainable productive capacity for economic growth. The simplified narrative has no room for an understanding of poverty as related to the underlying power relations within and between countries and the asymmetries in the global economy. It leaves no room to draw attention to the issues that have long been and remain on the agenda of developing countries and in international economic negotiations, such as the lack of voice in the World Bank, World Trade Organization (WTO) and other institutions of global governance. Similarly, it remains silent on the issues that have long been and remain on the agenda of critics of standard macroeconomic frameworks for their distributional consequences.

Narratives are powerful in communicating ideas that in turn shape policy agendas. Goals play an essential role in transforming a complex and intangible concept—development—into tangible and concrete objectives that help communicate the concept. In the process, goals transform the concept into a narrative that can be used to argue for policy, such as to justify development aid. The choice of goals thus helps define the narrative. As 2015 draws near, global development goals should be renewed but also redesigned to recapture the development narrative as the pursuit of development as articulated in the 2000 MD through inclusive globalization, which could be expressed as "human development",[2] or as "sustainable, equitable and human rights-based development."[3] This chapter highlights the 10 most pressing issues to be considered in this redesign, and proposes directions for a new set of global goals. First, though, I start with an explanation of why the MDGs must be understood as a narrative—rather than a development strategy—and why recapturing that narrative is important.

The MDGs: a narrative of international development, not a national development strategy

MDGs as the overarching objective

The MDGs have driven a consensus on ending poverty as the overarching goal of international development.[4] The MDGs have become the legitimized framework for defining what this means, accepted by national governments, bilateral and multilateral donor agencies, international development non-governmental organizations (NGOs), national civil society groups, regardless of views that any of these actors might hold individually about their relevance. The MDGs have become the reference point around which international debates about development revolve, in both professional and public forums. The success of development efforts is judged by whether the 2015 goals are being met. Since they were introduced in 2001, the UN, the World Bank and numerous other international bodies have monitored MDG implementation and issued annual reports with detailed data. International Monetary Fund (IMF) staff country reports such as appraisal of financing under the Poverty Reduction and Growth Facility (PRGF) systematically include the prospects for achieving the MDGs along with key macroeconomic performance indicators. UN meetings to review progress in achieving the MDGs have become both frequent and high profile political events that are significant for countries' prestige and international standing. Political leaders make speeches defending policy initiatives with the warning: "without such and such action the MDGs will not be achieved." Economists write research papers on macroeconomic policy choices and evaluate them against their contribution to achieving the MDGs. Local NGOs advocate national budget reforms "to achieve the MDGs," even though they may be highly critical of these goals, because they are the accepted standard to evaluate policy. Media reports on poverty refer to failing to achieve the MDGs to demonstrate the pervasiveness of abject poverty. In other words, the MDGs have become a convenient shorthand to define what they mean by the purpose of development and of ending poverty.

The MDG narrative meets the criteria of a norm that has become well established according to the trajectory of international norm dynamics elaborated by Finnemore and Sikkink.[5] Norms emerge, then cascade, and then reach the final stage of becoming "institutionalized."[6] At this stage, norms take on "a taken-for-granted quality and are no longer a matter of broad public debate."[7] The mechanisms that keep the norms alive at this stage are "habit" and "institutionalization." The main actors are the professions and bureaucracy who uphold and adhere to the norm in order to conform to a recognized standard. In contrast, it is the idealistically committed "norm entrepreneurs" who drive the emergence of a norm, and states and organizations that promote its "cascade."

Policy approaches

Emerging after two decades of acrimonious contestation over the Washington Consensus policies that divided the international development community during the 1980s and 1990s, the consensus on poverty might signal a shift in policy prescriptions of the World Bank, IMF and the donor community in their dialogues with aid recipients. The MDGs might be interpreted as the embrace of what Simon Maxwell termed in the debates of that time, the "New 'New Poverty Agenda',"[8] departing from the conditionality-driven Washington consensus policies of the 1980s to a people-centered human development agenda that gained momentum in the 1990s, especially through the series of UN development conferences.[9]

Yet, the MDG-led development decade has not seen the emergence of new thinking about poverty reduction strategies. Furthermore, during this decade, while many bold commitments were made, such as for doubling of development aid to Africa at the Gleneagles Summit in 2005, they have largely not been implemented and no significant international poverty initiatives were launched. As the title of the UN MDG Gap Task Force 2011 report, "The Global Partnership for Development: Time to Deliver," makes clear, donor countries have fallen far short of implementing their Goal 8 targets for aid, trade, debt and technology.[10] The only tangible progress made so far has been in reducing the debt burden of the poorest countries. Multilateral trade talks—the Doha Development Agenda, labeled the "development round"—have become deadlocked, largely over differences between developing and developed country positions on agricultural subsidies in the developed countries.[11] After an initial upturn at the beginning of the decade, aid commitments reached a plateau and are expected to decline again from 2009 in the context of the global financial crisis and economic recession.[12] Thus, while the MDGs have forged a new consensus on poverty as the overarching objective of development, they did not drive major changes in the means to achieve them. It was possible to achieve a consensus on the MDGs precisely because no one would disagree with the moral imperative of ending abject poverty, even if they did not agree on the means to achieve that objective.

Elsewhere,[13] I have explained how this happened by analyzing the origins of the MDGs. To summarize, they emerged as a means to create a united community to defend international development as a global project, particularly development aid. Throughout the 1980s and 1990s the controversies over the Washington Consensus not only pitted the NGOs and academics against the World Bank and IMF, but UN agencies such as UNICEF (the UN Children's Fund) as well as some stakeholders within national governments were advocating alternatives.[14] The MDGs provided a narrative that could unify this divided community. It was important, particularly for the UN leadership and development ministers of major bilateral donors, to put an end to these controversies because they faced declining public support for international development. With the end of the Cold War, geopolitical interests no longer sustained support for aid budgets. The poverty narrative was a convincing rationale to win over the parliaments and publics.

These motivations led bilateral donors to adopt the International Development Goals (IDGs), the list of six quantitative goals with timeframes for achievement, in three areas: economic wellbeing, social development, and environmental sustainability and regeneration.[15] These goals had been effective in articulating the meaning of international cooperation for development and had gained traction in raising awareness in the donor countries. They were a concrete articulation of a consensus donor vision of development published in the 1996 statement of the Development Assistance Committee (DAC) of the Organisation for Economic Co-operation and Development (OECD), entitled "Shaping the 21st Century: The Contribution of Development Cooperation." The DAC gave three reasons why rich countries should support development:

(i) the humanitarian purpose of ending dire dehumanizing poverty; (ii) enlightened self-interest in a world free of threats of terrorism, global disease, political instability, and uncontrolled migration; and (iii) solidarity for joint action to solve common challenges such as environmental sustainability.

Ending poverty was a narrative that could both unify the community and energize support,[16] but the IDGs could not be "owned" by all stakeholders since they were invented by the bilateral donors. The MDGs built on the IDGs to build a broader consensus including the Bretton Woods institutions, UN agencies and national governments. The MDGs could build a narrative behind which dissenting stakeholders could stand united and argue for development aid. The success of the MDGs can be attributed precisely to the fact that they allowed the protagonists in the 1980s and 1990s debates over structural adjustment—IMF, World Bank, US Treasury, UNICEF, NGO networks, and academics on both sides of the issue—to agree on the purpose of development while disagreeing on the means. It allowed bilateral development ministers who needed to support, and were supported by, all of these dissenting stakeholders to get out of the dilemma.

In the aftermath of the controversies over the Washington Consensus policies that led even its proponents to declare the consensus "dead,"[17] one clear direction on which there was considerable consensus was on the importance of the social dimensions of development, and the need to reduce absolute poverty. The MDGs provided a new consensus, not on strategy, but as an "overarching framework" for international development. The MDGs defined the ends, but not the means, and thus provided a powerful storyline to communicate to the general public and politicians in donor countries the urgency of providing assistance to end abject poverty. That said, Washington Consensus policies did not disappear. Rather, they continued as a part of a broader agenda, behind the headline of the MDGs.

It is therefore not surprising that the last decade has seen little in the way of new proposals by the World Bank and on new policy strategies to foster economic growth combined with social justice that addresses poverty, inequality and the fulfillment of human rights. For sure, important studies have been published and there have been many departures from the structural adjustment programs of the 1980s. Social investments and protection including initiatives such as conditional cash transfers have emerged as important priorities, but the orthodoxies behind those approaches—namely the pursuit of macroeconomic stability as a key objective and the liberalization of the economy as a leading strategy—have endured. At the same time, some of the countries most successful in reducing poverty and inequality, such as China and Brazil, have pursued policies outside that framework.

Aid architecture: new narrative, new instruments, old policies

The MDGs are a key feature of the narrative of development aid and the new aid architecture that was put in place in the late 1990s. The MDGs define poverty reduction as the objective of development and provide a justification for development cooperation on humanitarian grounds. The consensus over the MDGs also forms a basis for a relationship defined as *partnership* between donors and recipients. The partnership can be constructed on the basis of a shared vision of a world without poverty, to be pursued within the MDG framework, with a strategy defined in national Poverty Reduction Strategy Papers (PRSPs) that would be prepared by national governments through a participative process. The partnership is to be guided by principles of mutual accountability and respect for national ownership. Donor support would be provided to implement the PRSPs through the IMF's new PRGF, along with other multilateral and bilateral support and debt relief under the Highly Indebted Poor Country (HIPC) debt reduction initiative.

These instruments, introduced towards the end of the 1990s, retained the core policy elements of the instruments that they replaced. The PRSPs and the PRGF replaced the Policy Framework Papers to spell out policy reform agendas. These policy reforms conditioned release of financing under HIPC and PRGFs that replaced structural adjustment loans. The DAC's Paris Declaration principles of ownership and mutual accountability would guide partnerships between donors and developing country governments, but the underlying economic/development strategies remained macroeconomic stabilization and economic liberalization. To this the MDGs added a basic needs agenda, emphasizing priorities for social investments and commitments for partnership.

The MDG narrative and the definition of poverty and development

It is important to note that the MDGs were not politically agreed as the consensus objectives of development. The MDGs derived from the MD, adopted at the Millennium Summit in 2000, in which world leaders identified poverty and development, along with peace and security, democracy and human rights, as the common objectives of the twenty-first century. The MD, like other UN declarations, serves as a statement of broad objectives and principles that should guide the world community.

It is therefore a normative statement, rather than a blueprint for action. The MDGs were introduced in the Secretary-General's implementation plan for the MD, the "Road Map," in 2001.[18] The MDGs were thus intended to be benchmarks for monitoring implementation of the Declaration's development and poverty objectives.

The process of translating an objective that is broad, normative, and multi-faceted into a set of quantitative indicators is a treacherous one. The MDGs are powerful in communicating a vision because they express in clear and concrete terms what is meant by ending poverty. They are powerful in communicating serious intent because they use time-bound numeric goals. In the process, they inevitably reduce a complex social and human condition—poverty—into a simplified set of numeric indicators.

The essence of the MD is a renewed commitment to the universal values of freedom, equality, solidarity, tolerance, respect for nature, and shared responsibility, which are the central values of the UN Charter and of universal human rights. However, such values are intrinsically difficult to translate into numbers and are in fact absent from the MDGs. The fine wording of the Declaration and its statement of ethical principles, commitment to the right to development and empowerment are overshadowed by the MDG goals of halving the proportion of people living on less than US$1 a day, and cutting maternal and child mortality. As Ashwani Saith aptly put it, the process can be described as losing universal values in the translation to MDGs.[19]

The translation was a process of simplification and reification. The quantitative goals of the Declaration made concrete vague and intangible commitments: "We will spare no effort to free our fellow men, women and children from the abject and dehumanizing conditions of extreme poverty, to which more than a billion of them are currently subjected."[20] The UN Secretary-General and his advisors believed that numeric goals would be a way to strengthen the Declaration as a memorable and historic document that would have significant public impact.[21] For this purpose, simplification was an imperative, since "less is more." Thus the goal was to limit the number of goals to just a few that could be easily memorized and recited.[22] The MDG drafters fought the pressure and temptation to be comprehensive and include all the important dimensions of development and poverty in its outcomes, process, and causes. The goals needed to be "memorable" and powerful in communicating the message to the general public and in broad aggregate policy debates.

The MD is a statement of a "human rights-based" vision of development as both an end and a process. It conceptualizes poverty as a dehumanizing human condition, in the human rights and capabilities perspectives rather than in the utilitarian perspective of material deprivation. The central concerns are with poverty as an affront to human freedom and dignity. The Declaration commits to the realization of the right to development and to the principles of freedom, equality, solidarity, tolerance, respect for nature, and shared responsibility. It thus reflects a human rights perspective on poverty as a problem that imposes obligations on states and the international community to put in place adequate social arrangements to work towards its elimination.

The MDGs are an important advance on the purely money-centric definition of poverty and accommodate some of the multidimensional human perspectives on poverty. Their widespread adoption as a norm signifies a consensus on poverty as broader than income poverty, as a human condition, and as multidimensional. Nonetheless, the MDGs transform the meaning of poverty as an affront to human dignity in the human rights and capabilities perspective, rob it of the essential concerns with human agency and ethical demands on social institutions, and reconfigure the concept to a set of numerical and essentially *material* wants in a utilitarian perspective. It represents poverty as multi-dimensional *material* deprivation—lack of income, water, education and health services—that is stripped of the ethical commitments and human agency that are essential elements of the human rights and capabilities perspectives. In short, the MDGs define combating poverty simply as meeting certain basic—material—needs.

The power of numbers and redefining development

Thus the MDGs introduced a powerful new, easily digestible, narrative of development, design to appeal to "publics and parliaments" in rich countries. As the literature on the sociology of numbers explains,[23] numbers are used by authorities to organize and communicate social priorities and create incentives. The deployment of numbers in this way is a powerful mechanism of social communication. It has the capacity to simplify complex concepts (such as poverty), and render intangible objectives concrete (such as expressing poverty as living on less than $1 a day). This is what makes numbers such powerful tools; however, in the process they can reinterpret and redefine complex and intangible concepts. By reducing the complex challenges of development to a list of eight goals, the MDGs speak directly to the conditions of human life deemed morally unacceptable. In the process, the MDGs have come to be substituted for the complex concept of poverty, and redefined the very meaning of development and created a discourse of development as poverty reduction. However, this simplification has reduced development to poverty reduction, leaving out the notion of development itself.

Development can be defined in many ways but the concept is much more than the removal of abject poverty. As Margaret Anstee's contribution to this volume shows, the idea emerged in the late 1940s as a project of the international community in the context of the post-war de-colonization process, aimed at bringing economic independence to newly independent states. It has been understood as a process of national transformation that enhances the capacity of economies to grow, and societies to expand the opportunities that people have.[24] In concrete terms, the MDGs limit the scope of "development" to ending human poverty, encompassing essential basic needs, leaving out essential dimensions of a broader conception of development, either as economic transformation, or as the enlargement of people's choices. It also leaves out agendas for people's empowerment, justice and rights, the structural transformation of economies, and the asymmetries of global economic arrangements. Charles Gore makes similar points in arguing that developing countries made a "Faustian bargain" in the MDG compact with the donors, accepting the commitment to ending poverty but giving up the idea of national development.[25]

The policy implications of the MDG narrative are to give priority to basic social services and social protection, or a simplified form of the "basic needs" agenda. There can be nothing objectionable in this agenda except its narrow breadth. It ignores the new understanding of poverty that developed over the 1990s as a human, lived experience, and the causes of poverty as embedded in social and political structures. There was a considerable rethinking about poverty in terms of the concept, its measurement, causes and strategies. Drawing on this new thinking, the World Bank's *World Development Report* of 2000 concluded that a fundamental cause of poverty was that individuals lacked power. It prescribed empowerment, security and opportunity as the three pillars of a poverty reduction strategy. The MDG-led basic needs agenda does not reflect these lessons and echoes the earlier agenda of the 1980 *World Development Report*, which prescribed growth and social investment as the core elements of a strategy.[26]

Ten critical issues

Should the MDGs continue after 2015? There is no doubt that the MDGs have had an important positive impact on raising public awareness and solidarity about poverty. They have also shown the value of a common

framework and reference for debate amongst the thousands of stakeholders in the international community. The language of goals—time-
bound, quantitative targets—has been powerful for these purposes as
well as in providing the means to monitor progress and assess the
magnitude of challenges.

The new goals should correct the distortions in the definition of development introduced by the MDGs and recapture the normative vision
of the MD. The redesign should aim to shape a narrative of development
as more than meeting basic needs to encompass a broader agenda of
pro-poor growth and human development. To do this, a new set of goals
should by necessity address the following:

1 Inequality within countries

The MDGs do not address inequality within countries. Only one of the
eight goals deals with relative disparities and this is related to disparities between men and women. A defining trend since 1980 has been
the growing income inequality within countries in both poor and rich
countries, though this trend has been reversed in Latin America since
2000.[27] The MDGs are intended to be a select set of the "Internationally
Agreed Targets" that include all the goals agreed in the UN development
conferences of the 1990s.[28] A number of them addressed inequality, marginalization and the most vulnerable. They were not, however, incorporated
in the MDGs.

Reducing inequality merits a place as an important goal in itself (see
Frances Stewart's contribution to this volume, Chapter 9). It has intrinsic
importance on ethical grounds. It is a factor that can be an obstacle to
growth and human development. The goal could be monitored since
indicators and data are available for a large number of countries, such
as income distribution (shares of gross domestic product (GDP) by income
quintiles; Gini coefficient), and rural-urban disparities in income and
human outcomes, as well as access to social infrastructure.[29]

2 Pro-poor growth and employment

The MDGs do not include employment as a goal; some indicators
were added in 2005 to respond to this omission. MDG-led discourse
has also neglected growth and wider development strategies. While the
1990s was a period of active debate about economic strategies, with
controversies over diverse macroeconomic strategies such as trade liberalization, capital account liberalization, and investment policies, among
others, there has been less debate about macroeconomic strategies since

the post-2000 era of MDG-led development discourse. The MDG discourse has emphasized social investments and social protection. These are important for education, health, water and sanitation. Employment and incomes, however, depend less on direct government investments than on growth and growth that is pro-poor, where the benefits of growth accrue to the poorer populations. As already mentioned, increasing inequality has been part of the consistent themes of the recent decades with the exception of some countries of Latin America. Analyses of these countries show interesting policy approaches that combine macroeconomic policies that aim at stability, labor market policies that improve incomes of the poor, as well as social protection measures such as the conditional cash transfer programs of Mexico and Brazil.

3 Democratic governance and people's participation

Much has been learned about the process of poverty eradication within countries over the last 50 years and a very rich literature of development economics and multi-disciplinary development studies has been created. Recent research on poverty has expanded beyond a focus on low incomes to the broader set of inter-related economic, social and political variables. An important conclusion of this rethinking has been that poor people remain poor because they lack a voice in decision-making; that is, they are powerless. Moreover, the multiple dimensions of poverty—lack of education, poor health, lack of resources and capital, lack of access to public infrastructure—all reinforce one another. Poverty reduction strategies require not only economic and social policies but also political empowerment.

4 Climate change

Over the decade since the MDGs were adopted, we have come to recognize the urgency of combating climate change to forestall deep consequences for humanity for generations to come. The impacts of climate change are likely to hit many of the poorer developing countries: rising sea levels are projected to lead to major land losses; rising temperatures are forecast to lead to losses in agricultural productivity, particularly in sub-Saharan Africa. This, in turn, will lead to higher food prices. Between 2000 and 2006 climate disasters are estimated to have affected some 262 million people annually, over 98 percent in the developing world.[30] Moreover, the consequences will be particularly severe for people living already precarious lives who have fewer resources to manage risks and limit losses. Action to mitigate the setbacks to human development progress, to rethink growth and development trajectories to one that is sustainable, is not only urgent, it requires international cooperation around a consensus set of priorities.

5 Global governance reforms

While developing countries have become increasingly assertive in global forums such as the WTO and the international financial institutions (IFIs), there has been no systematic reform of global institutions with the exception of the emergence of the G-20. There are a number of other areas of structural reforms in global governance that are needed to create a more democratic process. The recommendations of the Stiglitz commission on the global financial and economic architecture presented to the UN General Assembly in June 2009 should be pursued. Quantitative goals could be set for indicators such as voting shares in the Bretton Woods institutions.

6 Quality, not quantity of aid, and issues of aid dependence and more radical reforms

Aid is important for the MDGs because countries that are farthest from the goals are dependent on external resources for financing development. Many of the absolute poor live in South Asia and in some parts of Latin America, but many live in very poor countries of sub-Saharan Africa and other least developed countries which are highly aid dependent. Almost the entire capital investment budgets of these countries are financed by external aid. Aid dependence has nefarious effects: for example, it weakens states and the democratic accountability of governments to their people; it makes coordination of economic management complex; and it leads to unpredictability of resource flows. Budget aid can be an important step towards reducing the negative effects of aid dependence.

Many of the efforts to improve aid effectiveness in the last decade have focused on strengthening reporting to donors rather than to the people of the recipient country. This is understandable, but it does not help build democratic accountability among populations. Given the severe limitations on the administrative capacity of governments, investing in accounting to external donors has high opportunity costs. New forms of generating development finance aid that can be more consistent with developing a democratically accountable state are needed. Efforts to increase the proportion of budget aid would help. New sources of financing development—such as taxes on international financial transactions—also have potential.

7 New approaches to financing research and development for critical technological needs of poor people

One of the major challenges of globalization is to create incentives for technological innovation to meet the needs of poor people and to expand their access to existing technologies. Technology alone is never a single magic bullet for progress, but technological innovation can overcome the constraints of income and institutions to solve obstacles to improving human lives. It is hard to think of any major human progress of the last century that was made without an input of innovation. Investments in innovation are an urgent priority for today's most enduring problems of poverty. Medicines and treatments can save and prolong lives. Higher performing varieties of crops and farming methods can improve the productivity of small-scale farmers. Yet investment in agricultural research has been on the decline for the last two decades.[31] Clean energy sources for over a billion people in the world who rely on biomass such as dung and crop residues as a fuel source are needed to address both environmental and health consequences, including the high rate of deaths related to respiratory diseases. Low-cost, solar powered computers adapted to the conditions and needs of isolated rural populations can break the barriers of information.

The critical obstacle to these needs is not science but policy initiatives to finance investments and broaden access in a world of strong global intellectual property protection. Intellectual property creates incentives for inventors but the needs of the poor do not translate into market demand and restrict access. For example, 90 percent of the investment in medical research and development is devoted to the disease burden of 10 percent of the world's population. Policy innovations require private partnerships. Many proposals—such as prizes to create incentives, and airline taxes to finance access—are being discussed and some are being piloted, but a large-scale system has yet to be implemented.

8 Clarifying the purpose—as monitoring benchmarks applicable at the global level

The MDGs originated from a normative process of defining what the world should look like as set out in the 2000 Declaration. They did not originate from a technocratic national planning process. As already explained, the MDGs were introduced as tools to monitor the implementation of the normative commitments to end poverty understood as a commitment to equality, solidarity and human rights. However, much of the debate about MDGs mistakes them as planning tools. Interpreted in this way, the MDGs have come under heavy criticism from all perspectives. Economists have shown numerous methodological weaknesses in the way that the targets were set. Clemens and his co-authors show that the levels are implausible for many countries in the light of historical experience.[32] Easterly argues that they are arbitrarily set without a consistent methodology.[33] Charles Gore and Ashwani Saith argue that the MDGs are misdirected and ignore the key issues of systemic reforms in the global economy and challenges of development and transformation (rather than poverty reduction).[34] Feminist Peggy Antrobus points out that they are blind to the political dimensions of poverty and dismisses them as a "major distracting gimmick."[35] Many NGOs in middle-income countries decry them as the "Minimum Development Goals" that set the agendas back in their countries because many of the goals have already been achieved there. The UN Office of the High Commissioner for Human Rights (OHCHR) argues that the MDGs set targets that are lower than standards of internal law, or do not reflect core principles and norms of equality, participation, non-discrimination, and transparency. UN agencies have also criticized the MDGs for leaving out too many pressing priorities and for not reflecting the full breadth of the agendas being pursued which were agreed at global conferences in their specific areas—such as health, education, and decent work.

9 Correct the metric for national performance monitoring— making progress

Interpreted as planning goals, the UN, World Bank and other international monitoring reports on MDGs assess progress by the criteria of whether the goals are likely to be achieved. This approach is helpful in showing how much has been accomplished and how much more needs to be done. However, when used as an accountability measure, and applied at the country level, this approach is biased against countries with low starting points. The MDGs set targets very high for many countries in relation to their historical record.[36] Easterly argues that the choices made in defining the targets build in a bias against Africa as a region, leading them to be dubbed (falsely) "failures."[37] Together with co-author Joshua Greenstein,[38] I have argued that the appropriate measure to monitor government performance on MDGs is the rate of progress made, not the level of achievement. Focus on the level of achievement leads to perverse results where countries that started at high levels of poverty and are making rapid progress are labeled "off track" and failures, and countries that started at low levels of poverty and are making very slow progress are labeled successes.

10 *Adapting targets to national contexts*

One of the most contentious issues in monitoring MDG progress is whether they should be applied globally only, regionally, or at the country level. While some argue that "adapting" the targets would lead to compromising the ambition of commitments made, others argue that it makes no sense to apply a single universal standard to countries with widely divergent conditions. In practice, some countries have adapted the targets. However, the official UN and World Bank monitoring reports assess progress, country by country, by applying the targets uniformly, and by the criterion of whether progress is on track to achieving the 2015 target.

The question is not addressed in the MD and the MDGs, leaving the issue open to interpretation. It is interesting to note that earlier global goals set by the UN were more explicit in the intention to set goals at the global level, while urging countries to set their own goals appropriate to their national conditions. Interpreting the MDGs as planning goals and assessing performance by whether the targets would be achieved is particularly erroneous when applied at the country level. Not only do they have very different starting points, but countries of the world face hugely diverse constraints and capacities, in financial, institutional and human dimensions. The MDGs need to be recast at the national level to set ambitious but realistic targets.

Conclusion: recapturing the narrative

To recapture the narrative of development as a process of national development and expansion of human dignity as envisioned in the MD, and give recognition to empowerment as a necessary priority, what might the new global goals look like? If the list were to be limited to 12 goals, it could include the following dimensions:

- economic growth and diversification;
- income poverty and employment;
- hunger;
- education;
- health, including child and maternal mortality, reproductive rights, global diseases;
- equality and removal of discrimination including gender equality;
- climate change and environmental sustainability;
- democratic participation and accountability in national governance;
- systemic reforms in global governance structures and regulation;
- greater participation of the least developed countries in global trade, investment, technology and migration;

- creating global public goods essential to human rights; and
- security in the public and private spheres.

The targets and indicators for each of these goals should systematically reflect the ethical commitments of equality, empowerment and solidarity. For example, indicators for climate change should draw attention to the effects of climate change on the most vulnerable people and countries, while indicators for hunger should draw attention to food security rather than aggregate availability of food. The systemic reforms in global governance would include an ambitious agenda including progress in creating arrangements to mobilize new forms of financing development and new forms of incentivizing investments in technology to meet the basic needs of poor people.

The MDG narrative as the overarching objective of international development emerged in part from the desire by the leadership to forge a consensus over and above the dissensions over development policy. However, basic questions persist about the deep structural causes of poverty and inequality that reside in the structures of global and national economies, and the impact of macroeconomic frameworks that are deepening inequalities. With a few national exceptions, the trend over the last decade has been to deepen inequalities within countries. While there is clearly a reordering of global economic and political power structures, the OECD countries remain in firm control of decision-making in the governance of international trade and finance.

The MDG decade has seen little in the way of proposals for new approaches to fostering economic growth combined with social justice that addresses not only poverty but also inequality and the fulfillment of human rights. Numbers transform complex social descriptions into abstract, simple, precise descriptions of the social world, but in the process reduce them and leave out many issues of importance. The MDGs are a strategy for describing what is meant by the MD's commitment to spare no effort to "free our fellow men, women and children from the abject and dehumanizing conditions of extreme poverty." In reducing this concept to quantitative goals, however, the MDGs not only shed meaning, they impose a particular interpretation on our understanding of poverty. A new set of quantitative goals is needed to reset the narrative of development as sustainable, equitable and human rights-based development.

Notes

1 As the United Nations (UN) and other monitoring reports document, important progress has been made across the goals since 2000, but the pace

has varied. At the global level the likelihood of the 2015 targets being met is mixed. Progress is "on track" to achieve the 2015 targets for income poverty, gender equality and access to clean water, while they are "off track" for maternal mortality. For schooling, nutrition and child mortality, progress is "off track," but less severely than for maternal mortality. More importantly, the pace of progress has not been hastened in most countries of the world for the 24 indicators for which data are available. See Sakiko Fukuda-Parr and Joshua Greenstein, "How should MDG Implementation be Measured: Faster Progress or Meeting Targets?" *Working Paper 63*, International Policy Centre for Inclusive Growth (2010), www.ipc-undp.org/pub/IPCWorkingPaper63.pdf.

2 By human development, I refer specifically to the concept as defined in UN Development Programme (UNDP) *Human Development Reports* based on the concept of capabilities articulated by Amartya Sen. Human development is a process of expanding choices and freedoms that people have to live lives they value. It incorporates expansion of capabilities in multiple dimensions and recognizes the importance of growth as a means, sustainability and equity between generations.

3 I owe this term to the discussions at the UNDP/Overseas Development Institute (ODI) workshop on MDGs held in Cairo, Egypt, on 26–27 October 2011.

4 Richard Black and Howard White, *Targeting Development: Critical Perspectives on the Millennium Development Goals* (London: Routledge, 2004).

5 Martha Finnemore and Kathryn Sikkink, "International Norm Dynamics and Political Change," *International Organization: International Organization at Fifty: Exploration and Contestation in the Study of World Politics* 52, no. 4 (1998): 887–917.

6 See Sakiko Fukuda-Parr and David Hulme, "International Norm Dynamics and 'the End of Poverty': Understanding the Millennium Development Goals (MDGs)," *Global Governance* 17, no. 1 (2011): 17–36, for a full elaboration of the spread of the poverty norm, applying the Finnemore-Sikkink model of international norm dynamics.

7 Finnemore and Sikkink, "International Norm Dynamics," 9.

8 Simon Maxwell, "Heaven or Hubris, Reflections on a New 'New Development Agenda'," *Development Policy Review* 21, no. 1 (2003): 5–25.

9 MDGs were not invented anew in the Millennium Declaration but are in fact a select set of goals set by UN conferences of the 1990s. They are a product of a process that opened up the UN to the energy of civil society actors from across the world, advocating an alternative policy agenda to the dominant policies of liberalization advanced as "Washington Consensus" and global market integration. They critiqued the distributional and human impact of liberalization policies and raised issues of poverty, inequality, human rights, and the asymmetries of global governance including issues of trade, debt, technology, finance, and developing country voice in decision-making. Much of this critique was part of new research that extended the analysis of poverty to relational and structural issues such as voice, accountability and empowerment, and reflected in the World Bank's 2000 *World Development Report*. The adoption of MDGs as consensus goals of development by the entire development community, embraced by the most powerful bilateral donors and Bretton Woods institutions, might be seen as victory, a culmination of the move to adopt a full-scale, human-centered development paradigm and a human development agenda.

10 United Nations, MDG Gap Task Force Report 2011, "Global Partnership: Time to Deliver," www.un.org/en/development/desa/policy/mdg_gap/index. shtml.

11 James Scott and Rorden Wilkinson, "The Poverty of the Doha Round and the Least Developed Countries," *Third World Quarterly* 32, no. 4 (2011): 611–27.

12 United Nations, MDG Gap Task Force Report 2011, "Global Partnership: Time to Deliver."

13 Fukuda-Parr and Hulme, "International Norm Dynamics."

14 UNICEF's critical analysis of the social consequences of adjustment, particularly through cuts in social spending, was one of the most powerful voices in these debates. See Andrea Cornia, Richard Jolly and Frances Stewart, eds., *Adjustment with a Human Face: Protecting the Vulnerable and Promoting Growth* (New York and Oxford: Oxford University Press, 1998).

15 OECD DAC, *Shaping the 21st Century: The Contribution of Development Co-operation* (Paris: OECD, 1996), 6.

16 For example, Lord Mark Malloch-Brown, who, as UNDP Administrator in 2000, played a central role in moving to build the Millennium Declaration into the MDGs and an implementation plan, recounts that the divide between the UN and the World Bank over structural adjustment controversies needed to be bridged (author's interview with Malloch-Brown, London, 27 June 2008).

17 For example, James Wolfensohn, President of the World Bank, observed: "the Washington Consensus has been dead for several years and has been replaced by all sorts of consensuses." Quoted in Simon Maxwell, "Washington Consensus is dead: long live the meta-narrative!" ODI Working Paper 243 (2005), www.odi.org.uk/resources/docs/2476.pdf.

18 *Road Map Towards the Implementation of the United Nations Millennium Declaration*, Report of the Secretary-General presented to the UN General Assembly, A/res/55/2.

19 Ashwani Saith, "From Universal Values to Millennium Development Goals: Lost in Translation," *Development and Change* 27, no. 6 (2006): 1167–99. For a comprehensive critique of MDGs from the human rights perspective, see OHCHR 2008, *Claiming the MDGs.*

20 United Nations Millennium Declaration, A/res/55/2. Resolution adopted by the General Assembly, New York.

21 Author's interviews with: John Ruggie, Cambridge, Mass., 6 August 2008; Malloch-Brown, London, 27 June 2008.

22 Author's interviews with: John Ruggie, Cambridge, Mass., 6 August 2008; Malloch-Brown, London, 27 June 2008.

23 See particularly: Sally Engle Merry, "Measuring the World: Indicators, Human Rights and Global Governance," *Current Anthropology* 52, no. 3 (April 2011): 83–94; Mary Poovey, *A History of the Modern Fact: Problems of Knowledge in the Sciences of Wealth and Society* (Chicago, IL: University of Chicago Press, 1998); Theodore M. Porter, *Trust in Numbers: The Pursuit of Objectivity in Science and Public Life* (Princeton: Princeton University Press, 1995).

24 See David Clarke, *The Elgar Companion to Development Studies* (Cheltenham, UK: Edward Elgar, 2006).

25 Charles Gore, "The MDG Paradigm, Productive Capacities and the Future of Poverty Reduction," *IDS Bulletin* 41, no. 1 (2010): 70–79.

26 The World Bank's *World Development Report* decadal issues on poverty can be considered indicative of the latest thinking of the day in the mainstream international community.

27 Giovanni Andrea Cornia, "Economic Integration, Inequality and Growth: Latin America vs. the European economies in transition," DESA Working Paper No. 101 ST/ESA/2011/DWP/101, January 2011.

28 UN Department of Economic and Social Affairs, *The United Nations Development Agenda: Development for All* (New York: United Nations, 2007).

29 Sakiko Fukuda-Parr, "Reducing Inequality—The Missing MDG," *IDS Bulletin* 41, no. 1 (2010): 26–35, Falmer: Institute of Development Studies, University of Sussex.

30 UNDP, *Human Development Report 2007/2008* (Oxford: Oxford University Press, 2008), 16.

31 World Bank, *2008 World Development Report* (Washington, DC, 2008).

32 Michael Clemens, Charles Kerry and Todd Moss, "The Trouble with the MDGs: Confronting Expectations of Aid and Development Success," *World Development* 35, no. 5 (2007): 735–51.

33 William Easterly, "How the Millennium Development Goals are Unfair to Africa," *World Development* 37, no. 1 (2009): 26–35.

34 Charles Gore, "The MDG Paradigm, Productive Capacities and the Future of Poverty Reduction," *IDS Bulletin* 41, no. 1 (2010): 70–79; Ashwani Saith, "From Universal Values to Millennium Development Goals": 1167–99.

35 Peggy Antrobus, "Critiquing the MDGs from a Caribbean Perspective 1," *Gender and Development* 31, no. 1 (2005): 94–104.

36 Clemens *et al.*, "The Trouble with the MDGs."

37 Easterly, "How the Millennium Development Goals are Unfair to Africa."

38 Sakiko Fukuda-Parr and Joshua Greenstein, "How should MDG Implementation be Measured: Faster Progress or Meeting Targets?" *Working Paper 63*, International Policy Centre for Inclusive Growth, www.ipc-undp. org/pub/IPCWorkingPaper63.pdf.

3 From the Millennium to Global Development Goals

Ramesh Thakur

From 1000 AD to 1800 AD, Asia, Africa and Latin America—comprising today's developing countries—accounted for 65–75 percent of world population and income. China and India dominated the world economy and Turkey dominated the Islamic world. Europe surged to world dominance through the industrial, transport and communications revolutions, and the ideology and practice of colonialism. Nostalgic imperial revisionism about the spread of civilization notwithstanding, between 1870 and 1950 Asia's per capita income plummeted from one-half of Western European levels to one-tenth.[1] Developing countries have been bouncing back since 1950. As a consequence, a much-needed global rebalancing—economic, political, and even moral—is in train.

The normative thrust of this chapter is to promote social democracy and market economics in the developing countries for inclusive, representative and empowering governance with built-in accountability mechanisms. The basic political actor in today's world is the sovereign state. The prerequisite to enduring and sustainable order, stability, development and growth is an efficient, functioning and effective state. However, the state is both more legitimate and more effective in its elemental tasks when it is democratic, inclusive and organized on principles and structures of good governance. Many of these can be informed by international debate and best practice, but no system of governance will survive and thrive if it is a foreign import. Instead it must connect to, and build on, local traditions, belief systems and governance practices. At the same time isolation and disengagement from global norms is no more an option in today's world than is delinking from the global economy or rejecting globalization.

The primary purpose of the United Nations (UN) at inception in 1945 was the maintenance of international peace and security. With decolonization, the size and nature of UN membership changed dramatically. The urgent priority for the newer countries was to jumpstart national integration, state building and economic growth which had been fractured, stunted and distorted under colonial rule. The short-hand description for this, to be achieved with the help of an actively interventionist state, was development, which therefore became the second great normative agenda of the UN. The historic Millennium Declaration (MD) contained a balance between the security and development agendas. The latter were translated into measurable targets to be achieved by 2015 and adopted as the Millennium Development Goals (MDGs).

In this chapter I contextualize the MDGs within the debates on development studies and the importance of good governance before offering my analysis of the accomplishments and shortfalls of the MDGs. This then serves as the springboard to recommendations for the vision and terms of a replacement set of Global Development Goals (GDGs) after 2015. Compared to the MDGs, I argue, the GDGs should rebalance state empowerment and international assistance to prioritize the former in order to highlight national ownership of the process and national responsibility for the outcome.

Development

Among developing regions, the primary focus of this chapter—as indeed of this book—is on Africa, for the simple reason that on most measures, African countries are disproportionately clustered in the group of developing countries. Their dire plight, even in comparison to other developing countries of Asia, is graphically captured in Tables 3.1 to 3.6.

The examples of Asian successes notwithstanding, with few exceptions African countries are still firmly anchored in the lagging group of developing economies. Whether we look at per capita income (Table 3.1), multidimensional poverty (Table 3.2), or human development (Table 3.3), African countries are a long way behind. The multidimensional indicators of poverty in South Asia, for example, are significantly worse than East Asia but considerably better than the truly shocking statistics from sub-Saharan Africa. India, Pakistan and Bangladesh are still a world removed from the likes of Guinea, Ethiopia, Central African Republic, Mali, Burkina Faso, Burundi, and Niger. Moreover, more than half the population in several African countries lives below the income poverty line of purchasing power parity (PPP) US$1.25 per day—in Tanzania, Rwanda, Guinea, and Liberia, the proportion living below the poverty line is 70 percent and higher. Even Afghanistan—a conflict-ridden state and at the bottom of the index in Asia—has a Human Development Index (HDI) value of 0.349, compared to 0.140 for Zimbabwe.

Table 3.1 State capacity, selected Asian and African countries (2008)

	GNI/c (PPP US$)	Tax (% of GDP)	FDI (% of GDP)	ODA (% of GNI)	Remittances (% of GDP)
Asia					
Afghanistan	1,419	5.8	2.8	45.8	–
Bangladesh	1,587	8.8	1.2	2.4	11.3
Cambodia	1,868	8.2	7.9	8.1	3.1
China	7,258	9.4	3.4	0	1.1
India	3,337	12.9	3.6	0.2	4.3
Indonesia	3,957	12.3	1.8	0.2	1.3
Korea, South	29,518	16.6	0.2	–	0.3
Laos	2,321	10.1	4.1	10	0
Malaysia	13,927	16.6	3.3	0.1	0.9
Mongolia	3,619	23.2	13	4.8	3.8
Myanmar	1,596	3.3	–	–	–
Nepal	1,201	10.4	0	5.6	21.6
Pakistan	2,678	9.8	3.3	0.9	4.3
Philippines	4,002	14.1	0.8	0	11.2
Sri Lanka	4,886	14.2	1.9	1.8	2.3
Thailand	8,001	16.5	3.6	0.3	0.7
Vietnam	2,995	–	10.6	2.9	7
Africa					
Angola	4,941	–	2	0.5	0.1
Burundi	402	–	0.3	43.9	0.3
Congo, Democratic Repub.	291	6.3	8.6	15.6	–
Ethiopia	992	10.2	0.4	12.5	1.5
Ghana	1,385	22.9	12.7	8.1	0.8
Guinea	953	–	10.1	7.6	1.9
Kenya	1,628	18.9	0.3	4	5.6
Liberia	320	–	17.1	185	6.9
Mali	1,171	15.6	1.5	11.4	3.9
Niger	675	11.5	2.7	11.3	1.5
Nigeria	2,156	–	1.8	0.7	4.8
Rwanda	1,190	–	2.3	21.1	1.5
Senegal	1,816	16.1	5.3	8.1	9.7
Sierra Leone	809	10.8	−0.2	19.2	7.7
South Africa	9,812	27.7	3.7	0.4	0.3
Tanzania	1,344	–	3.6	11.7	0.1
Uganda	1,224	12.8	5.5	11.7	5.1
Zimbabwe	176	–	3	–	–

Source: (UNDP, *Human Development Report 2010—The Real Wealth of Nations: Pathways to Human Development* (New York: Palgrave Macmillan, 2010), tables 1 and 15, 143–47, 202–05)

The UN has recognized the distinctive weaknesses, vulnerabilities and development challenges of least developed countries (LDCs) since 1960. They satisfy three criteria: annual per capita income of less than US$905; impoverished human assets as measured by low levels of education, literacy, nutrition and health; and high economic vulnerability as measured by population size, agricultural, forestry and fishery dependency, export concentration and instability, and exposure to natural disasters. Of the 48 LDCs, 33 are in sub-Saharan Africa, 14 in Asia and one is in Latin America and the Caribbean.

The fact that in 2012 there should still be a total of 48 countries classified as least developed speaks graphically to the broken paradigms and unfulfilled promise of development. In the 1960s the dominant development paradigm was modernization theory, the key emphasis was on post-colonial development including economic growth and political order, and the main critique came from dependency theory. In the contemporary discourse, including the implicit philosophical underpinnings of the MDGs, the dominant paradigm has been the liberal peace enterprise, the key emphasis is on post-conflict stabilization and reconstruction through "nation-building," and the main critique comes from critical theory.

The origins of the concepts and discourse of development studies are rooted in the historical encounter between the European and non-European. The abundance of terms to refer essentially to the same group of countries reflected dissatisfactions with each: backward, developing, undeveloped, underdeveloped, less developed, under-developing, Third World, southern, low income, traditional. In these days of political correctness, perhaps we should call them "the economically challenged" or "the industrially embarrassed."

To be sure, there are important shared characteristics in many developing countries: poverty; small, subsistence, agrarian economies dependent on a narrow range of products in international exchanges, often just one or two cash crops like coffee, cotton, rubber or sugar; low levels of life expectancy and literacy; and simplified political and bureaucratic structures. Despite superficial similarities, variations among developing countries are just as significant as among developed ones, but globalization, industrialization and the penetration of technology into the farthest reaches of quotidian life are generating pressures towards social and institutional homogeneity.

For most developing countries at independence, the private sector had neither the money nor the expertise to finance industrial development on the desired scale and pace. Gunnar Myrdal famously described Asia as a continent trapped in unequal exchange with the West.[2]

Table 3.2 State priorities

	Public expenditures (% of GDP)				Perception of safety (%)
	Education	Health	Military		
	2000–07	2000–07	2008	Social: Military*	2006–09
Asia					
Afghanistan	–	1.8	1.9	–	37
Bangladesh	2.4	1.1	1.0	3.5	82
Cambodia	1.6	1.7	1.1	3.0	60
China	1.9	1.9	2.0	1.9	74
India	3.2	1.1	2.6	1.7	74
Indonesia	3.5	1.2	1.0	4.7	83
Korea, South	4.2	3.5	2.8	2.8	60
Laos	2.3	0.8	0.4	7.8	79
Malaysia	4.5	1.9	2.0	3.2	49
Mongolia	5.1	3.5	–	–	40
Myanmar	1.3	0.2	–	–	81
Nepal	3.8	2.0	2.0	2.9	43
Pakistan	2.9	0.8	2.6	1.4	44
Philippines	2.6	1.3	0.8	4.9	66
Sri Lanka	–	2.0	3.6	–	72
Thailand	4.9	2.7	1.5	5.1	65
Vietnam	5.3	2.8	2.4	3.4	80
Africa					
Angola	2.6	2.0	3.0	1.9	53
Burundi	7.2	5.2	4.0	3.1	63
Congo, Democratic Repub.	–	1.2	1.4	–	47
Ethiopia	5.5	2.2	1.4	5.5	49
Ghana	5.4	4.3	0.7	13.9	69
Guinea	1.7	0.6	–	–	48
Kenya	7.0	2.0	1.9	4.7	35
Liberia	2.7	2.8	0.6	9.2	34
Mali	3.8	2.9	1.9	3.5	77
Niger	3.7	2.8	–	–	73
Nigeria	–	1.7	0.8	–	51
Rwanda	4.1	4.9	1.5	6.0	80
Senegal	5.1	3.2	1.6	5.2	63
Sierra Leone	3.8	1.4	2.4	2.2	53
South Africa	5.1	3.6	1.3	6.8	20
Tanzania	6.8	3.5	1.1	9.4	46
Uganda	3.8	1.6	2.3	2.3	51
Zimbabwe	4.6	4.1	–	–	41

Source: (UNDP, *Human Development Report 2010—The Real Wealth of Nations: Pathways to Human Development* (New York: Palgrave Macmillan, 2010), tables 10 and 15, 180–83, 202–05)
Note: * (Education + Health) divided by (Military)

Table 3.3 Human Development Index, 1980–2010

	Value				Average annual growth	Rank
	1980	1990	2000	2010	1980–2010 (%)	2010
Asia						
Afghanistan	–	–	–	0.349	–	155
Bangladesh	0.259	0.313	0.39	0.469	1.99	129
Cambodia	–	–	0.412	0.494	–	124
China	0.368	0.46	0.567	0.663	1.96	89
India	0.32	0.389	0.44	0.519	1.61	119
Indonesia	0.39	0.458	0.5	0.6	1.43	108
Korea, South	0.616	0.725	0.815	0.877	1.18	12
Laos	–	0.354	0.425	0.497	–	122
Malaysia	0.541	0.616	0.691	0.744	1.06	57
Mongolia	–	–	–	–	–	–
Myanmar	–	–	–	–	–	–
Nepal	0.21	0.316	0.375	0.428	2.37	
Pakistan	0.311	0.359	0.416	0.49	1.52	125
Philippines	0.523	0.552	0.597	0.638	0.66	97
Sri Lanka	0.513	0.558	–	0.658	0.83	–
Thailand	0.483	0.546	0.6	0.654	1.01	92
Vietnam	–	0.402	0.505	0.572	–	113
Africa						
Angola	–	–	0.349	0.403	–	146
Burundi	0.181	0.236	0.223	0.282	1.47	166
Congo, Democratic Repub.	0.267	0.261	0.201	0.239	–0.37*	–
Ethiopia	–	–	0.25	0.328	–	157
Ghana	0.363	0.399	0.431	0.467	0.84	130
Guinea	–	–	–	0.34	–	156
Kenya	0.404	0.437	0.424	0.47	0.5	128
Liberia	0.295	–	0.294	0.3	0.005	162
Mali	0.165	0.187	0.245	0.309	2.1	160
Niger	0.166	0.18	0.212	0.261	1.51	–
Nigeria	–	–	–	0.423	–	142
Rwanda	0.249	0.215	0.277	0.385	1.45	152
Senegal	0.291	0.331	0.36	0.411	1.15	144
Sierra Leone	0.229	0.23	0.236	0.317	1.09	158
South Africa	–	0.601	–	0.597	–	110
Tanzania	–	0.329	0.332	0.398	–	148
Uganda	–	0.281	0.35	0.422	–	143
Zimbabwe	0.241	0.284	0.232	0.14	–1.81*	169
OECD	0.754	0.798	0.852	0.879	0.51	–

(Continued on next page)

Table 3.3 (continued)

	Value				Average annual growth	Rank
	1980	*1990*	*2000*	*2010*	*1980– 2010 (%)*	*2010*
East Asia and Pacific	0.383	0.46	0.559	0.643	1.73	–
South Asia	0.315	0.387	0.44	0.516	1.65	–
Sub-Saharan Africa	0.293	0.354	0.315	0.389	0.94	–
LDCs	0.251	0.292	0.325	0.386	1.44	–
World	0.455	0.526	0.57	0.624	1.05	–

Source: (UNDP, *Human Development Report 2010—The Real Wealth of Nations: Pathways to Human Development* (New York: Palgrave Macmillan, 2010), table 2, 148–51)
Note: * The two worst performers over the 30 years, 1980–2010.

One major strand of development theory held that the only solution for developing Asia was to adopt state-led and -directed industrial policies, Soviet-style planning, frontier protection for import-substitution policies, and infusions of foreign capital and expertise. The state would play the decisive role in the production and distribution of material goods. There was agreement on the desirability of rapid economic growth under a feasible rate of resource mobilization, on the need to improve infrastructure, and on industrial expansion and diversification. The framework for processing these goals into policy outputs was often an elaborate planning machinery with the concomitant concept of the state occupying the commanding heights of the economy.

The concept of aggregate growth, using such measures as gross domestic product (GDP), gross national product (GNP), or national income, dominated policy and scholarly debate in the initial years. As dissatisfaction grew with the assumptions and prescriptions of growth-through-modernization theory, analysts tried to think of alternative measures that would better capture the reality of social development. The most influential new measure was the human development index (HDI) constructed by the UN Development Programme (UNDP) in the early 1990s as a composite index of life expectancy, adult literacy and per capita income measured in PPP. The HDI acknowledged that GNP was a necessary but flawed measure of wellbeing, and its own composite index gave a snapshot of welfare as well as wealth.

The concept of human security[3] as an analogue to human development, both of which began to be promoted actively by the UN system from the mid-1990s, helped to soften the hard edges and harsh consequences of the World Bank's structural adjustment directives. Despite initial skepticism, UN alternatives to adjustment became increasingly accepted over the years, culminating in the broad notion of development in the MDGs.

Globalization

With the end of the Cold War, the neoclassical consensus returned to the idea that all economies can achieve growth and development with free markets and open trade and investment policies. Developing countries have been severely buffeted by the crosswinds of globalization and the resulting "end of geography" in a flat world. Globalization is both desirable and irreversible, having lifted standards of living throughout the world. However, the benefits and costs of linking and delinking are unequally distributed. Industrialized countries are mutually interdependent; developing countries are largely independent in their economic relations with one another but highly dependent on industrialized countries. Brazil, China and India are starting to change this equation.

The flow of capital is highly asymmetrical. Over the last two decades, overseas development assistance from the rich to the poor countries has totaled US$50–80 billion per annum. In the same period $500–800 billion of illegal funds were sent annually from poor to rich countries.[4] Thus for every dollar of aid money over the table, the West gets back 10 dollars under the table and, for good measure, lectures the rest on corruption. There has been a growing divergence in income levels between countries and peoples, with widening inequality among and within nations—in effect a redistribution of wealth from the poor to the rich. Assets and incomes are more concentrated. Wage shares have fallen, profit shares have risen, and capital mobility alongside labor immobility has reduced the bargaining power of organized labor (most workers simply do not have the option available to capital to move to other economic activities and legal-political jurisdictions that promise higher returns). Thus the benefits of growth do not trickle down to laborers in the workforce; costs and prices have globalized-cum-equalized (converged) rather more "efficiently" than incomes and employment.

The rapid growth of global markets has not seen the parallel development of social and economic institutions to ensure balanced, inclusive and sustainable growth. Labor rights have been less sedulously protected than capital and property rights, and global rules on trade and

Table 3.4 Inequality and deprivation

	Income gini coefficient (2000–2010)	Multidimensional poverty index (2000–08)*			Gender inequality	
		MDPI	Pop at MDP risk (%)	Pop <US$1.25 PPP per day (%)	Value	Rank
Asia						
Afghanistan	–	–	–	–	0.797	134
Bangladesh	31.0	0.291	21.2	49.6	0.734	116
Cambodia	44.2	0.263	20.2	25.8	0.672	95
China	41.5	0.056	6.3	15.9	0.405	38
India	36.8	0.296	16.1	41.6	0.748	122
Indonesia	37.6	0.095	12.2	29.4	0.68	100
Korea, South	31.6	–	–	–	0.31	20
Laos	32.6	0.267	14.1	44.0	0.65	88
Malaysia	37.9	–	–	–	0.493	50
Mongolia	36.6	0.065	20.7	2.2	0.523	57
Myanmar	–	0.088	17.6	–	–	–
Nepal	47.3	0.35	15.6	55.1	0.716	138
Pakistan	31.2	0.275	11.8	22.6	0.721	112
Philippines	44.0	0.067	11.1	22.6	0.623	78
Sri Lanka	41.1	0.021	14.4	14.0	0.599	72
Thailand	42.5	0.006	9.9	<2.0	0.586	69
Vietnam	37.8	0.075	12.0	21.5	0.53	58
Africa						
Angola	58.6	0.452	10.7	54.3	0.627	–
Burundi	33.3	0.53	12.2	81.3	–	79
Congo, Democratic Repub.	44.4	0.393	16.1	59.2	0.814	137

Table 3.4 (continued)

	Income gini coefficient (2000–2010)	Multidimensional poverty index (2000–08)*			Gender inequality	
		MDPI	Pop at MDP risk (%)	Pop <US$1.25 PPP per day (%)	Value	Rank
Ethiopia	29.8	0.582	5.2	39.0	–	–
Ghana	42.8	0.14	21.4	30.0	0.729	114
Guinea	43.3	0.505	9.4	70.1	–	–
Kenya	47.7	0.302	23.2	19.7	0.738	117
Liberia	52.6	0.484	9.5	83.7	0.766	131
Mali	39.0	0.564	7.3	51.4	0.799	135
Niger	43.9	0.642	4.0	65.9	0.807	136
Nigeria	42.9	0.368	15.7	64.4	–	–
Rwanda	46.7	0.443	14.0	76.6	0.638	83
Senegal	39.2	0.384	11.6	33.5	0.727	109
Sierra Leone	42.5	0.489	11.1	53.4	0.756	125
South Africa	57.8	0.014	3.9	26.2	0.635	82
Tanzania	34.6	0.367	23.0	88.5	–	–
Uganda	42.6	–	–	51.5	0.715	109
Zimbabwe	50.1	0.174	24.6	–	0.705	105
OECD	–	–	–	–	0.317	–
East Asia and Pacific	–	–	–	–	0.467	–
South Asia	–	–	–	–	0.739	–
Sub-Saharan Africa	–	–	–	–	0.735	–
LDCs	–	–	–	–	0.746	–
World	–	–	–	–	0.56	–

Note: * Calculated based on survey data on household deprivation in health, education and living standards.

finance are inequitable to the extent that they produce asymmetric effects in rich and poor countries. The deepening of poverty and inequality—prosperity for a few countries and people,[5] marginalization and exclusion for the many—has implications for social and political stability among and within states.

Globalization has also let loose the forces of "uncivil society" and accelerated the transnational flows of terrorism, human and drug trafficking, organized crime, piracy, and pandemic diseases. The growth in transnational networks of global uncivil society threatens both state institutions and civil society in many countries.[6]

The outright rejection of globalization and a retreat into autarky is neither practical nor desirable: who wants to be the next Myanmar or North Korea? Equally, though, who wants to be the next Iceland, Greece or Ireland? The notion that endless liberalization, deregulation and relaxation of capital and border controls will assure perpetual self-sustaining growth and prosperity has proven to be delusional. The challenge is to accentuate the positives and discount the negatives of globalization.

Governance

Governance has both intrinsic and instrumental importance. Globally validated in the Millennium Declaration, it is intrinsically valuable as a foundational element of human development and instrumentally critical to providing the systemic enabling environment for the achievement of MDGs. "Good governance" incorporates participation and empowerment with respect to public policies, choices and offices; rule of law and independent judiciary to which the executive and legislative branches of government are subject along with citizens and other entities; and standards of probity and incorruptibility, transparency, accountability and responsibility. It also includes institutions in which these principles and values are embedded.

Markets and democracy

Development economists can be divided into those who trust unregulated markets to deliver the public good of development and those who put their faith in government intervention. The obvious growth, poverty alleviation and redistributive successes of East Asian economies have been used by both sides to bolster their case. Interventionists argue that the key to the success of the Asian dragons was selective trade protection and an enlightened industrial policy. Free marketeers respond that among developing countries the Asian dragons had small government, open trade regimes, competitive exchange rates and low inflation.

The end of the Cold War was a triple defeat of the Soviet Union: as the superpower rival of the United States, as the font of communism and as the standard bearer of the command economy. The enterprise of state-making since the early 1990s reflects these broader contextual realities. Yet historically, as Ha-Joon Chang argues, all major developed economies used interventionist policies—tariffs, capital controls, protection of infant industries—when ascending the ladder to prosperity, and then decided to kick away the ladder, rewrote the rules of international trade and commerce to forbid the remaining poor countries from following in their paths, and used international institutions like the World Bank, the International Monetary Fund (IMF) and the World Trade Organization (WTO) as global enforcers of these tough new rules.[7]

For example, Australia is widely regarded as one of the very few developed countries to have survived unscathed by the financial crisis of 2008–10. Two major reasons for this are the series of liberalizing and deregulating policy reforms instituted by governments of all parties in the 1980s and 1990s, and the robust prudential regulatory and surveillance instruments put in place to monitor economic activities. Yet for all the economic border control reforms, tariffs and subsidies remain in place as part of the country's industrial policy. The federal government provided AUS$17.3 billion in gross support to industries for the financial year 2009–10: $9.4 billion via tariffs, $4.1 billion in tax concessions, and $3.7 billion in budgetary outlays. Provincial governments provide an additional $4 billion annually in industry policy.[8] On the other hand, the story of the $10 billion collapse of the Australian wool industry, despite tariff walls and other government interventions in the twentieth century, is a cautionary tale of the perils of industrial policy.[9]

If East Asia shows the benefits of state intervention, South Asia was the poster region for the ills of dirigisme. India's planned economic development proved unable to improve the standard of living and quality of life of its citizens and unable to compete in the global marketplace. Only after the reforms begun by Manmohan Singh as Finance Minister in 1991 was India able to exploit its comparative advantages: a people who work hard, achieve high rates of saving because though poor they are thrifty, and at home and abroad have demonstrated successful entrepreneurship and initiative.

The key question is which approach to balancing relations between citizens, society, market, state and the global economy can produce the greatest gains in delivering performance and results. In the last three decades China has produced the biggest rise in incomes for the largest number of people in history. India followed China's economic liberalization 13 years later and its deepening engagement with the world economy still lags China's by a decade. Democracy would appear to be irrelevant to their common failure before, and their parallel success after, economic reforms. For example, a common political system cannot explain the great variation in economic performance among India's different states—from the agricultural and industrial powerhouses of Punjab, Gujarat and Maharashtra to the impoverished coffers, wasting infrastructure, deep poverty and endemic caste violence of the BIMARU states (Bihar, Madhya Pradesh, Rajasthan and Uttar Pradesh in the Hindi heartbelt of central India).[10] Rather, the explanation lies in the mix of policies and quality of governance.

Markets require governance; good governance is not possible without democracy, civil society and civic virtue. Liberal democracies and market economies rely for long-term success on similar attributes of good governance: competition, information, property rights, sanctity of contracts, independent judiciary, multi-skilled and well-educated workforces and citizenry, efficient and transparent legal system, prudential regulatory systems, merit-based recruitment and promotion, and executives who are accountable to shareholders for the mistakes they make as well as answerable to the courts for the legality of their actions. Democracies better facilitate the achievement of the necessary social compromises between capital and labor, efficiency and equity, and growth and equality. There is also a parallel argument for striking the right balance between markets that deliver freedom and prosperity and communities that sustain cultural and social values.

Democracy, economic growth and poverty alleviation are neither self-generating nor self-guaranteeing. Governments can be fallible and markets are often imperfect. It is better to let the people decide and reap the consequences of their choices. Their capacity and will to learn, from mistakes and successes alike, is greatly strengthened if they are themselves responsible for making crucial life-changing decisions on their economic and political futures.

The indicators in Table 3.5 can help to establish some measurable regional norms of democracy, human rights and press freedom. These should be reflected in the post-2015 GDGs. In some sectors the state will continue to have to assume the main responsibility: in providing the indispensable legal and political context, ensuring law and order, protecting property rights, creating the necessary infrastructure, dispensing primary healthcare and education, and insuring citizens against life's disasters. The role of the state and its relationship to the market came

Table 3.5 Political and economic freedoms and choices

	Satisfaction with freedom of choice (%)	Democracy score (0–2)[a]	Human rights violations score (1–5)[b]	Press freedom (index)[c]	Democratic decentralization score (0–2)[d]	Ease of doing business (rank/183)[e]
Asia						
Afghanistan	63	1	5	54.3	0	167
Bangladesh	62	0	4	37.3	0	107
Cambodia	93	1	2	35.2	–	147
China	70	0	4	84.5	2	79
India	66	2	4	29.3	1	134
Indonesia	75	2	3	28.5	2	121
Korea, South	55	2	2	15.7	1	16
Laos	84	0	1	92.0	1	171
Malaysia	83	1	2	44.3	–	21
Mongolia	42	2	3	23.3	1	73
Myanmar	–	0	5	102.3	–	–
Nepal	58	2	4	35.6	2	116
Pakistan	31	2	4	65.7	1	83
Philippines	87	2	4	18.3	2	148
Sri Lanka	74	2	4	75.0	2	102
Thailand	84	2	3	44.0	2	19
Vietnam	73	0	3	81.7	2	78
Africa						
Angola	69	0	3	36.5	0	163
Burundi	43	2	4	29.0	2	181
Congo, Democratic Repub.	54	1	5	53.5	0	175

(Continued on next page)

Table 3.5 (continued)

	Satisfaction with freedom of choice (%)	Democracy score (0–2)[a]	Human rights violations score (1–5)[b]	Press freedom (index)[c]	Democratic decentralization score (0–2)[d]	Ease of doing business (rank/183)[e]
Ethiopia	35	1	3	49.0	1	104
Ghana	74	2	2	6.0	—	67
Guinea	67	0	4	28.5	—	179
Kenya	58	2	4	25.0	—	98
Liberia	72	2	2	15.5	—	155
Mali	49	2	2	8.0	2	153
Niger	88	2	3	48.5	—	173
Nigeria	51	2	4	46.0	0	137
Rwanda	77	1	2	64.7	1	58
Senegal	54	2	3	22.0	0	152
Sierra Leone	72	2	3	34.0	0	143
South Africa	73	1	3	8.5	2	34
Tanzania	54	1	2	15.5	—	128
Uganda	76	1	3	21.5	—	122
Zimbabwe	41	1	4	46.5	—	157

Source: UNDP, *Human Development Report 2010—The Real Wealth of Nations: Pathways to Human Development* (New York: Palgrave Macmillan, 2010), table 6, 164–67; and *Doing Business: Economy Rankings* (Washington, DC: International Finance Corporation and World Bank, 2010), www.doingbusiness.org/rankings

Note: [a] 0 is nondemocratic, 1 is democratic with no alternation, 2 is democratic; [b] 1 is fewest, 5 is most human rights violations; [c] A lower score indicates more freedom of press; [d] 0 is no local elections, 1 is legislature elected but executive appointed, 2 is legislature and executive locally elected; [e] Economies are ranked on their ease of doing business, with a higher ranking denoting that the regulatory environment is more conducive to starting and operating a local firm. The index averages the country's percentile rankings (from 1 to 183) on nine equally weighted topics: starting a business, dealing with construction permits, registering property, getting credit, protecting investors, paying taxes, trading across borders, enforcing contracts, and closing a business.

sharply back into focus in the aftermath of the Western (mistakenly called global) financial crisis of 2008–10 as the policy discourse saw a split between the deficit and stimulus hawks. The dominant policy response was to promote austerity by cutting deficits through reductions in welfare spending (taking from the poor). The policy neglect of job creation saw the number of people worldwide who were unemployed reach 212 million in 2009.[11]

Emerging market economies have successfully implemented many first-generation reforms to integrate with the global economy. They are yet to implement the politically more sensitive second-generation reforms of dismantling domestic subsidies, cutting regulatory and licensing requirements, adopting pro-growth taxes with a widened tax base, and so on. Economic and political institutions remain weak and inefficient, raising business costs and constricting consumer and citizen choices. High barriers to intra-regional flows of capital, goods, services and labor also stifle competition and competitiveness.

The benefits of business-friendly policy measures, while real, can also be exaggerated. The World Bank Group's *Doing Business* report, produced annually since 2003, measures the ease and difficulty of a local entrepreneur to start, operate and close a small or medium-sized business when complying with the relevant regulations. The indicators are partial, not comprehensive. They do not examine workforce skills, job security, infrastructure or macroeconomic conditions. Even so, the assumption is that countries that strengthen transparency and property rights and improve the efficiency of commercial dispute resolution at the level of the firm will improve economic outcomes at the national level. Bearing in mind the twin caveats that correlation is different from causation, and that some of the most impressive national growth performances in the past two decades have occurred in some of the toughest business regulatory environments, it does seem to be the case that region by region, higher income cohorts correspond with more business-friendly regulatory regimes (Table 3.5). Acknowledging the policy import of this, in 2009–10 two-thirds of developing economies made it easier to do business, doubling the rate from when the surveys began.[12] Since 2003, 75 percent of the world's economies have made it easier to start a business in the formal sector.

However, the record is highly uneven within and across regions. Against the average rank of the high-income Organisation for Economic Co-operation and Development (OECD) countries of 30, East Asian and Pacific economies ranked an average of 87, South Asia 117, and sub-Saharan Africa 137. In 2009–10, 59 percent of the sub-Saharan African economies reformed business regulations and institutions, compared to 75 percent in Asia-Pacific and 63 percent in South Asia.[13]

Corruption

Corruption rankings measure the extent to which the state is captured by elites and vested interests who use public power for private gain. Corruption is more pervasive in developing countries (Table 3.6), where its effects are also most destructive and savage.[14] They would do far better to eliminate corruption through their own efforts than seek handouts from the rich countries in the form of foreign aid. Corruption robs civic life of public virtue and instills cynicism and rage among citizens. The generally high rankings of Singapore, Hong Kong and Japan underline the critical importance of public probity in escaping from the poverty trap and in wealth creation.

Corruption is principally a governance issue—a failure of institutions and stewardship of public life, a lack of capacity to manage social, economic and political affairs by the rules of the game and with the help of effective checks and balances. The policy framework for eradicating high levels of corruption is appropriate laws that criminalize and impose adequate penalties. The institutional framework includes well resourced, well paid and well trained police, civil service and judiciary. In addition, there is a need for civil society involvement in monitoring and holding to account public authorities. There is also a key role for developed countries. The UN anti-corruption treaty should help. General Assembly Resolution 65/1 (22 September 2010) on the MDGs stressed the importance of "fighting corruption at both the national and international levels" (para. 52). With much more robust surveillance and regulatory instruments and state capacity, the developed countries could monitor, detect and punish bribe-giving firms and individuals, and also return illicit money parked in their banks and financial institutions to the people from whom it was stolen by corrupt politicians, officials and generals.

The MDGs

The eight main development goals and 21 related targets grouped into the MDGs have been commonly accepted throughout the UN system as a framework for guiding development policies and assessing progress towards poverty reduction and sustainable human development. As such, the MDGs articulate a strategic vision for mobilizing the international community for action. They changed the discourse from inputs to targets that were common to all development agencies; facilitated the engagement of the private sector in poverty alleviation; and have proven to be a tool for social mobilization and a system of political as much as economic governance benchmarks.

Table 3.6 Corruption scores and ranks, 2001 and 2010

	2001		2010	
	Score	*Rank (N=99)*	*Score*	*Rank (N=178)*
Asia				
Afghanistan	–	–	1.4	176
Bangladesh	0.4	91	2.4	134
Cambodia	–	–	2.1	154
China	3.5	57	3.5	78
India	2.7	71	3.3	87
Indonesia	1.9	88	2.8	110
Korea, South	–	–	5.4	39
Laos	–	–	2.1	154
Malaysia	5.0	36	4.4	56
Mongolia	–	–	2.7	116
Myanmar	–	–	1.4	176
Nepal	–	–	2.2	146
Pakistan	2.3	79	2.3	143
Philippines	2.9	65	2.4	134
Sri Lanka	–	–	3.2	91
Thailand	3.2	61	3.5	78
Vietnam	2.6	75	2.7	116
Africa				
Angola	–	–	1.9	168
Burundi	–	–	1.8	170
Congo, DR of	–	–	2.0	164
Ethiopia	–	–	2.7	116
Ghana	3.4	59	4.1	62
Guinea	–	–	2.0	164
Kenya	2.0	84	2.1	154
Liberia	–	–	3.3	87
Mali	–	–	2.7	116
Niger	–	–	2.6	123
Nigeria	1.0	90	2.4	134
Rwanda	–	–	4.0	66
Senegal	2.9	65	2.9	105
Sierra Leone	–	–	2.4	134
South Africa	4.8	38	4.5	54
Tanzania	2.2	82	2.7	116
Uganda	1.9	88	2.5	127
Zimbabwe	2.9	65	2.4	134

Source: Transparency International, *Corruption Perceptions Index 2001*, and *Corruption Perceptions Index 2010*, www.transparency.org
Note: Excluding Hong Kong, Japan, and Singapore as outliers. Averages are per country, not per capita.

One may well question the fascination with targets. It makes sense for private-sector companies to set financial targets with clear lines of accountability for meeting them and matching incentives and penalties, but how similar are national and international public policy to the operations of for-profit companies? Inevitably there is a large element of arbitrariness in how the MDG targets were selected—why "x" per-cent and not "y" or "z" percent? Targets by themselves provide no guidance on how they are to be met—they are more in the nature of exhortations. "We must do better" is a slogan, not a policy. No penalty is known to have been put in place on any UN official for the failure to meet any MDG target. The UN professional bias always is to see a glass as half full; to engage in self-congratulation on how far we have come, not how far short we are from the stated destination.

Quantitative targets do not automatically capture social goals of inclusive growth, reduced inequality, and improved learning outcomes. For example, increased domestic spending and foreign aid can improve access to schools, but only efficient and responsive educational institu-tions will convert this into improved learning and health outcomes. Nor does a rise in per capita income capture the affordability of food and fuel if global production falls, if there is also a resulting scarcity, and price spike. Even where indicators are largely positive in the aggregate, they can conceal significant pockets of deprivations among ethnic, lin-guistic or religious minorities who survive on the margins of mainstream society.

The MDGs represent a global consensus on development policies and targets even in the absence of a common understanding of what constitutes development or agreement on the strategies for achieving it. They are neither radical nor overly ambitious, being the minimum neces-sary to restore dignity and give practical expression to the call to cleanse the world of fear and want. They are also mutually reinforcing and inter-twined. Eradicating extreme poverty, for example, would help to reduce infant mortality, improve maternal health, and better ensure environ-mental sustainability. Similarly, achieving universal primary education, combating endemic diseases and empowering women would contribute to eradicating poverty.

The MDGs are a quintessentially UN achievement: setting aside disagreements on contested concepts in favor of reaching agreement on shared goals and milestones. As such, they constitute a primary nor-mative mandate which validates many of the operational agendas. They also provide the agreed country framework for development planning. The MDGs are the chief template for measuring a country's development progress against agreed benchmarks, for policy and strategy dialogues among a variety of development agencies—the UNDP, the World Bank, the IMF, the regional banks, even bilateral donors—and between them and individual countries. They define and validate the terms of the relationship between the industrial and developing countries, setting forth the reciprocal rights and obligations as well as the time-bound targets and performance indicators.

The MDGs also represent a quintessential UN shortcoming because there is little to be done to ensure compliance. The United Nations can provide policy advice and technical assistance, collect and collate data, identify shortfalls as well as progress, issue appeals and exhortations, and try to embarrass a country that fails to provide education to girls or meet its aid targets. However, it cannot impose its preferences and policies on sovereign member states.

MDG achievements include successes in combating extreme poverty, improving school enrolment and child health, reducing child deaths, expanding access to clean water, controlling malaria and other tropical diseases, and expanding access to HIV/AIDS prevention, treatment and care. On the other hand, new HIV infections still outnumber those starting treatment; progress has been slow in reducing maternal mortality or improving maternal and reproductive health, reaching full employment and gender equality, and advancing women's empowerment. Progress on some MDGs has been so fragile that the gains can easily be reversed.

Global Development Goals

As noted in the Johannesburg Statement on the Millennium Development Goals appended to this book, the MDG experience since 2000 has proven the value of the goals in affirming the global commitment to worldwide poverty reduction and eradication. To consolidate and build on their undoubted successes and address pressing new global concerns, a new set of GDGs should be articulated, comprising measurable targets and indicators, while confronting the shortfalls and gaps in MDG achievements.

On 22 September 2010 the UN General Assembly adopted Resolution 65/1 entitled "Keeping the Promise: United to Achieve the Millennium Development Goals."[15] In it, the heads of state and government welcomed the progress made since 2005, "while expressing deep concern that it falls short ... " As one would expect from such a political document, it was rhetoric-rich, expressing the conviction that the MDGs can be achieved, even in the poorest countries, "with renewed commitment, effective implementation and intensified collective action ...

strengthened institutions ... increased mobilization of resources ... increased effectiveness of development cooperation and an enhanced global partnership for development." Many motherhood statements were reiterated, including the importance of good governance, the rule of law, human rights, gender equality and women's empowerment (paras. 11–13).

In addition, there were also some important substantive statements, starting with the affirmation that based on "universal membership, legitimacy and unique mandate," the UN "plays a vital role in the promotion of international cooperation for development and in supporting the acceleration of the implementation of the internationally agreed development goals" (para. 14). The "internationally" agreed aspect of the agreed development goals is the true and historic significance of the MDGs, as recognized in the Johannesburg Statement on the Millennium Development Goals.[16] That can be the promise and attraction of the GDGs, which, like the MDGs, will have to be interconnected and mutually reinforcing (para. 15). Emphases on the importance of equity, social inclusion, reduction of inequalities, adoption of social protection floors, promotion of universal social benefits, the adoption of proactive employment-generating and pro-poor policies, expanding opportunities for women and girls, strengthening their protections and promoting their empowerment—that is, on social policies as well as on economic growth—is a notable feature of Resolution 65/1 (see especially para. 23). Similarly, while recognizing the "role of trade as an engine of growth" and the need to reform and modernize the international financial institutions (paras. 40, 42), the resolution acknowledged that countries may have "to evaluate the trade-off between the benefits of accepting international rules and commitments and the constraints posed by the loss of policy space," because the scope for domestic policies in the areas of trade and investment is now increasingly framed by "international disciplines, commitments, and global market considerations" (para. 37).

If we look back at Table 3.2 on poverty, deprivations, income and gender inequalities, two things stand out. First, persisting poverty is a major obstacle to reducing income and gender inequalities. Second, social inequalities are often clustered in sub-regions, suggesting that they are socially and culturally rooted. In turn, this indicates the need for coordinated regional efforts to tackle common problems of inequality based on inherited norms of social behavior and ingrained states of mind.

Asians were deeply displeased with the IMF's crisis management in the Asian financial crisis of 1997–98. An important shift in the global economic order has occurred in the decade since. The accumulation of large currency reserves as self-insurance and the domestication of debt cushioned emerging countries from the systemic shocks of the recent financial crisis. Asia has continued to focus on pursuing growth and development through domestic savings and capital accumulation, increased private and aid flows, and improved market access for its goods. As Razeen Sally noted in the 2011 Hayek Lecture, today's Asian Drama is "the exact opposite of Myrdal's diagnosis and prognosis," a dynamism unleashed by the liberalization and deregulation of internal markets, external trade and services, of product and factor markets, and of domestic and foreign investment.[17] Asia's success, in turn, was at the heart of the uniquely successful combination of globalization, growth and prosperity between 1980 and 2008. With 60 percent of the world's population, Asia had accounted for a mere 20 percent of global GDP in PPP dollars. That had doubled by the end of the century and could account for half of global GDP by 2050 at market exchange rates. The divergence in economic performance between the developed and emerging economies in the face of the financial crisis since 2008 has accelerated the long-term trend towards convergence between the West and emerging markets, especially in Asia.

After the Western financial crisis, the resulting loss of faith in Western prescriptions led many countries to look for an alternative model to replace the discredited Washington Consensus: the free-market, pro-trade and globalization policies promoted by the Washington-based financial holy trinity of the US Treasury, the IMF and the World Bank. Some developing countries want to discard it in favor of the recipe for faster growth and greater stability of the "Beijing Consensus" of a one-party state, government-guided development, strictly controlled capital markets and an authoritarian decision-making process that can think strategically for the long term, make tough choices and long-term investments, and not be distracted by daily public polls.[18] Thus during his trip to China, South Africa's President Jacob Zuma said that the "discipline" of China's political system should be studied as a potential recipe for the economic growth of Africa and other developing countries.[19]

China's continuing rise and the more recent economic successes of Brazil and India have also revived interest in the notion of a "developmental state," with differing needs, strategies and growth trajectories than the so-called "Anglo-American" model. With the former, the goals of strengthening state capacity, promoting social cohesion, maintaining territorial integrity and political independence, resisting encroachments on national sovereignty, and achieving economic growth to underpin and bankroll material progress and human development receive top priority.

State capacity

The GDGs should emphasize the importance and role of a capacitated state as the main driver of development. The modern state is the most substantial manifestation of political power that has been depersonalized, formalized and integrated into the greater social whole.[20] The state embraces the network of authoritative institutions which make and enforce collective decisions throughout a country. Most postcolonial societies pursued state-building, nation-building and economic development simultaneously. At times they worked against one another, leading to crises of state legitimacy and the weakening of state institutions.

One of the most important requirements, therefore, is state capacity: the creation of government with legislative and executive powers that can be exercised effectively to allocate resources and values authoritatively, and of structures (civil service, judiciary, police, army) supported by an ideology that legitimates the role of neutral state authority in maintaining social order through prescribed procedures and the rule of law. Conversely, a state will be judged to be weak, sometimes to the point of being a failed state, if it fails to establish a monopoly on legitimate violence, law and order breaks down, and basic services can no longer be delivered.

Gross national income (GNI) per capita is one important indicator of state capacity (Table 3.1). Although high income levels are not a sufficient measure of state capacity, a minimum threshold is a prerequisite to a capacitated state. The OECD average GNI/capita is PPP US$37,077; East Asia and the Pacific, $6,403; South Asia, $3,417. While the world average is $10,631, the average GNI/capita of sub-Saharan African countries is a meager $2,050. The state has to play an active role in building the legal and institutional infrastructure of a market economy as well as a social democracy, so that public power is exercised for the public good to ensure public safety, educate and train citizens and the workforce, enforce contracts, protect property rights, safeguard labor rights, promote human rights, conserve the environment, look after public health, protect national security, and so on.

For most of these, an efficient and fair tax system is essential as the main source of public revenues. As US Supreme Court Justice Oliver Wendell Holmes said, taxes are the price of civilization: "Ultimately tax is the most sustainable source of finance for development and the long-term goal of poor countries must be to replace foreign aid dependency with tax self-sufficiency."[21] Tax revenues as a proportion of GDP range from a low of 10 percent for the United States to a high of 36 percent for Denmark; most European countries seem to be in the 20–30 percent range (Table 3.1).

East Asians range between 8 percent for Cambodia and 23 percent for Mongolia, with most clustering in the mid-teens. By comparison, Africans have a significantly lower tax collection as a proportion of GDP.

Moreover, for citizen incomes to translate into adequate public revenues, the state must collect taxes from a broad base. Many developing countries are hampered in fiscal redistribution efforts by a low tax base compounded by low incomes and a large, untaxed informal sector. Indirect taxes are also more difficult to manage than direct taxes and create built-in incentives for tax evasion. Developing countries must undertake tax reforms to widen and strengthen the tax base in order to reduce dependence on indirect taxes, foreign aid and remittances. Furthermore, a narrow tax base means that high net worth individuals develop fears of still higher, punitive tax rates. This spurs them to park still more of their capital and build up wealth outside the country in order to shield their assets from the tax authorities—hence the need to strengthen tax administration and crack down on tax evasion.

The effectiveness, efficiency and integrity of public administration is also at stake in curbing the illicit outflow of capital through activities such as corruption, transactions involving contraband goods, criminal activities, and tax evasion. Illicit outflows from developing to developed countries increased from US$369 billion in 2000 to $1.26 trillion in 2008, with the annual illicit outflows ranging from $725 billion to $810 billion.[22] In the 1990–2008 period a total of $197 billion flowed out of the 48 LDCs, mainly into developed countries, worth 4.8 percent of GDP. African LDCs account for 69 percent of all illicit flows, followed by Asia and Latin America with 29 percent and 2 percent, respectively.[23] Moreover, the problem is getting worse, not better. The illicit flows from LDCs increased from $9.7 billion in 1990 to $26.3 billion in 2008.[24]

Illicit capital outflows impede government efforts to mobilize resources for economic development, fund critical social programs and balance public expenditures and tax revenues. Capital flight necessarily lowers the rate of domestic savings, which in turn increases the dependency of emerging economies on external sources of capital (investment, overseas development assistance (ODA), remittances). Moreover, they contribute to a net transfer of resources from poor to rich countries. Thus Kenya's Central Bank Governor Njunna Ndung'u noted in October 2007 that capital flight from sub-Saharan Africa was close to half a trillion dollars, more than double its aggregate external liabilities.[25] There is also a significant link between capital flight and the growth of external debt through the "revolving door effect."[26]

The 2010 MDG summit committed the international community "to curtail illicit financial flows at all levels."[27] Possible solutions to the problem of illicit flows include measures to correct trade mispricing (which occurs with collusion between exporters and importers on invoices), for example through systematic customs reform, adoption of transfer pricing regulations, and enhanced enforcement capacity. There is also a critical role for the international community, starting with a systematic exchange of tax information between governments on non-resident individuals and corporations. There should also be a global harmonization of transfer pricing regulations and norms and the development of an international accounting standard.

The GDGs should examine the ratio of taxes, foreign direct investment (FDI) inflows, ODA and inward remittances, and establish a benchmark balance. The MDGs had set targets for increased ODA flows as a proportion of the GDP of donor countries. The GDGs should balance this with targets for decreased ODA inflows in the recipient countries as a proportion of total government revenue.

Poverty and conflict

Paul Collier has argued that 50 failed states that are home to the poorest 1 billion people on Earth pose the central challenge of development.[28] They have been falling further and further behind the majority of the world's people, often experiencing an absolute decline in living standards. In the *Foreign Policy* failed states index, 14 of the top 25 and 27 of the top 50 countries are from Africa, compared to three and 11, respectively, from Asia (excluding the Middle East, Central Asia and Oceania).[29] Collier analyzed the causes of failure, pointing to a set of traps that ensnare these countries, including civil war, a dependence on the extraction and export of natural resources and bad governance. Standard solutions do not work: aid is often ineffective and globalization can actually make matters worse, driving development to more stable nations. What the bottom billion need from rich countries, Collier concluded, is preferential trade policies, new laws against corruption, and even carefully calibrated military interventions.

Similarly, the World Bank's annual report notes that 1.5 billion people live in countries affected by repeating cycles of political and criminal violence, and that the least developed, conflict-afflicted and fragile states have had the greatest difficulty in achieving even a single MDG target. More than 90 percent of civil wars so far this century have occurred in countries that had already experienced a civil war in the previous 30 years. The best form of conflict *prevention*, therefore, is conflict resolution. Moreover, in countries suffering from protracted violence, poverty rates on average are 20 percent higher. To complete the vicious cycle, countries that score poorly on government effectiveness, rule of law and corruption have a 30–45 percent higher risk of civil war and also show a significantly higher risk of criminal violence.[30]

The policy implication is therefore clear: institutionalized good governance that delivers citizen security, justice and jobs. Institutional transformation is difficult to achieve in less than a generation (15–30 years). Economic development policies have to be crafted that are consciously pro-poor, prioritizing employment over austerity, and focusing on job-creating schemes like large-scale public works; expanding access to education, training and retraining, upskilling, access to finance and credit; and addressing infrastructure bottlenecks. For these programs to be effective across a broad spectrum of sectors, they must be socially inclusive, with women and marginalized groups being involved in their design and implementation. Otherwise the communities will remain trapped in endlessly repeating cycles of instability, criminal violence and group conflict.

Noting an "unfortunate divorce of poverty and inequality" in international development policy, Yusuf Bangura argues that "poverty is closely related to inequalities of class, ethnicity and gender, which are ... dysfunctional for development." He adds that "High levels of inequality make it harder for the poor to participate in the growth process; restrict the expansion of the domestic market; may raise crime levels or cause violent conflict; and may create institutions that lock the poor into poverty traps."[31] Thus development policies must not only promote economic growth but also, simultaneously, combat inequalities (of income, ethnicity, gender, region) on the explicitly political dimensions of public policy, both domestic (national governments) and international (development agencies and donor governments). Exceptionally in the West, in the northern European countries, especially Scandinavia, employment-centered growth strategies, progressive taxation and universal-cum-comprehensive social policies, based on a better balance between the state and the market and labor-management compacts, have kept inequalities in check. The notion of growth is central to the construction of economically viable states that lift people from poverty; the notion of equity is equally central to the construction of inclusive societies and shared citizenship. The GDGs should embrace, not ignore or exclude, agricultural and industrial policies whereby the terms of exchange between labor and capital are set, regulated and refereed by the state.

Foreign aid

The long-stated goal of 0.7 percent of GDP as ODA remains on the books but is unlikely to be reached anytime soon. In the meantime, aid as an instrument of development policy remains fiercely contested. Does it facilitate economic growth, institutional resilience and good governance, or foster international welfare dependency, give recipient governments an alibi for their own shortcomings, and assuage donor countries' consciences for continuing serious barriers to trade and labor from developing countries?

The international debate over the role, efficacy and importance of ODA is well captured in three influential books in recent times. Jeffrey Sachs argues that the goal of development assistance is to help the world's 1 billion poorest people—who are caught in a poverty trap—reach the first rung on the ladder of economic development. Rather than a handout, ODA is an investment in global economic growth that will strengthen the security of all nations.[32] However, William Easterly contends that successful poverty reduction programs are usually achieved through indigenous, ground-level planning, not through well-intentioned but policy-distorting ODA that can sometimes worsen the plight of poor economies.[33] Dambisa Moyo, too, supports a tough love policy that would stop the tide of money that, however well intentioned, promotes corruption in government and dependence in citizens.[34] Instead of aid, she advocates foreign investment, new bond markets, microfinancing, and revised property laws.

Based on the above analysis, and recalling the stated goal of transferring ownership of process and responsibility for outcome to developing countries themselves, my recommendations for the GDGs would be:

- Invest in physical infrastructure;
- invest in social infrastructure (health, education, social protection) to improve HDI indicators, with particular focus on female literacy and primary and secondary education;
- invest in the administrative infrastructure of the rule of law;
- establish flexible, pragmatic and adaptable power-sharing arrangements to give all groups and sectors a stake in political and economic orders;
- establish networks of well resourced and high quality, locally owned and operated think tanks, applied research institutes and universities as rich sources of contestable policy advice that will promote national ownership of the development discourse;
- create markets and policy and institutional frameworks to ensure an efficient and competitive market economy;
- carry out rigorous assessments of lead sectors for appropriate industrial policies by country and sub-region, while emphasizing growth that is inclusive, balanced and sustainable with a focus on creating jobs;
- improve ease of doing business indicators;

- establish targets for tax as a percentage of GDP, the proportion of the population that must pay taxes in a broadened tax base, rates of taxation that are reasonable rather than punitive, an efficient balance between direct and indirect taxes, and a robust tax collection machinery;
- promote consciously pro-poor policies that incorporate poverty reduction, intergroup and gender equality promotion as integral components of economic growth strategies;
- set targets for health and education expenditure as a multiple of defense expenditure;
- map and establish national integrity systems to reduce/eliminate corruption; and
- adopt ODA reduction targets.

A curvilinear commitment to outflows by donor countries over 15–20 years, where aid rises but then plateaus before tapering off, might prove more beneficial than a simple linear commitment to increase aid/ GDP. Rich countries should rather deregulate and liberalize the international labor market so that incomes track price equalization across borders; reduce/eliminate agricultural subsidies in high income countries; lower and dismantle tariff and non-tariff barriers to imports from the least developed/lowest income countries; relax intellectual property rights for medicines to them; and enact and enforce tough anti-corruption laws and lift banking secrecy laws that hide ill-gotten gains stolen from the poor.

Only then will we have global development worth shouting about.

Notes

1 Deepak Nayyar, *Developing Countries in the World Economy: The Future in the Past?* (Helsinki: UN University World Institute for Development Economics Research, WIDER Annual Lecture 12, 2009), 41.
2 Gunnar Myrdal, *Asian Drama: An Inquiry into the Poverty of Nations* (New York: Twentieth Century Fund, 1968).
3 See S. Neil MacFarlane and Yuen Foong Khong, *Human Security and the United Nations: A Critical History* (Bloomington: Indiana University Press, 2006).
4 Raymond Baker (Director of the Washington-based Global Financial Integrity), "The Ugliest Chapter in Global Economic Affairs Since Slavery," speech delivered on 28 June 2007, www.gfip.org/index.php?option=com_co ntent&task=view&id=109&Itemid=74.
5 People in the developed countries are wealthier, healthier, better educated and live longer than they ever have before.
6 See Jorge Heine and Ramesh Thakur, eds., *The Dark Side of Globalization* (Tokyo: United Nations University Press, 2011).

7 Ha-Joon Chang, *Kicking Away the Ladder: Development Strategy in Historical Perspective* (London: Anthem Press, 2002), and *23 Things They Don't Tell You about Capitalism* (New York: Bloomsbury Press, 2010).

8 Figures provided in Rowan Callick, "The free-trade principle is accepted wisdom in our modern economy, yet protectionist rhetoric won't die," *The Australian*, 31 August 2011.

9 See Charles Massy, *Breaking the Sheep's Back* (Brisbane: University of Queensland Press, 2011).

10 "Bimaru" is a pun on the Hindi word for the sick.

11 *Doing Business: Economy Rankings* (Washington, DC: International Finance Corporation and World Bank, 2010), 2, www.doingbusiness.org/rankings.

12 *Doing Business*, 8.

13 *Doing Business*, 2.

14 See C. Raj Kumar, *Corruption and Human Rights in India: Comparative Perspectives on Transparency and Good Governance* (New Delhi: Oxford University Press, 2011).

15 UN document A/RES/65/1, 19 October 2010.

16 See Appendix to this book.

17 Razeen Sally, "Liberty outside the West," Lecture for the Hayek Tage, Freiburg, 10 June 2011.

18 Zhongying Pang, "China's Soft Power Dilemma: The Beijing Consensus Revisited," in *Soft Power: China's Emerging Strategy in International Politics*, ed. Mingjiang Li (Lanham, MD: Lexington Books, 2009), 125–42; and Stefan Halper, *The Beijing Consensus: How China's Authoritarian Model Will Dominate the Twenty-first Century* (New York: Basic Books, 2010).

19 Geoffrey York, "South African president heaps lavish praise on authoritarian China," *Globe and Mail* (Toronto), 25 August 2010.

20 Gianfranco Poggi, *The State: Its Nature, Development and Prospect* (Stanford: Stanford University Press, 1990).

21 Dev Kar, *Illicit Financial Flows from the Least Developed Countries: 1990–2008* (New York: UNDP Bureau for Development Policy, May 2011), 4, www.gfip.org/index.php?option=com_content&task=view&id=374&Itemid=70.

22 See Dev Kar and Karly Curcio, *Illicit Financial Flows from Developing Countries: 2000–2009* (Washington, DC: Global Financial Integrity, January 2011), iff-update.gfip.org.

23 Kar, *Illicit Financial Flows from the Least Developed Countries*.

24 Kar, *Illicit Financial Flows from the Least Developed Countries*, 3.

25 Quoted in Kar, *Illicit Financial Flows from the Least Developed Countries*, 6.

26 See Niranjan Chipalkatti and Meenakshi Rishi, "External Debt and Capital Flight in the Indian Economy," *Oxford Development Studies* 29, no. 1 (2001): 31–44; Leonce Ndikumana and James K. Boyce, "Congo's Odious Debt: External Borrowing and Capital Flight in Zaire," *Development and Change* 29, no. 2 (1998): 195–217.

27 UN General Assembly Resolution 65/1, "Keeping the Promise: United to Achieve the Millennium Development Goals," para. 78(j); A/RES/65/I, 19 October 2010.

28 Paul Collier, *The Bottom Billion* (Oxford: Oxford University Press, 2007).

29 www.foreignpolicy.com/articles/2011/06/17/2011_failed_states_index_interactive_map_and_rankings. The index ranks 177 countries using 12 social, economic and political indicators and more than 100 sub-indicators gathered

from publicly available documents and other quantitative data. The index should be treated with caution. The 2011 index ranked both China (72) and India (76) worse than Libya (111).

30 World Bank, *The World Development Report 2011: Conflict, Security and Development* (Washington, DC: World Bank, 2011).

31 Yusuf Bangura, "Inequality and the Politics of Redistribution," *European Journal of Development Research* 23, no. 4 (2011): 531.

32 Jeffrey Sachs, *The End of Poverty: Economic Possibilities for Our Time* (New York: Penguin, 2006).

33 William Easterly, *The White Man's Burden: Why the West's Efforts to Aid the Rest Have Done So Much Ill and So Little Good* (Oxford: Oxford University Press, 2007).

34 Dambisa Moyo, *Dead Aid: Why Aid is Not Working and How There is a Better Way for Africa* (New York: Farrar, Straus and Giroux, 2009).

4 Women and the MDGs

Too little, too late, too gendered

Sophie Harman

The United Nations (UN) Millennium Development Goals (MDGs) represent an ambitious set of indicators, initiatives and calls to action. Specific goals such as MDG 6 to combat HIV/AIDS, malaria and other diseases have seen ambition surge in the creation of new actors and sources of finance primed to address the issues and respond effectively to the indicators. Yet other goals have been found wanting, specifically MDG 5 to improve maternal health and MDG 3 to promote gender equality. These goals have seen increased interest since 2010, but the previous 10 years of neglect suggests something quite telling about the relationship between the MDGs and women. Not only have these goals been somewhat neglected, but efforts to deliver on the other goals have in part undermined work towards gender equality and improving the lives of women through the reassertion of gendered norms of women as carers and mothers. Women have occupied a fundamental position in the delivery of the MDGs, yet their labor is seen as freely given. This chapter argues that despite the MDGs outlining ambitious plans for women— their equality, their health and that of their children—the goals have in fact been too little, too late and too gendered. Women have become the stubborn issue of development that fails to go away yet remains vital to its success.

The chapter explores the role of women in the MDGs and how interventions—projects, policies, poverty alleviation tools, and institutions— established to reach the goals have been too little and too late and have undermined efforts to help women living in poverty. It does so by first outlining the inclusion of women in the MDGs, the priority areas around issues of gender inequality and how the UN system has responded to such priorities. Second, the chapter focuses on the too little and too late by exploring the lack of action on MDG 5, the lack of gender in strategies for maternal and child health and the role of the UN Fund for Women (UNIFEM), now UN Women. Third, the chapter considers how the MDGs have been too gendered in delivery and strategy in their embedding of gender norms between men and women. This section explores how re-enforcement of gender norms—specifically women as carers and mothers—has delayed progress in poverty alleviation rather than heightened it. The chapter then situates the issue of women and gender with wider institutional problems pertaining to the MDG process before offering several recommendations for how the future development agenda beyond 2015 could benefit women living in poverty.

Women in the MDGs

Previous to the MDGs women were included in the development process through the 1995 Beijing Declaration and Platform for Action that recognizes women's rights and gender equality as human rights fundamental to peace and development.[1] Women's rights have been advanced within the UN by various legal declarations and initiatives on the status of women such as the Convention on the Elimination of All Forms of Discrimination against Women (CEDAW), the Declaration of the Elimination of Violence Against Women, and the Declaration on the Right to Development within the UN's Declaration on Human Rights. As part of the UN, such declarations are binding on member states and compel the various bodies of the UN to action. Key UN agencies that are central to poverty alleviation and development include specialized units on women and gender—such as the Gender and Development section of the World Bank and the UN Girls Education Initiative housed in the UN Children's Fund (UNICEF)—established to eliminate gender inequality and to promote the rights and roles of women in all aspects of social, political and economic life. It is through these declarations, institutional responsibility and UN projects such as five-year plans for the advancement of women that women were included in the development process prior to the MDGs. However, despite such inclusion these issues and projects tended to occupy a sideline in development policy-making and processes, with women and gender being tacked on to existing projects. Since the introduction of the MDGs, specialized projects, units, and conventions have emerged to attempt to fully integrate women into the everyday workings of the UN and the wider development community.

In statement of intent, at least, women became the core objective of the MDGs. Women and gender are specifically highlighted as a stand-alone issue in MDG 3 to promote gender equality and empower women and feature in targets 1.B, full and productive employment for all, including women, and 2.A, both boys and girls having complete primary education.[2] Such inclusion indicates specific recognition on the part of the UN and the international community of the link between gender inequality and poverty. The goals are framed in a specific way to focus on the experiences of women living in poverty and to recognize women as fundamental to the development process. This is evident in the emphasis and support placed on training and developing the skills and campaigns of women as political candidates, increasing women's access to micro-finance and specific skill development for paid employment, and campaigns to end violence against women.[3] Commitment to such initiatives by a range of UN agencies—the UN Population Fund (UNFPA), UNICEF, UN Women, UN Educational, Scientific and Cultural Organization (UNESCO) and the World Bank—in funding and leadership shows the broad-based institutional support for women within the UN system.

The biggest sign of intent is the inclusion of a specific goal to promote gender equality and empower women. MDG 3 emphasizes the need to increase rates of female employment in decent, paid work; decrease the amount of women working in informal employment,[4] and promote women's access to top-level jobs by understanding and addressing the barriers to them; and support women's inclusion in political positions and government through quotas and special measures.[5] A fundamental part of MDG 3, which cuts across many of the other eight goals, has been the emphasis on eliminating gender disparity in education, specifically girls' access to and continued uptake of primary and secondary education. The emphasis on women and girls in development similarly cuts across MDG 2, which stresses equality in access to primary schooling for "boys and girls alike," and MDG 6, which recognizes the role of education of women in the prevention of HIV transmission and giving women greater economic and social options.[6] MDGs 4 and 5 have significant implications for women, specifically pregnant women and women who are mothers or carers. The three health goals (4, 5 and 6) all emphasize the reproductive aspect of women's health and thus the position of women as central to the development agenda.

Some progress has been made in reaching these goals. People living with HIV are living longer, prevalence rates are down and new infections are seemingly in decline.[7] Child mortality has seen a 28 percent drop since 1990 and more pregnant women living in rural parts of developing countries are receiving "skilled assistance."[8] Beyond these measurable statistics, women have become much more visible in the development process. Women are the main tools of new or innovative forms of development delivery such as micro-finance projects and conditional cash transfers. Women are seen as the main providers of community care for health and implementation of HIV/AIDS initiatives[9] and as such occupy multiple positions in this regard. Yet according to the UN's own research, those MDGs that have a direct impact on the lives of women living in developing countries have been found wanting. There are still more men in paid employment than women, men occupy the top jobs, and most politicians are men, with women disproportionately represented in informal work.[10] There has been little progress in reducing levels of teen pregnancy, and huge disparities between the level of neonatal care afforded to the rich and poor and those living in rural settings remain.[11] There has been "little or no progress in recent years" in reducing child mortality,[12] and maternal health has suffered from poor health infrastructure and inadequate financial support.[13] This lack of progress towards those goals that specifically affect women can be explained by the implementation of the MDGs being too little, too late and too gendered.

Too little, too late

2009/10 marked a turning point for maternal and child health. Previously unaddressed beyond efforts to reduce mother-to-child transmission of HIV, there has been a re-assertion of effort through the Global Strategy for Women's and Children's Health (2010); UNFPA's Safe Motherhood Strategy; the World Bank's Reproductive Health Action Plan 2010–15, *Better Health for Women and Families*; the Global Consensus on Maternal and Neonatal Health (2009); and the new Department of Maternal, Newborn, Child and Adolescent Health within the World Health Organization (WHO), launched in 2011. These strategies, alongside various statements of intent by bilateral donors such as the UK Department for International Development (DFID),[14] suggest a shift in political will and intent towards reaching these previously neglected goals. However, such policies have come at a time that is arguably too late to implement before the 2015 deadline and have come into play during a period of financial crisis and austerity. Though attention to maternal and child health is currently at its height since 2000, reductions in public spending in North America and Western Europe during the current period of financial austerity will have a direct affect on the money available for overseas aid. Funding towards HIV/AIDS programs has started to decline and is set to decrease further.[15] This will impact on the number of children born with HIV and the maternal health of their mothers as efforts to support prevention of mother-to-child transmission and funding to support treatment and drug purchasing are cut. In many countries the significant sums of money directed to

HIV/AIDS have been used to support community health centers and resources. Many women only visit or are able to access such health centers and see medical professionals because of wider anti-retroviral programs and services for HIV prevention. Two and a half million children under the age of 15 are living with HIV;[16] a cut in funding to HIV-specific initiatives will see a reversal of MDGs 4, 5 and 6.

Beyond budget cuts, the policy frameworks and project strategies to promote maternal and child health do not go far enough in recognizing gender and the difference in how women experience healthcare. Difference and the experience of healthcare has recently been the central focus of maternal health campaigns, and efforts towards decentralization and more community-based health delivery has been evident. Yet this is not for all women, just for pregnant women and mothers. MDGs 4 and 5 have become increasingly conflated with strategies to implement them. Global strategies for women's and children's health are not specific to maternal health but follow a similar pattern to multi-sectoral interventions developed within HIV/AIDS and neglected disease strategies. These strategies were initially developed and put into practice by the World Bank through programs such as the Multi-Country AIDS Program (MAP).[17] Such projects emphasize the role of multiple state and non-state actors in the planning and delivery of services, decentralization and the earmarking of specific funds to enhance civil society engagement. UNFPA's Safe Motherhood Strategy, the World Bank's *Better Health for Women and Families*, the Global Consensus on Maternal and Neo-natal Health (2009) all bear clear similarities to such high-profile AIDS projects: they clearly follow the same multi-sectoral framework, have similar indicators and lack a gender- or women-specific approach to addressing the issue of maternal and child health.[18] In a way, such a similarity should not be a problem as MDG 6 arguably presents one of the more successful goals and therefore it seems common sense to use a similar strategy. Yet this is problematic as it suggests that not enough has been done to address these goals in a manner that is issue and context specific or cognizant of the differences between women and men. Moreover, research suggests that multi-sectoral forms of participation have tended, in practice, to be bureaucratic, confused and highly centralized by the donors and architects of the project.[19] Hence these strategies are not country, issue or gender specific or locally driven. Instead a blueprint model has been adopted and adapted to fit the issue. Strategies to combat maternal health have to address the complexities and specific needs of this health concern for them to be effective.

A key explanation for the lack of gender-specific strategies to address maternal and child health has been the absence of a lead agency with a strong mandate and political support within the UN to address women's issues. Up until January 2011 the agency responsible for the empowerment of women and the promotion of their rights was UNIFEM. Despite recognizing the need for interventions that acknowledge gender, difference and women's experience, UNIFEM lacked financial, institutional and political support to effectively carry out a mandate for women independent from larger agencies such as the UN Development Programme (UNDP). UNIFEM was sidelined from decision-making by exclusion from key meetings at both headquarters and country level.[20] UNIFEM was not a co-sponsor of the Joint UN Programme on HIV/AIDS (UNAIDS) that coordinates the UN's response to HIV/AIDS and hence mother-to-child transmission. Beyond UNIFEM, women and gender units within other agencies such as the World Bank have faced similar issues of sidelining and tokenistic integration within development projects and policies. Involvement of women and gender issues is often dependent on the type of project, individual interest, concern for gender projects and awareness of specialized support within a specific agency, and constant interaction and pressure on the part of the women and gender representative.[21] The lack of presence in meetings, in country, with governments, and independence from other UN agencies restricted the ability of UNIFEM and other women-specific agencies to raise fully the profile and voice of women both within the UN and within member states.[22]

Effort to address these institutional shortcomings is evident in the formation of UN Women in January 2011. UN Women has a mandate to promote gender equality and empowerment by helping intergovernmental bodies create norms, standards and policy, supporting member states to implement such standards and holding the UN system to account.[23] In terms of mandate, approach and staff it is similar to UNIFEM, yet a crucial difference is its autonomy within the UN system from UNDP, which although collaboration is paramount to the working operations of the UN, provides space for women's issues to be consistently raised within the system and UN Women with their own seat at the table of development discussions. Yet, the old problems of relations with sovereign states and effective gender mainstreaming that takes into account women's lives and difference between people, whether men or women, when delivering the MDGs remain. For UN Women to be successful requires a combination of building an effective and clear policy and program profile, fostering internal relations and networking outside of the UN to secure external support and pressure for change. Alone, UN Women's voice will not be heard and the activities of UN Women will similarly become too little, too late.

Too gendered

Part of the wider problem underpinning the too little, too late has been the embedding of gender roles by the very programs and policies set to empower women out of poverty and the successful realization of the MDGs. This is evident in poverty alleviation strategies that have focused on various forms of social protection and micro-finance as well as projects and programs aimed at specific goals such as MDGs 1, 4, 5 and 6. The inclusion of women in the development process often reasserts women's position in unpaid work and the informal economy that rests on gendered assumptions of women as carers and mothers, and actually sees women as secondary to the development process as they prioritize the lives and needs of others first. This section considers the gendered nature of poverty alleviation strategies in general before focusing more specifically on how such gender roles manifest themselves within MDG-specific interventions.

Since the mid-1990s the development community has been increasingly interested in the role of social protection as a form of reducing intergenerational poverty and giving more power in decision-making and aid spending directly to people. Social protection in the form of social assistance such as housing benefits, social insurance such as free health care for the elderly and labor market regulation have been dominant features of social policy around the world since the end of World War II,[24] and have underpinned much development practice and aid giving. However, new forms of social protection such as cash transfers given directly from international aid agencies to families in need of support have been seen as a "revolution from the global south"[25] that have the potential for real long-term change in the fight against poverty. These programs emphasize intergenerational poverty reduction through increased school uptake, the promotion of access to primary healthcare, provision of food and nutrition, and giving the poor the ability to make their own decisions about where to spend aid money. Hence, cash transfers are provided to poor households as an efficient means of assisting or facilitating demand for public services that would equip individuals with the basic capabilities of education, nutrition and primary healthcare and thus more equal opportunities in life.[26] These transfers have come to constitute a prominent feature of poverty reduction strategies throughout Latin America, involving hundreds of thousands of households, and billions of dollars of investment.[27] The scope and budgets of these projects are so large in part because of their perceived success. Development practitioners, specialists and politicians have all been keen to highlight the positive outcome of such projects and their potential for future practice.[28] In this sense they are very much seen by agencies such as UNICEF and the World Bank as a key tool in ending poverty and the successful realization of the MDGs. Fundamental to the success of these projects have been women.

New forms of social protection such as cash transfers are predominantly given to women, who are perceived to be more reliable in spending money on the human development of their children than men.[29] For many this has been seen as a source of empowerment for women as they have greater control over family budgets and household spending and promote education, empowerment and self-esteem in young girls. They have thus been a central vehicle in which to assist in the delivery of MDGs 1 and 3. However, for others cash transfers perpetuate the notion that women are the solution to the male problem of inter-generational and family poverty[30] and in application have come to support gender norms of women as carers and asymmetric gender roles.[31] In placing women as the central recipients of personal aid budgets, cash transfers represent an extension of what Chant calls the "feminization of poverty alleviation,"[32] wherein women bear the burden of responsi-bility and become the site of international development initiatives.[33] The view that social protection projects lead to women's emancipation from poverty just through their participation is thus somewhat proble-matic. It presupposes that the main role of women in poverty allevia-tion is to prioritize the lives and needs of others and to implement the strategies devised by governments and international aid agencies. Their freedom and input into decision-making only exists within the narrow framework of a specific government project. Women's inclusion in micro-finance and social protection strategies continues to position "poor women" as community-focused and family-based, reinforcing gender stereotypes and distinctions between men and women in terms of repro-duction, with little consideration of women's lives and needs. Under-pinning such a position are two gender norms that have become intrinsic to the development process: (i) that women are mothers and carers first and women second; and (ii) that women give their labor for free. These two norms are particularly evident when considering the role of women in the realization of MDGs 4, 5 and 6.

Framing women primarily as mothers or carers in the goal process is particularly evident in the equating of women's health with maternal and child health in MDGs 4, 5 and 6. The MDGs position women and their health as only important in their role in childbearing and child-rearing. The strategies for maternal health and child health share the same priorities, types of intervention, and overlapping mandates between the agencies that are set to deliver them. This is evident in the common strategy for areas in maternal and child health such as the Global Strategy for Women's and Children's Health and the formation of joint Departments and policy approaches that tend to conflate the two issues. Within each of the strategies developed since 2010 to address maternal health and child health there is no direct reference to how women experience healthcare differently.[34] The MDGs recognize the importance of caring for pregnant women and mothers and the urgent need to address the needlessly high rates of maternal mortality, yet they also do so to the exclusion of women's other needs. Whilst the MDGs have been forward looking in addressing women's maternal health, in conflating much of this with children's health they have adopted and promoted a gender norm within the goals that only recognize women in development for their role in childbearing and childrearing, or in other words social reproduction. This emphasis sidelines other efforts to empower women in roles beyond the family and social reproduction, in the production of private capital, which they have claim to and presence in public life through government positions. Women are seen as fundamental to the development process, but only within a narrow gendered frame that sees their role as the production and protection of children and carers within the community.

The role of carers within the community is particularly evident in regards to MDG 6, to combat HIV/AIDS and other diseases. Similar to MDGs 4 and 5, there have been considerable efforts on the part of the international community to address the disproportionate rates of female HIV prevalence. Globally there are more women living with HIV than men. This difference is particularly acute in sub-Saharan Africa. Women are disproportionately infected and affected by HIV not just because of physiological factors but by gender inequality.[35] The last 10 years have seen a strong emphasis on community-based decision-making and project delivery as a means of combating HIV/AIDS. At the forefront of this have been women who act as peer educators and home-based carers, looking after their family and neighbors affected by the disease. HIV/AIDS has given women a quadruple burden of responsibility as they now have to look after their own family, work, care for the orphans of their extended family and local community, and engage in community action such as home-based care.[36] This burden is endemic throughout Africa, and is often a great strain on grandmothers.[37] Women give this labor—home-based care, peer education, pastoral care of orphans and vulnerable children—for free. Despite advocacy campaigns on the part of agencies such as the Stephen Lewis Foundation to pay for such labor, the majority of agencies responsible for combating HIV/AIDS and delivering the MDGs assume that women will perform such tasks for free. Despite these roles, women's participation in community decision-making and formal bodies such as community or district AIDS councils is not proportionate to the work they do.

What is somewhat pertinent about the gender roles ascribed to women within the MDG process is the absence of men and boys. Men feature in discussions of how the goals should affect men and women, boys and girls equally and pay attention to both, but strategies to involve men in the development process are lacking. This can be explained in several ways. First, men are already considered to be active in the design and implementation of development strategies and thus special dispensation towards them is not necessary. Second, development activities are not attractive to men, as other than decision-making and agenda-setting roles, project delivery and implementation tends to be unpaid. Alternatively, and third, development delivery is seen as an extension of women's work and role in unpaid social reproduction. Taken together, these factors show a need for wider recognition to increase women's activity beyond the family and the informal economy as well as the role of men within the family and the communities in which they live. This recognition is evident in the directives and statements in support of the goals, specifically MDG 3,[38] yet these statements in practice are somewhat separate from the policies and projects designed to improve the role of women.

Despite some evidence that the UN system recognizes the problem of women's unpaid labor and role in social reproduction, and the need to see how interventions affect men and women differently, in effect this has not been interwoven in the *delivery* of MDG strategies. In practice, it is women, not gender, and a very specific type of "woman" that is emphasized in delivering the goals. The combination of the emphasis on women, their role as mothers and carers, and the assumption that their labor is free in the practical delivery of MDGs 4, 5 and 6, undermines any gains or the successful realization of MDG 3. Seeing women's labor as freely given traps women in these roles and reduces space for their wider inclusion in political office and community decision-making, or involvement in paid labor and good jobs. For parts of the UN to promote the need for formal, paid employment of women, and then for other parts of the UN to engage women in free unpaid services, contradicts the overarching aims of the MDGs for women and in so doing reduces the potential of the goals to fully combat poverty.

Vogue goal-setting and the UN system

The problem of the MDGs being too little, too late, and too gendered on the issue of women and poverty alleviation is symptomatic of a lack of acknowledgment as to how the successful realization of different goals inter-relates and in some areas undermine or contradict the overarching goal. This is evident in the funding portfolio of specific agencies, the tendency for funding to cluster around "vogue" development issues, and the problem of goal-based strategies for development, all of which are endemic within the UN system.

A key factor in explaining the sidelining of women and gender from the MDG process has been the ability of key agencies to attribute significant funds to specific issues that fit within their institutional objectives. With the exception of UNICEF, UN agencies are able to make large statements of intent, but lack the funding capacity for on-the-ground projects. This is where institutions with special status in the UN such as the World Bank have been able to sway certain agendas and prioritize specific interventions through the large-scale funding support they are able to offer. Agencies such as UNIFEM and UNFPA have set targets for and advocated greater investment in maternal and child health for the last 40 years, yet widespread action did not come fully onto the agenda until the World Bank pledged significant funds through its 2010–15 *Better Health for Women and Families*, a US$1.3 billion project that saw a substantial 59 percent increase towards maternal health funding on recent years.[39] A key problem for UNIFEM was that it lacked the budget to implement and fund specific projects in pursuit of its overarching objectives, hence could only tack on to or frame its objectives in the wider agenda of those actors with the budgets to implement. Of course, agencies such as the World Bank have UN specialized status and are thus mandated to work in support of the wider UN system and high-profile objectives such as the MDGs. This tends to be the case in practice at the country and headquarter level, but can also vary across country, issue and individual personality as rivalries, jealousy and claims to ownership of success come to the fore. In practice, partnerships among and within agencies can be hierarchical and dependent on country presence, timing, knowledge exchange and budget.[40] The result of this is that those agencies with large funding portfolios and presence have greater say on which development issues and strategies are prioritized.

The priority afforded to certain development initiatives is indicative of a wider problem within the MDG process: vogue development aid. Vogue development aid refers to the ability of key actors within the development community to focus on a specific issue or set of issues and galvanize political will and financial support for such an issue. This can occur through the setting of clear objectives, seed funding, or effective issue framing. Within the MDGs, specific goals have been framed in a particular way to elicit wider support and global attention towards the cause. This is often seen to be the case with HIV/AIDS. The international community built around HIV/AIDS successfully made the case for support among the political community through framing the issue as more than a development problem but one of international security[41] and a disease that is having an enormous impact on the lives of children in developing countries. Whilst both of these frames can be seen as true to a certain extent, they are also true for other MDGs that have received less attention. The HIV/AIDS response was effective in snowballing political will and support to combat the disease and position it as something exceptional, a comprehensive development concern. Yet HIV/AIDS is now going out of fashion, with maternal and child health coming into vogue. As gender equality undercuts an array of development issues, it is thus difficult to maintain the relevance of gender beyond the role of women in specific issues such as HIV and maternal health as women become too complex to address. Whilst the rhetoric of the UN towards "one UN" or "delivering as one" would suggest an integrated system that addresses inter-related issues as a whole,[42] in practice the eight goals are often addressed as individual entities.

The issue of addressing specific goals alone or at best with cross-over benefits and influence is part of a wider issue of goal-setting as a means of promoting development. On the one hand this form of goal-setting allows the international community—UN agencies, governments, civil society, private donors and individuals—to be held to account, it gives a real measure of progress and a clearly defined agenda towards which to work. Yet it also excludes that which cannot be measured, and importantly does not address development as a cohesive whole that has inter-related processes, impacts and outcomes. Gender is stubborn in its inability to be neatly compartmentalized into a specific goal or objective, and where efforts to do so exist, they have been undermined by competing goals. Numerous issues that are central to the realization of the eight goals—infrastructure, road-building, training of specialized staff, education, and sanitation systems, and so on—are omitted from the MDG process. For example, provision of access to neonatal care requires the building of health centers in rural communities, safe and affordable transportation to health centers, nutritional support, and the training and payment of community-based midwives and provision of incentives to keep those trained experts in developing countries. Hence a key challenge for MDG 5 is the provision of effective, community-responsive healthcare systems, and long-term investment in the health workforce. Though in practice agencies have tried to use funding towards the MDGs to tackle some of these broader infrastructure issues, investment is still desperately required and initiatives to do so have, in the main, been found wanting. The trick is how to balance much-needed investment in infrastructure with specific targets and emergency development concerns.

To 2015 and beyond

Despite this critique of the MDGs being too little, too late and too gendered to fully confront the position of women living in poverty, there are several small and large adjustments that could be made. The first would be to recognize women's role in social reproduction and the implementation of development strategies. To fully achieve MDGs 1, 2, 3, 4, 5 and 6, the development community needs to value and rethink how they see such roles, and understand that women's labor is currently freely given to assist in the implementation of the goals and in so doing is anathema to their overarching objectives. As such, core parts of development budgets should be cognizant and remunerative of women's unpaid work. Such recognition would foster greater progress in women gaining access to paid, full-time employment as their skills become identified as such and the care economy becomes less stigmatized and less gendered. Gender equality can only be achieved through more than equal pay—equal recognition of women's and men's work and the breaking down of boundaries between them. The UN system should not work to exacerbate this: where interventions rest on women's labor they should be paid.

Whilst the goals provide a good mechanism for measurement and holding different actors to account, greater space needs to be given to that which cannot be measured. For the MDGs to be successful the UN must integrate specific goals with more horizontal development projects that engage with infrastructure. Infrastructure can take on a variety of forms including, but not limited to: judicial systems that promote equal land rights; transportation and road-building that allows people to access health and education facilities; and integrated local support centers where people can access prescription drugs and advice on a range of social issues. Working with the government and society of a state, donors and development practitioners need to address the infrastructural issues that limit the successful realization of the MDGs. Provision of basic services must be fundamental to development.

Efforts by the UN to fully address gender issues through the introduction of UN Women should be supported by member states, specialized agencies, civil society and private actors internal and external to the UN. Support should come from budgetary commitments that allow UN Women to identify and implement a strategic vision and collaborations with civil society, academics and the private sector that help position the agency as an effective source of knowledge and expertise. For the disproportionate infection rates and burden of HIV on women to be fully recognized, UN Women must become a co-sponsor of UNAIDS. Fundamentally, the issue of women has to be at the cornerstone of all discussions of development, thus UN Women has to be fully represented in key decision-making forums within the UN. Attitudes towards women, gender and UN Women need to see women as something more than a stubborn issue that is best addressed through maternal and child health strategies or anti-violence programs. Strategies and projects to implement such initiatives must recognize differences between women and men, and women in different cultures, societies, classes, heritages and countries. Reducing the complex and varied nature of the lives of women living in poverty to homogenous responses restricts any full engagement with their needs and experiences.

Conclusion

The MDGs have been too little, too late and too gendered to help the lives of women living in poverty. Policies, projects and strategies to address maternal health have come 10 years too late and do not go far enough in taking into account women's lives, experiences, gender, and the differences between maternal health and child health. Recent strategies bind issues of maternal and child health together and replicate existing health interventions into areas such as HIV/AIDS. This is problematic as it sidelines women's experience from the process and does not recognize the specific needs and arrangements for different health concerns.

Inclusion of women in the MDG process is too gendered. It is gendered in regards to the widespread recognition of the role and position of women in delivering development for free. Women are the central focus of projects and programs that are designed to break intergenerational poverty and deliver on goals for child health, nutrition and education, the result of which has been the positioning of women in unpaid care roles that presupposes their labor is freely given and reasserts gender norms of women as carers or women as mothers. It is women's role within the development process, not their lives, that has become central. Women's needs are seen as secondary to those of their children, family and society within the MDGs. The permeation of such gender norms in the delivery of MDGs 1, 4, 5 and 6 has contradicted and undermined the successful realization of all the goals, especially MDG 3.

The too little, too late, and too gendered aspects of the MDGs can be explained by the processes and institutions responsible for their effective delivery. Institutions mandated to combat gender inequality and promote the lives of women such as UNIFEM have been under-funded and under-represented, and, similar to gender strategies, have come too late. UN Women was formed in 2011, just four years before the MDG deadline. The lack of institutional presence has limited the voice for women within the UN. Although the UN supposedly represents men and women equally, evidence suggests the need for an agency to raise the issues of women and gender at high-level meetings and garner wider support. The ability of UN Women to do so will depend on both internal and external alliances, knowledge expertise and effective issue framing.

Issue framing reflects the culture of vogue development aid that has been built around the MDGs. Goal-setting has led to the prioritization of specific issues within the UN to the exclusion of others. Such exclusion can refer to specific MDGs over others—for example HIV/AIDS over maternal health—or the sidelining of wider issues such as infrastructure. Goal-setting and vogue development aid has led to the MDGs being addressed on an individual basis rather than a cohesive whole. This has specific implications for women as their involvement in reaching some of the goals, notably MDGs 1, 2 and 4, has undermined the realization of other goals, specifically MDGs 3, 5 and 6. For the MDGs to be realized and to have a better impact on the lives of women, development must be understood in broader terms than eight specific goals. These goals are important, but they lead to swings in priority and funding allocation from one goal to another. Ultimately this will lead to the neglect of these specific issues altogether as the fashion for development swings back towards infrastructure and the continued sidelining of women's needs.

Change towards greater gender equality is possible within the future development agenda beyond 2015, but only if women are recognized for not only their role in delivering better development for the lives of others, but the different lives they lead and their needs. For this to occur, women have to be seen beyond issues of childbirth, childrearing, and HIV/AIDS, and the gender norms endemic to the MDG process recognized. The UN has the ability to lead the way with this in supporting the work of UN Women and fully recognizing and rewarding women's work in delivering the goals. As the UN highlights, women are at the centre of development and poverty alleviation strategies, but focusing on the free work of women obscures greater understanding of their lives and needs. It is the needs of all women that must be at the centre of the development agenda beyond 2015.

Notes

1 UN, *Beijing Declaration and Platform for Action* (New York: UN, 1995), www.un.org/womenwatch/daw/beijing/pdf/BDPfA%20E.pdf.

2 UN, *Develop a Global Partnership for Development*, www.mdgmonitor.org/goal8.cfm.

3 www.un.org/millenniumgoals/pdf/MDG_FS_3_EN.pdf.

4 Informal employment can refer to a number of things. This chapter uses Razavi's understanding as "very *different* kinds of work, some akin to survivalist strategies with low returns that people resort to when economies stagnate, while other kinds of informal work (piece-rate, wage-work) are integrated with and contribute to processes of accumulation of a national or global scale" (Shahra Razavi, "The Gendered Impacts of Liberalization," in *The Gendered Impacts of Liberalization*, ed. Shahra Razavi (Oxon, UK: Routledge, 2009), 16).

5 UN, *Promote Gender Equality and Empower Women* (New York: UN, 2010), www.un.org/millenniumgoals/pdf/MDG_FS_3_EN.pdf.

6 UNAIDS, *Women and Girls*, www.unaids.org/en/strategygoalsby2015/womenandgirls.

7 UN, *The Millennium Development Goals Report* (New York: UN, 2010), www.un.org/millenniumgoals/pdf/MDG%20Report%202010%20En%20r15%20-low%20res%2020100615%20-.pdf#page=22.

8 UN, *The Millennium Development Goals Report*, 22.

9 Sophie Harman, "The Dual Feminisation of HIV/AIDS," *Globalizations* 8, no. 2 (2011): 213–28.

10 UN, *The Millennium Development Goals Report*.

11 UN, *The Millennium Development Goals Report*.

12 UN, *The Millennium Development Goals Report*, 27.

13 UN, *The Millennium Development Goals Report*, 34.

14 DFID, *Reproductive, Maternal and Newborn Health*, www.dfid.gov.uk/Global-Issues/Emerging-policy/Reproductive-maternal-newborn-health.

15 Betsy McKay, "AIDS funding slides," *The Wall Street Journal* (16 August 2011), online.wsj.com/article/SB10001424053111903339290457651080073806 5130.html?mod=googlenews_wsj; and Sarah Boseley, "In spite of the Bruni glitzkrieg, Aids funding is set to decline," (October 2010), www.guardian. co.uk/society/sarah-boseley-global-health/2010/oct/06/hiv-infection-aids.

16 www.unaids.org/globalreport/Epi_slides.htm.

17 Sophie Harman, "The Causes, Contours and Consequences of Multisectoralism," in *Governance of HIV/AIDS: Making Participation and Accountability Count*, ed. Sophie Harman and Franklyn Lisk (Abingdon: Routledge, 2009), 165–79; Sophie Harman, *The World Bank and HIV/AIDS: Setting a Global Agenda* (Abingdon: Routledge, 2010).

18 UNFPA, "Safe Motherhood," www.unfpa.org/public/home/mothers; World Bank, *Better Health for Women and Families: The World Bank's Reproductive Health Action Plan 2010–2015* (Washington: World Bank, 2010).

19 Harman, "The Causes, Contours and Consequences"; Harman, *The World Bank and HIV/AIDS*.

20 Harman, "The Dual Feminisation."

21 Interview with Waafus Ofosu-Amaah, Senior Gender Specialist, World Bank, 28 April 2006, Washington, DC; Harman, *The World Bank and HIV/AIDS*.

22 Harman, "The Dual Feminisation."

23 UN Women, "About us," www.unwomen.org/about-us/about-un-women.

24 Theodore R. Marmor, ed., *Poverty Policy: A Compendium of Cash Transfer Proposals*, 2008 edn (USA: Transaction Publishers, 2008).

25 Armando Barrientos and David Hulme, "Social Protection for the Poor and Poorest: An Introduction," in *Social Protection for the Poor and Poorest: Concepts, Policies and Politics*, ed. Armando Barrientos and David Hulme (Basingstoke: Palgrave Macmillan, 2008); Joseph Hanlon, Armando Barrientos and David Hulme, *Just Give Money to the Poor* (Sterling: Kumarian Press, 2010).

26 Natalia Caldes and John Maluccio, "The Cost of Conditional Cash Transfers," *Journal of International Development* 17 (2005): 151–68; Alain deJanvry and Elisabeth Sadoulet, "Making Conditional Cash Transfer Programs More Efficient: Designing for Maximum Effect on the Conditionality," *The World Bank Economic Review* 20, no. 1, (2006): 1–29; Paul Gertler, "Do Conditional Cash Transfers Improve Child Health? Evidence from PROGRESA's Control Randomized Experiment," *Health, Health Care and Economic Development* 94, no. 2 (2004): 336–41; Seth Gitter and Bradford Barham, "Women's Power, Conditional Cash Transfers, and Schooling in Nicaragua," *The World Bank Economic Review* 22, no. 2 (2008): 271–90; Emmanuel Skoufias and Vincenzo Di Maro, "Conditional Cash Transfers, Adult Work Incentives and Poverty," *Journal of Development Studies* 44, no. 7 (2008): 935–60.

27 Sarah Bradshaw, "From Structural Adjustment to Social Adjustment," *Global Social Policy* 8, no. 2 (2008): 188–207; deJanvry and Sadoulet, "Making Conditional Cash Transfer Programs More Efficient"; Skoufias and Di Maro, "Conditional Cash Transfers."

28 Sarah Barber and Paul Gertler, "Empowering Women to Obtain High Quality Care: Evidence from an Evaluation of Mexico's Conditional Cash Transfer Programme," *Health Policy and Planning* 24 (2009): 18–25; Tania Barham and John Maluccio, "Eradicating Diseases: The Effect of Conditional Cash Transfers on Vaccination Coverage in Rural Nicaragua," *Journal of Health Economics* 28 (2009): 611–21; Armando Barrientos and David Hulme, "Chronic Poverty and Social Protection: Introduction," *European Journal of Development Research* 17, no. 1 (2005): 1–7.

29 Gitter and Barham, "Women's Power."

30 Bradshaw, "From Structural Adjustment to Social Adjustment."

31 Maxine Molyneux, "Conditional Cash Transfers: A 'Pathway to Women's Empowerment'?" *Pathways to Women's Empowerment* Working Paper 5 (Brighton: Institute of Development Studies, 2008).

32 Sylvia Chant, "Re-thinking the 'Feminisation of Poverty' in Relation to Aggregate Gender Indices," *Journal of International Development* 7, no. 2 (2006): 201–20.

33 Sarah Bradshaw and Ana Quiros Viquez, "Women Beneficiaries or Women Bearing the Cost? A Gendered Analysis of the *Red de Protecion Social* in Nicaragua," *Development and Change* 39, no. 5 (2008): 823–44; Maxine Molyneux, "Mothers at the Service of the New Poverty Agenda: Progresa/Oportunidades, Mexico's Conditional Cash Transfer Programme," *Social Policy and Administration* 40, no. 4 (2006): 425–49; Maxine Molyneux, *Change and Continuity in Social Policy in Latin America: Mothers at the Service of the State?* Programme on Gender and Development, Paper No. 1 (Geneva: UNRISD, 2007).

34 The only acknowledgement of these types of issues can be found in the appendices of the World Bank's Action Plan for Maternal Health, see Sophie Harman, *Global Health Governance* (Abingdon, UK: Routledge, 2012) for further detail.

35 Harman, "The Dual Feminisation."
36 Harman, "The Dual Feminisation."
37 For further information on the role of grandmothers, see the grandmothers campaign run by the Stephen Lewis Foundation, www.grandmotherscampa ign.org/index.php?option=com_content&task=view&id=12&Itemid=46&limi t=1&limitstart=1.
38 UN, *The Millennium Development Goals Report*, 24.
39 World Bank, "Reproductive Health and the World Bank: The Facts," web. worldbank.org/WBSITE/EXTERNAL/TOPICS/EXTHEALTHNUTRITIO NANDPOPULATION/EXTPRH/0,contentMDK:22965013~menuPK:376 861~pagePK:148956~piPK:216618~theSitePK:376855,00.html.
40 Harman, *The World Bank and HIV/AIDS*.
41 Colin McInnes and Kelley Lee, "Health, Security and Foreign Policy," *Review of International Studies* 32, no. 1 (2006): 5–23.
42 "Delivering as one" has long been an issue within the UN: see www.un.org/ events/panel/resources/pdfs/HLP-SWC-FinalReport.pdf, and Margaret Joan Anstee, *Never Learn to Type* (Chichester, UK: John Wiley and Sons, 2003).

5 MDGs meet religion

Past, present, and future

Katherine Marshall

In late August 2000, one of the largest ever assemblies of world religious leaders, and the first ever at the United Nations (UN) in New York, gathered in the UN General Assembly hall. The Millennium World Peace Summit, right on the eve of the historic UN gathering of world leaders that marked the turn of the millennium, focused on world peace; however, poverty and environment were prominent on the agenda and, like the subsequent UN Millennium Summit, the aim was to agree on concrete and binding commitments worthy of such a landmark. The religious leader summit was marred by disputes, notably over the last-minute un-invitation of the Dalai Lama, visible interreligious tensions (especially among Hindus and Christians), and poor organization, but the fact that the event occurred was a wake-up call that world religions saw themselves and were seen by many as central actors in world affairs.[1]

Despite the inspirational images and messages of world religious leaders assembled at the heart of the UN, in practice they had marginal roles in the crafting of the Millennium Development Goals (MDGs) themselves. The terrorist attacks on the United States the following September deflected from the positive impetus created by the earlier assembly of religions, where the language was of peace and harmony. September 11 reinforced negative images that portrayed religion, generically, as tending towards extremism and heightened notions of a clash of civilizations with religion a divisive force. Nonetheless, the subsequent decade has witnessed a building momentum to engage religion in international affairs, and has seen growing numbers of religious and interreligious institutions embracing the MDG framework. A live and demanding issue today is how to engage this sprawling, complex world of institutions, ideas, and actors more actively and effectively in reflections and actions on poverty, equity, and peace-building agendas, now and looking ahead. This chapter reviews the linkages and disconnects among faith and secular actors on the ideals and mechanisms behind the

MDGs, highlights obstacles that have stood in the path of purposeful partnerships, focuses on contemporary tensions around the meaning and priority of human rights in the MDG context, and reflects on how faith actors could and should be engaged as attention turns to strategies, goals, and priorities beyond 2015.

Looking at the MDGs in 2011

The Johannesburg Declaration on the Millennium Development Goals highlights the historic breakthrough that the MDGs represent. As the Statement puts it: "The MDGs captured the normative consensus on the nature and meaning of development and articulated measurable and timetabled indicators. They corrected the skewed focus on markets and stabilization, redirecting attention and efforts towards the reduction of poverty and the promotion of human development. They served as a powerful tool for mobilising governments, the UN system and civil society" (see Appendix 2).

The covenant that the MDGs represent—a global moral compact that commits world nations, collectively, to act to end global poverty—is as valiant and valid today as it was in 2000. The boldness of the MDG vision, and of its corollary—the determination to hold all nations to account on progress and results—can readily be lost in the fractious disputes that occur over optimal measures of progress, differing judgments on success or failure, and sheer disappointment at slow progress towards what are rather minimal goals. Bland repetitions and exhortations are all too common and blunt the message, as do predictable doomsday commentaries or implausible declarations of victory. There is merit, therefore, in underlining the historic nature of the year 2000 call of world leaders to common action and the significance of their shared commitment. The MDGs represented an historic breakthrough in the unequivocal commitment to development as a matter of justice, in the ethical tenor of the language of the Millennium Declaration (MD), and in the adoption of the businesslike principle that progress must be measured, and that accountability must be assigned and rigorously pursued. At a global level, there has never been anything like it.

Annual reviews of progress towards the MDGs involve two significant if predictable parts. The first is the emergence of impressive reporting mechanisms. Far more than in the past, progress and shortfalls are pinpointed, and the fingers are pointed to those institutions seen as responsible for the shortfalls. The specificity of the goals and their necessary focus ensures that there is sustained attention on poverty and human development, notwithstanding pressures to shift focus, for example in

2011, to the European financial crisis and other pressing demands. Reflecting back on the nascent stages of the MDGs, the early heroic estimates of financing needs and groping for specificity in goals in light of conflicting statistics, progress is impressive. Yet the challenge of keeping the MDGs fresh and inspirational, a positive light to move towards and a discipline to goad action, has proved far more difficult than the authors could have imagined. Nowhere is this more apparent and more telling than in the response of faith communities to the MDG framework.

"There will always be poor people in the land. Therefore I command you to be openhanded toward your brothers and toward the poor and needy in your land." This assertion in the "Book of Deuteronomy" of the *Old Testament Bible* (15:11) is a reminder that an intrinsic element in the history of approaches to poverty was the historically realistic conviction of its inevitability. It also illustrates the call to charity based on compassion and religious virtue, with no suggestion that such charity is a matter of justice or that it stands a chance of bringing poverty to an end.

Poverty was understood as an inevitable, unchangeable facet of the human condition and people, across many faiths, were enjoined to help the poorest among them, especially the particularly vulnerable categories of widows and orphans. Historically, charity was seen in many traditions as benefiting as much the moral condition of the giver as the real and lasting welfare of the receiver.

This idea that poverty is inevitable is deeply rooted in many faith traditions. So the idea of ending poverty as a central and achievable goal has taken root rather slowly. It seems that it has yet to take a firm hold in political or public imaginations and understanding. The view that poverty is inevitable, in some fashion "earned" or merited, and that helping "the poor" is simply a voluntary, altruistic act of charity, is still widely held. Such assumptions color discourse and may sap some essential elements of the MDG framework, which is built on respect for the rights of all and a conviction that ending poverty is truly possible. The link between core religious teachings and attitudes towards poverty is important as a factor that explains in part the somewhat tepid support for the MDGs. That is a factor in why there was, at the outset, no rush by the religious leaders to embrace the MDGs. The disconnects extend further. Visions and understandings of poverty as due to complex systemic causes, with its backdrop in economics-speak, cast in rather technocratic language dominated by statistics, jar in the world of Sunday sermons and Friday prayers. The MDGs are anchored in defining and sticking to tangible goals, measuring the results of actions and programs, fixing on selective priorities, and constant, rigorous reporting.

The "business culture" and businesslike, disciplined approach that is an integral part of the vision and especially the accountability mechanisms of the MDGs can seem more bureaucratic than inspirational, more mundane than prophetic. This can be rather off-putting to those whose language of discourse is quite different.

Partnership may be the most elusive of the MDG goals, hard to communicate but harder still to translate into practice. There is a drumbeat of grumbles from less financially endowed partners about the need for true balance and true partnership in relationships, especially between "givers" and "receivers" of funds, and for predictability and persistence in partnership arrangements so that they do not stop and start abruptly, driven by one-sided decisions. The lofty language and promise of new kinds of partnerships raised hopes of a manna of new funds. The complex patchwork of international development finance has shifted, but not dramatically, so many hopes for radical change have been disappointed. To many faith actors, for example those struggling to meet the needs of AIDS orphans or to run overcrowded schools, the promises of new partnerships raised what were plainly, in retrospect, rather unrealistic hopes and this remains a source of tension. To many working at community level, the image is of large institutions flush with funds supporting bloated bureaucracies and slick consultants and briefcase non-governmental organizations (NGOs), while those laboring in the vineyards, that is among poor people, see little benefit despite the promises.

The MDGs are supposed to upend development finance logic but that message has yet to take hold in a meaningful way, even within professional "development" circles and among the informed public. Instead of asking, "what can we afford" or "what are we, in the goodness of our charitable hearts, willing to give," the MDG logic asks what financial resources are needed to achieve the minimum goals and moves on from there. Essential programs should, following this logic, never again be starved for funds. This new logic is clearly still an aspiration, and financial constraints have loomed ever larger with successive economic and financial crises and the demands of security and disasters like earthquakes, floods, and wars. The goal that richer nations will give 0.7 percent of their gross domestic product (GDP) for development is a barometer for some European countries but is rarely part of the North American discourse, especially at budget decision times.

Furthermore, overemphasizing the aggregate statistics of goals and targets in discussions about MDG demands and progress can numb sensibilities and lend an abstract aura to the goals. As one preacher commented, "how can I preach a sermon that explains that 'only' half of my congregation will be poor after 15 years?" Reducing any MDG, much less the whole structure, to simplified financial flows is such an over-simplification of complex realities that it can stymie real understanding and action. Financial resource flows through overseas development assistance (ODA) are vital and that point needs constant refreshing, but the public financial resources committed to the MDGs are not in themselves sufficient. Making the arguments about the need for development aid with sophistication and plausibility is always a challenge.

Thus, the MDGs, while they offer a magnificent moral scaffold, have proved to be a tough intellectual and, still more, political sell. With wide variations among countries and sectors and rather flimsy and often slippery data, the simplifying messages of MDGs can be distorting and, when they are parodied, as they sometimes are, as the "minimum development goals" (too little, leaving out so much), can detract from the essence and boldness of the vision. The MDGs *per se* rarely spark compelling political or moral discourse. Too simplistic an approach can foster confusion or deflect needed attention from some of the missing dimensions in the MDG framework: climate change, higher education, shelter, and equity and distribution within and among nations, as examples. It is a paradox: the MDGs reflect an historic and bold commitment but they can sound short-sighted and timid. The upshot has been a slow uptake of formal commitments to the MDGs by faith institutions, and a somewhat tepid approach to faith partnerships, notwithstanding the Goal 8 call to work together across all sectors.

This picture has changed. Religious communities in different parts of the world have adopted the MDGs as a core principle and a basis for advocacy and action. Among the most engaged communities are the Anglican Communion and the American Episcopal Church, a group of Evangelical churches linked together as the Micah Challenge, and two major global interfaith organizations, Religions for Peace and the Council for the Parliament of the World's Religions. The successful One Campaign has engaged faith partners as a central part of its mobilization and advocacy campaigns. The Anglican Communion approach is exemplified in a website that features the MDGs.[2] It translates into a wide range of actions within individual congregations and the denominations and communion as a whole. The Micah Challenge,[3] launched at the UN, takes its inspiration from the "Book of Micah": "He has shown you O man what is good. And what does the Lord require of you? To act justly, and to love mercy, and to walk humbly with your God" (Micah 6v8). The capacity of evangelical preachers to translate the MDGs into inspirational language is without parallel. Religions for Peace has worked with the UN Development Programme (UNDP) on toolkits that guide local faith communities in advocacy and action,[4] and the Parliament of the World Religions focused a major part of its program at the Melbourne, Australia Parliament in December 2009 on fighting poverty, framed in the language and ideals of the MDGs.[5] The "ONE Sabbath" campaign is an example of skillful linking of faith and MDG advocacy.[6] In short, one can point to a wide range of initiatives that show an impressive array of efforts to translate the MDGs into prophetic terms, compatible with faith language and principles.

Yet a nagging sense remains that the disconnects, the missed opportunities to build ambitious partnerships that would truly engage the world religions, the professed goal of which is to help those in need and work for justice, outweigh the progress made since 2000. In many respects it is a story of missed opportunities.

Obstacles in the path to achieving the MDGs

Hopefully this picture of missed opportunities can change in the future and the recent embrace of MDGs by religious leaders and communities and their effective advocacy and community action point to large and largely untapped potential. Surely there are few more compelling advocates of the MDGs than Archbishop Desmond Tutu, who speaks often to the moral imperative that the MDGs represent.[7] To move forward, however, there is a need to explore the obstacles that have stood in the way of progress since 2000. Ten areas arising from the preceding analysis deserve particular focus in looking towards more active and effective engagement of faith communities towards the MDGs and, beyond, looking to a post-2015 framework.

First, flagging, diffuse commitment is a continuing challenge worthy of the prophetic voice that demanding religious voices can bring. The annual reporting and five-yearly hoopla (2005, 2010) that accompany major MDG reviews help to keep the spirit alive and serve as reminders of the magnitude and vision of the global commitment. However, with successive crises (financial, disasters, politics) confronting world leaders and the grind of local politics demanding attention and resources, international development still tends to tumble down the priority pecking order. This reality reinforces a nagging suspicion that the political commitment and will to achieve the MDG cause is rather shallow, too tentative to assure the constant attention and commitment that the MDGs need and demand. This applies to the "donor" world, thus political leaders in the nations that provide aid. It applies still more to political leaders across a wide spectrum in poorer countries. There are remarkable examples of leaders who are deeply committed to ending poverty, driven and guided by strong visions of priorities and gritty determination to achieve results, but there are others for whom talk of ending poverty sounds more like an obligatory rhetorical flourish than a deeply held conviction.

Constant and creative efforts to reinvigorate the MDG message and build committed constituencies are needed because political will is of the essence. Whether the "white wristband," "End Poverty Now" variety of simple messaging is the right path today is open to debate: simple messages carry far in the social media age but may not advance the cause many steps along the road towards sustainable development. Celebrating and rewarding positive examples of committed leadership more deliberately, with resources, awards, and tributes, is part of the solution. Less patience with mediocrity and craven politics is another. Broader-based constituencies are essential, and it is fair to argue that today's constituencies are to a degree capable of appreciating much of the complexity and demands of the development process. Few social communities and groups of leaders are as skilled in framing messages and in mobilizing communities as religious leaders and institutions. The large and unexpected impact of the Jubilee 2000 debt campaigns, a quintessentially faith-inspired and -driven movement, and the Make Poverty History campaign of 2005 are cases in point.

Second, conflict remains a devastating obstacle in too many situations. Especially in Africa, around the "hotspots" of the Horn of Africa and Great Lakes region, progress towards development is almost impossible because war and violence shatter people, infrastructure, and trust. Tribal tensions in India are a worrying trend, as is the rise of populism, with its polarizing messages, in parts of Latin America. Worse, today's conflicts all too infrequently belong to that rare breed that settle important issues and clear the ground for some form of rebuilding. Instead, they seed misery and lasting resentment, and destroy what has been built with great effort. The likelihood of new conflicts is substantial when grievances are not addressed. Conflicts in poorer countries (witness Guinea, just to give one example) attract too little attention.

The worlds of "peace-building" and "development" are both critical for the challenge of addressing conflict and rebuilding, but they represent fields of study and action that are not well integrated. While both address the same problems, the disciplines and vocabulary tend to suggest that they move in different directions. Synergies and disconnects around actual work in conflict-affected communities are poorly mapped. Addressing conflict needs to be a more integral part of thinking about MDGs and development more broadly, and development needs to be more integrated into peacemaking and peace-building. A host of academic/intellectual and organizational issues follow from this challenge.

Among areas that deserve sharper attention are the roles that religious actors play in both the peace and development arenas. This applies with particular force for the groups of countries variously termed "bottom billion," "failing states," or "low-income countries" under stress. In virtually every such country or community, religion is a major factor, whether contributing to tension and conflict or providing services to communities (especially schools and clinics) despite state collapse and war.

Similarly, there is too little synergy among business and civil society actors and public national and international leaders on critical issues including natural resource development and accompanying tensions, food distribution and nutrition, pharmaceutical products, and the tensions that can be associated with them. Again, religious actors play important yet often unappreciated roles.

Third, awful governance needs to be acknowledged more forthrightly and dealt with and addressed with greater determination and skill, as it may be the single most important impediment to progress on the development agenda. Governance challenges cover a wide gamut, from undemocratic rule, gross incompetence and inefficiency, overly bureaucratic rules, restrictions on free debate and media coverage, and corruption. Poor governance saps programs and erodes will, and it wastes energies and resources. It is a far larger obstacle than many would recognize, even as it looms ever larger in the public perception of what development involves. Here, the potential to engage faith leaders, ideas, and communities more effectively in fighting corruption, particularly, is far greater than has been recognized.[8] If faith communities are, as many hope, to assume larger roles in delivering services and contributing directly to MDGs, especially for health and education, they themselves need to strengthen their governance systems and mechanisms for accountability.

Fourth, aid fragmentation is a large problem that demands both focused attention and thoughtful analysis and approaches. The Johannesburg Declaration lays out the goal and underlying principles clearly:

> Promoting national ownership by: (i) adapting the goals to national circumstances and priorities; (ii) creating mechanisms whereby external aid conforms to priority needs identified in national development plans prepared by the countries themselves; and (iii) putting in place financial aid and technical assistance to strengthen the analytical, policy development and programme delivery capacity of target countries.

Despite aid harmonization programs and declarations that reflect insight into the problems that out-of-control, even if well-intentioned, aid can represent, and ambitious international meetings in Rome, Paris, Accra, and Busan, much more effort is needed before anyone could plausibly argue that the ideals for aid harmonization and country ownership have been translated into practice. The sheer difficulty of bringing into some harmony large groups of donors with differing interests and styles is a first problem—it is hard even to point to clear successes today in the widely touted sector-wide approaches and programs. Another important factor is a real unease, some justified, some less so, about the capacity and direction of much-vaunted government leadership (not quite the same if often equated with country ownership). Better models, less rhetoric, and more leadership are called for. Solid mapping of what is happening on the ground, that goes beyond public facilities to those, for example, run by faith institutions, can use new technologies to help establish more clearly what is happening and where the coordination challenges are focused. Then those challenges can be addressed more effectively than they are today. This discussion highlights the extraordinary diversity and richness of work by faith institutions that is barely factored into the aid harmonization approach. In many countries this experience and associated financial flows are not captured in official data. Learning from best (and worst) practice takes place in a random fashion at best. It is hardly surprising, then, that the benefits of programs rarely add up to a larger and higher quality whole.[9]

Fifth, gender inequality is still the rule in too many ways and places, despite remarkable progress in some areas, especially education of girls. The development community needs to be more serious about gender equality, including domestic violence, rape in conflict situations and peacetime (even in schools), neglect of women's health challenges (especially but not exclusively maternal health), sharpening the focus, consistently and in practical ways, on adolescent girls, and increasing women's presence in all leadership positions (including business and religion). Progress on gender "mainstreaming" is impressive, and the 2011 World Bank/International Monetary Fund (IMF) annual meetings and the UN General Assembly were marked by much discussion about the priority of focusing on women. Yet, even though the 2012 *World Development Report* is on gender,[10] there is still a long way to go. Given both the images of many religious institutions as patriarchal and reluctant to embrace gender equality, and the complex realities of women's roles in religious communities, gender and religion needs to be a priority topic, both for the development community and for faith institutions.[11]

Sixth, navigating the shoals of lively debates about aid is an arduous challenge and many need help to make sense of the sharply polarized and polarizing communications: what works and what is simply money down a rat hole? Is free trade truly a better option for poor countries than large flows of government or private aid? Is microcredit the magic answer or a mythical magic bullet? Is a national strategy essential or simply a new cover for Communist-style central planning? Debating such issues is obviously important; different viewpoints have their validity and open discussion is a virtue. However, much of the debate does not seem to be informing programs and solutions, as ideally it should.

Many debates about aid tend to be rather circular and prone to stereotypes, and produce too little real dialogue geared to learning. Many suffer an acute time warp: debates about issues the framing of which dates back decades and which reflect poorly real advances in understanding. Here also many faith communities tend to find themselves caught, often at the margins, in fractious debates, with ideas and data that are outmoded, even as they have at their disposal rich sources of information about what is actually happening in their communities. The question is how to break out of the ruts, recognizing both the merits of different arguments and approaches (for example, the planners and seekers, hedgehogs and foxes), and their challenges and real drawbacks. Development programs and above all ideas have had significant impact over the long run, but clearly there are many failures. Only a part of these lie in technical design, more in implementation and sustained commitment to goals. Much development work is like white water rafting, often in turbulent waters. Without recognizing the complexities of the environment and the long-term nature of many programs, no amount of design, blind testing, and monitoring can assure success.

Seventh, the tendency of the development community to operate by successive fads (shifting from one popular idea, like rural development or empowerment, to another) seems to loom ever larger in today's culture of intense and rapid communication. Following fads, however, can impede solid reflection on lessons of experience, sensible blending of approaches, and humility in the face of complexity. Above all, it erodes sustainability and continuity. The faddist tendency is a constant complaint of faith communities working at community level, as they are bewildered to sit at the receiving end of shifting focus and vocabulary. The tendency to follow successive fads is related to the tendency to pile hopes and resources on "donor darlings," even when they veer off course. Of course some people's "fads" are others' innovative ideas. The new is seen to open new paths (and certainly fresh ideas are vital); new approaches can help assure that programs are not stuck with ideas the time of which has passed.

Yet one refrain voiced time and again by veterans of decades of development work is its complexity. Many challenges today have been challenges for decades and still defy simple solutions. Solid, incremental learning as well as brilliant breakthroughs are called for. Development is a marathon, not a sprint.

Perhaps the most striking recent example of practical impact of shifting development fashions is the "rediscovery" of the importance of agriculture in recent years, and "new" development strategies. Some of these ideas and strategies reflect new insights, but most are frankly reminiscent of thinking and approaches decades ago. One lesson to draw from the agriculture story is that the difficulties that stood in the way then— over-emphasis on state roles, unwillingness to stick with the demands of an agricultural research system well linked to extension, communicating well with women farmers, the pitfalls of managing agricultural extension which tends to be highly decentralized—are as real today as they were in earlier times. In effect, we have lost decades as programs fizzled and the development gurus moved on to different challenges. Similarly, capacity building, a sensible focus today, bears striking resemblance to much of the discussion around technical assistance challenges two decades ago. Experience is often the best teacher and as new ideas emerge the record of the past should not be ignored.

Eighth, education is touted as the nearest thing that exists to a magic bullet for development, and rightly so, but the focus has been too much on quantity, and it needs to shift to quality. Excellence should be the next demand, with more emphasis on defining what constitutes and what can achieve, quality. Another imperative is to reach the marginalized. Problems like absentee teachers and integrating public and private providers deserve more attention. Poor healthcare is also at the heart of poverty, everywhere, and deserves the priority it is receiving. The contentious back and forth between the respective merits of vertical and horizontal programs, however, needs to be pragmatically and quickly addressed. For both education and health, faith actors play important and often unappreciated and unanalyzed roles. It is puzzling how little real effort is going into capturing their vast experience in both sectors, in many countries.

Ninth, the administrative architecture and some of the paradigms behind the MDGs can be more a hindrance than a help when they do not take full account of local realities. The framework can encourage too much focus on money, and not enough on ideas, too much on numbers and quantitative results and too little on quality and the need for excellence. The ideals of partnership, essential as they are, can be over-generalized. The MDG architecture, constructed with much inspiration, technical expertise, and effort, offers a solid scaffolding that should be preserved. In looking to local realities, the experience of faith communities, often longer in time and more deeply rooted in communities than government, private companies, or NGOs, offers a source of ideas and also observations of impact and lessons of experience.

Tenth, bringing religion thoughtfully, systematically, and creatively into the MDG framework and apparatus is necessary, wise, and demanding. With Africa the world's most religious continent on many measures, with an extraordinarily dynamic and complex religious landscape, it is time to factor this reality far more into policy thinking at many levels for the MDG priority countries of Africa. Both governments and development institutions should be actively engaged. Both take far from a coherent and informed approach to religion and its conflict and development roles. What does that mean in practice? First, far better knowledge and information (where are the clinics, what are the messages religious service providers convey, what is their impact, what innovations are they introducing to address problems?) is needed. Second, there should be particular focus on high-potential sectors (education and health are especially large, but agriculture and water also offer possibilities), then creative and thoughtful efforts to work out sound partnership arrangements.

Rights versus responsibilities: a conundrum

Interconnectedness and rights are essential features of the MDG idea. The MDGs are global and local, they engage each affected community, and they engage the world's citizens as a whole. The core argument is that no one is secure unless all are secure, that in a globalized society the welfare of one community affects the whole. Running parallel is the notion that development is a human right, not charity, not a privilege or a voluntary gift, nor should it depend on a survival of the fittest contest for resources. The MDGs suggest that the welfare of the world's poorest citizens measures both our moral worth and future prospects. The MDGs are not an option; the intent is not a generous charitable impulse. They are a moral and practical imperative but also the precondition for a successful and peaceful future in a world where interconnections are a core reality.

The notion of a "right to development" is still an abstraction for many, rich and poor alike. Those who propound it tend to oversimplify to the point of implausibility (how meaningful is it simply to demand food for all?). The linkages between the complex and demanding elements that constitute the ways in which human rights and development are related trace a tortuous path. A complex web of responsibilities ties the ideals of human rights to those responsible for their protection. It is hardly surprising that human rights, widely accepted as foundational and inspirational, in practice spark plenty of debates and are subject to doubts, many of them unspoken.

Within the UN system, some describe human rights as the closest there is to a religion. Rights offer a unifying theme, a basis and mandate for action, an ethical framework for intervention and action. Thus it is worrying to hear that human rights are coming increasingly under fire. It is ironic that many (certainly not all) religious institutions and leaders are among those raising questions as to whether responsibilities trump rights and whether rights undermine cultural prerogatives and benefits. The most sensitive area by far is women's equality and reproductive rights, but even the mention of gender has become sensitive. The rights of children are seen by some groups as undermining parental and teacher authority.

Human rights are too central and too important, as a goal and a unifying theme, to allow the doubts and doubters to undermine the core of international consensus and standards. The questions raised obviously have importance and they deserve attention. What is most needed now is forthright dialogue and efforts to pinpoint the true areas of disagreement (Are there really any who oppose family values? What about equality for girls is truly in question?). The question is how and where to engage such a dialogue in ways that will move the debates forward.

Looking forward: visions, process, and strategic choices

We are reaching a fork between two paths that meet in 2015, with the choice where to move beyond. Now is the time to choose and set the future direction. The first path would continue directly forward with the current MDG structure, modified in some fashion (for example to take more explicitly into account lessons from experience and obvious new factors, notably the new appreciation of the vast demands of climate change). However, the basic idea would be to stick with what we have and build on what has been learned and achieved.

The second path would involve a rethinking and revamping. It would open the path to new goals and new approaches. It might, for example, take a far more regional approach (rather than global), with goals more specifically tailored to individual countries and situations. It could add new goals and deemphasize some areas of current focus. Ideally it would garner ideas from different groups, to build stronger ownership and make the process more participatory. This approach would open new possibilities, both in terms of approach to development priorities and as to how the global commitments that are reached are expected to translate into action.

It scarcely needs saying that the option of stopping in 2015, declaring victory or failure, is surely out of the question. As the process of thinking beyond the year 2015, in setting and framing goals, refining understandings of the complex partnerships involved, and reshaping the worthy frameworks for accountability and active learning, faith communities, ideas, leaders, and institutions obviously belong at the table.

Conclusion

The MDG challenge is one of humankind's boldest and most demanding adventures. It is inspirational in its vision of ending poverty and addressing inequalities, at national and community levels. It is demanding in its calls for measurement and accountability. Despite its visionary aura and sincere demands for discipline and naming of those responsible, making the MDGs a watchword and guide to international action remains a challenge. Among the challenges, both an indicator of sensitive areas and a weak link in the goal of new and creative partnerships, engaging religious institutions and leaders more proactively on the MDGs deserves priority.

Ironically, the unprecedented gathering of world religious leaders on the eve of the 2000 Millennium Summit offered an opportunity to engage this world in the global MDG effort. Hopes for engagement, at least in the early years, were largely disappointed, in part because the energies of the religious gathering took different directions, but also because 11 September 2001 so sharply deflected energies around religion and changed the terms of the debate. Both developments go a long way to explaining rather tepid initial religious engagement on the MDGs, as advocates and as actors. However, over the past few years important religious actors have taken on the MDG challenge, working actively on every MDG and target, even though not all this work is counted, and much is not fully appreciated. The experience underscores the importance of seeing faith actors as major partners in MDG implementation, addressing the obstacles that stand in the path, and engaging this complex set of institutions and ideas as the next stages of international commitments to ending global poverty are traced and turned into covenants and action.

Notes

1 I was a participant in the Summit, as a representative both of the World Bank and the World Faiths Development Dialogue (WFDD). See description in Katherine Marshall, "Development and Religion: A Different Lens

on Development Debates," *Peabody Journal of Education* 76, no. 3 & 4 (2001): 339–75, siteresources.worldbank.org/DEVDIALOGUE/Resources/PeobodyArticle4a.pdf.

2 www.e4gr.org/mdgs/fast_facts.html. See also Sabina Alike and Edmund Newell, ed., *What Can One Person Do? Faith to Heal a Broken World* (Church Publishing, 2005).

3 www.micahchallenge.org.

4 See toolkit at religionsforpeace.org/resources/toolkits/faith-in-action.html.

5 www.parliamentofreligions.org/news/index.php/tag/overcoming-poverty.

6 See as an example, www.christianpost.com/news/one-sabbath-campaign-taps-religion-to-fight-poverty-40920.

7 See, for example, this speech to a convention of lawyers: www.cms-cmck.com/Archbishop-Tutu-delivers-inspiring-commentary-on-moral-challenges-of-UN-MDGs-07-14-2009.

8 For a discussion of potential faith community contributions to the global anti-corruption effort, see Katherine Marshall, "Ancient and Contemporary Wisdom and Practice on Governance as Religious Leaders Engage in International Development," *Journal of Global Ethics* 4, no. 3 (2008): 217–29.

9 A WFDD review of the development work of faith institutions in Cambodia highlighted the fact that a wide range of religiously linked institutions are active on every single MDG, many making unique or distinctive contributions. Yet their work is largely unknown and unappreciated in the "aid community" because information systems are poor and biases towards religious institutions impede communication. For report on Cambodia analysis see repository.berkleycenter.georgetown.edu/101209CambodiaReport.pdf.

10 econ.worldbank.org/WBSITE/EXTERNAL/EXTDEC/EXTRESEARCH/EXTWDRS/EXTWDR2012/0,menuPK:7778074~pagePK:7778278~piPK:7778320~theSitePK:7778063~contentMDK:22851055,00.html.

11 Katherine Marshall, "Development, Religion, and Women's Roles in Contemporary Societies," *The Review of Faith & International Affairs* 8, no. 4 (2010): 33–40.

6 ECOSOC and the MDGs

What can be done?

Thomas G. Weiss[1]

The Economic and Social Council (ECOSOC) has long been the butt of jokes by friends and foes of the United Nations (UN). However, no other international forum brings together in quite the same way the economic, social, and environmental issues that are integral to development policy. Since 2006 and the approval of General Assembly resolution 61/16 on "Strengthening of the Economic and Social Council," this long-disparaged principal organ seems to have gained a second lease on life with special pertinence for monitoring the Millennium Development Goals (MDGs) as well as improving system-wide coherence. This chapter explores possible alterations in standard operating procedures that might benefit monitoring and implementing the MDGs.

Background

Discussions about reforming ECOSOC began shortly after it gathered for the first time, in 1946. UN member states approved structural changes in 1965 and 1973 (expanding membership from 18 to 27 and then to 54, the current size), but no increases in power have accompanied increases in size.

The boldest proposals for change consist of turning ECOSOC into a different sort of "council" akin to the Security Council, the UN's only principal organ that sometimes has teeth to back up "decisions" instead of merely making "recommendations." The Commission on Global Governance was the first visible group of eminent persons to propose such a change, in their 1995 report Our Global Neighbourhood.[2] As part of preparations for the September 2005 World Summit, the High-level Panel on Threats, Challenges and Change reiterated this call in their 2004 report *A More Secure World: Our Shared Responsibility.*[3] Not surprisingly, no such proposal was agreed, and ECOSOC lacks the wherewithal to secure compliance with its recommendations.

To be fair, there has been more adaptation by the UN over time than many recognize. Indeed, founders might well not recognize today what they created in 1945. In particular, ECOSOC's portfolio reflects a vast institutional and substantive terrain that covers not only an ever-expanding list of specialized agencies, programs, funds, and assorted bodies linked directly to economic and social development, but also an ever-growing list of agenda items. Because everything is linked to everything else, ECOSOC's purview of development policy now includes issues from security crises (which interrupt development) through peace-building efforts (which after war are stepping stones back toward a more normal development path). The council also seeks high-level engagement by member states with international financial institutions, the private sector, and civil society.

In short, there is virtually nothing that is not on ECOSOC's agenda, and this principal organ has a dizzying array of possible partners among its constituents. Moreover, it also suffers from the UN's wider culture in which process invariably trumps results. Apparently, if only we get the consultations and the processes right, then better outcomes will necessarily follow. Nothing better illustrates this non sequitur than the seemingly never-ending discussion of reforming the UN Security Council that took up about 95 percent of diplomatic energy before the 2005 World Summit, predictably to go nowhere. Conversations about ECOSOC reform suffer from the same malady.

By accretion ECOSOC has become what may be the UN's most unwieldy and least powerful deliberative body. Periodically a "new" ECOSOC is announced, but the updated version invariably reproduces the weaknesses of previous ones. Shortly after retiring from the UN and before becoming a minister in the United Kingdom, Mark Malloch-Brown quipped that the world organization is the only institution where, around water coolers or over coffee, reform is a more popular topic than sex.[4]

Can anything actually be done with ECOSOC, perhaps the only intergovernmental forum that brings together all of the economic, social, and environmental issues that are integral to development policy? I see little value added in trying to answer that question by assessing the pluses and minuses of possible but insignificant changes in pursuit of General Assembly resolution 61/16—for example, conversations around a different agenda for the Annual Ministerial Review (AMR) or the Development Cooperation Forum (DCF) or better links with the Peacebuilding Commission (PBC). Rather, I explore four broad-gauged changes in focus that could and should dramatically alter the ways that ECOSOC, and more broadly the UN, conducts business: closing down the North-South theater; pursuing consolidation; emphasizing comparative advantage not defensiveness; and realizing that policy ideas matter.

Closing down the North-South theater

A fundamental reason behind mediocre performances by ECOSOC and other UN bodies stems from the diplomatic burlesque that passes for negotiations on First Avenue in Manhattan or the Avenue de la Paix in Geneva.[5] The aging acting troupes from the industrialized North and from the developing countries of the global South provide the actors for Conor Cruise O'Brien's "sacred drama."[6] Launched in the 1950s and 1960s as a way to carve out some diplomatic space for countries on the margins of world politics, the once creative voices of the Non-Aligned Movement and the Group of 77 developing countries have become prisoners of their own rhetoric. These counterproductive groups—and the artificial divisions and toxic atmosphere that they create—constitute almost insurmountable barriers to diplomatic initiatives. Serious conversation is virtually impossible and is replaced by meaningless posturing in order to score points in UN forums and be reported by media at home.

Prime examples of marquee "stars" include former US Ambassador to the UN John Bolton and Venezuelan President Hugo Chávez. Former Canadian politician and senior UNICEF (UN Children's Fund) official Stephen Lewis wrote that "Men and women cannot live by rhetoric alone," but his characterization obviously does not apply to UN ambassadors and officials.

Moving beyond the North-South quagmire and toward issues-based and interest-based negotiations is an essential prescription for what ails ECOSOC and the UN. Fortunately, states have on occasion breached the fortifications around the North-South camps and forged creative partnerships that portend other types of coalitions that might unclog deliberations in ECOSOC and elsewhere.

Examples of wide-ranging partnerships across continents and ideologies include those that negotiated the treaties to ban landmines and to establish the International Criminal Court (ICC) as well as normative efforts to halt mass atrocities.[7] First, landmines mobilized a very diverse group of countries across the usual North-South divide as well as global civil society under the leadership of the World Federalist Movement and the usually reticent International Committee of the Red Cross. Second, the idea of a permanent criminal court had been discussed since the late 1940s but received a push after the ad hoc tribunals for the former Yugoslavia and for Rwanda; the shortcomings (including costs and the burden of evidence) demonstrated the need for a permanent court that could also act as a deterrent for future thugs. The 60-country, like-minded coalition gathered in Rome in 1998 represented a formidable and persuasive group that joined forces with the 700 members of the non-governmental organization (NGO) Coalition for an International Criminal Court, and the ICC treaty moved ahead vigorously in spite of strong opposition from several permanent members of the Security Council. Third, inconsistent "humanitarian intervention" had led to circular tirades about the agency, timing, legitimacy, means, circumstances, and advisability of using military force to protect human beings. Again, though, the North-South divide largely disappeared following the journey of the responsibility to protect (R2P) from an international commission to the World Summit to implementation in Libya so that R2P's central normative tenet is that state sovereignty is contingent and not absolute; it entails duties not simply rights. After centuries of largely looking the other way, sovereignty no longer provides a license for mass murder in the eyes of legitimate members of the international community of states.

These breakthroughs in security and human rights were also present in the economic arena for discussions about the Global Compact, which seeks to bring civil society and transnational corporations into a more productive partnership with the UN.[8] It is an effort to move beyond shibboleths about the dangers of the market and other neo-imperial designs from the global capitalist North that formerly were rejected automatically by the global South, and this type of openness to change and rejection of ideology suggests how ECOSOC, too, could evolve.

One bridge across the so-called North-South divide would involve enhanced transparency. While major problems still exist for any hard-nosed implementation of the Universal Periodic Review within the Human Rights Council,[9] a variation would be worthwhile for ECOSOC. Why not require a universal periodic review of commitments to the MDGs for the 54 elected members of the council? Rather than a voluntary system that allows member states merely to report what they wish on the topics that suit them, would it not make sense to move toward more transparency with independent and across-the-board scrutiny of the wealthy and poor, of industrialized and developing countries?

While they got a bad name during the Iraq War, serious international politics invariably mobilize "coalitions of the willing." Less posturing and role-playing is a prerequisite for the future health of the world organization. The results-oriented negotiations on landmines, the ICC, R2P, and the Global Compact suggest the benefits of more pragmatism and less ideology in international deliberations. Would such a reorientation not be possible for climate change, development finance, nonproliferation, reproductive rights, and terrorism? Within international institutions we should be seeking larger and more legitimate coalitions of the willing around specific policies. The residue of the tired North-South rhetoric of the past serves no one's interest and should be in history's dustbin rather than in the headlines. Within ECOSOC, policy debates and negotiations can and should reflect issues-based and interest-based coalitions.

Pursuing consolidation

It is hard to keep a straight face when examining documents and resolutions about "system-wide coherence," growing from the last major study commissioned by outgoing Secretary-General Kofi Annan, the 2006 report *Delivering as One*.[10] The overlapping jurisdictions of various UN bodies, the lack of coordination among their activities, and the absence of centralized financing for the system as a whole make bureaucratic struggles more attractive than sensible cooperation. The UN's various moving parts work at cross-purposes instead of in a more integrated, mutually reinforcing, and collaborative fashion. Not to put too fine a point on it, agencies relentlessly pursue cut-throat fundraising to finance their expanding mandates, stake out territory, and pursue mission creep. Fundamental change and collaboration are not in the bureaucracy's interest; turf battles and the scramble for resources are.

The UN's organizational chart refers to a "system," which implies coherence and cohesion. In reality that system has more in common with feudalism than with a modern organization. Frequent use also is made of the term "family," a folksy but preferable image because, like many such units, the UN family is dysfunctional.

Consolidation is anathema as officials rationalize futile complexity and react to incentives from donors to go their own way within a structure the design of which even Rube Goldberg could not have improved. Futile complexity and incentives explain why individual organizations focus on substantive areas often located in a different city from other relevant UN partners and with separate budgets, governing boards, organizational cultures, and independent executive heads. An almost universal chorus sings the atonal tune praising decentralization and autonomy, and ECOSOC is one of the main concert halls for this cacophony.

Yet the kind of reform that almost occurred in 1997 in the humanitarian arena illustrates what would be plausible if donors backed centralization with resources instead of speaking out of both sides of their mouths.[11] At that time, Maurice Strong proposed pulling together the

Office of the UN High Commissioner for Refugees with relevant parts of UNICEF, the World Food Programme (WFP), and the UN Development Programme (UNDP). That proposal lasted until the sky was falling, at least according to agency heads. "Coordination lite," the UN's perpetual solution to overlap, was supposed to improve delivery and protection. The powerless Office for the Coordination of Humanitarian Affairs resulted—a warmed-over version of a previous concoction, the Department for Humanitarian Affairs.

Without counting the World Bank and the International Monetary Fund (IMF)—de jure but not de facto components—over 50,000 UN officials spread out in 15 different headquarters country locations and in some 1,400 representative offices worldwide command annual budgets of some US$16 billion but are largely indifferent to other family members. They constitute ECOSOC's portfolio to foster so-called system-wide coherence. Competition and duplication necessitate ever more elaborate and expensive oversight. Current efforts revolve around creating "one UN" at the country level in order to reduce transaction costs by host governments. However, the collective memory is short. In the early 1990s, 15 unified offices were created in the former Soviet Union but rapidly were undermined by agency rivalry.

Opinion among development specialists reflects the desperate need for centralization and consolidation, although typically leaving the system alone is the only real option because inertia is so overwhelming. Support traditionally has been feeble for any real bureaucratic shake-up, but that may be changing. An independent survey conducted by the Future of the UN Development System (FUNDS) Project received over 3,000 responses from every part of the globe and from the private sector, NGOs, academia, and governments.[12] Respondents, 90 percent located in the global South, agreed that the UN's neutrality and objectivity were strong suits but decentralization was by far the defining weakness. Asked about 2025, over 70 percent agreed that there should be fewer UN agencies, with dramatic changes in mandates and functions, including stronger NGO and private-sector participation. Nearly 70 percent supported the appointment of a single head of the UN development system, although views were split about a single headquarters. Almost 80 percent sought a single representative and country program in each developing country.

ECOSOC's operating style itself is a microcosm of failed efforts at restructuring elsewhere. Proposals to create a single governing board for myriad special funds and programs, for instance, are met with guffaws. The decision to create UN Women in July 2010 was an encouraging institutional breakthrough of sorts. While no formal UN institution has ever been shuttered as an anachronism, at least UN Women consolidated four previously weaker and autonomous units. It would have been an even more crucial precedent had the consolidation also folded in the UN Population Fund (UNFPA) and avoided creating yet another governing body. Billed as an effort to pool resources and mandates, the new UN Women was not empowered with the largest operational agency with an impact on women's lives, and it created yet another executive board (albeit with non-traditional donors). Is it not possible to consolidate executive boards? Do we really require an eleventh one specifically to engage in gender theological disputes?

The UN system remains more wasteful and weak than it should be; indeed, much of what passes for "reform" amounts to wishful thinking. I could refer to ages of vintages and the newness of bottles, but perhaps a better metaphor is George Bernard Shaw's description of a second marriage, the triumph of hope over experience.

We need to get more from ECOSOC and the system through centralization and consolidation rather than hoping for the best from ad hoc serendipity and fortuitous personal chemistry. If donor countries would back their rhetoric with cash, then consolidation and centralization rather than endless chatter would result. The mobilization of "coherence funds" for use by UNDP resident coordinators for the eight country experiments with "delivering as one" were carrots to foster more centralization, but the jury is still out as to whether they have succeeded. Donors are inconsistent; their contrariness in the various corridors of UN organizations is legendary. The very countries that bemoan the world organization's incoherence also field delegations to different UN entities, which acquiesce in widening mandates and untrammeled decentralization of responsibilities to an increasingly chaotic and competitive field network.

Emphasizing comparative advantage not defensiveness

Rather than being defensive and feeling uneasy about the maturation of the G-20, ECOSOC needs to think hard about its own comparative advantage.[13] Rather than viewing the new powerhouse as a threat, the UN in general and ECOSOC in particular should think of the relationship as symbiotic rather than competitive. More generally, it is crucial to augment different country configurations for different problems and to stop insisting on fixed memberships, and especially universal participation, for every agenda item. "Minilateral" forums will not replace universal ones, but the former can galvanize progress in the latter.

To date, reactions in ECOSOC and elsewhere in UN circles have been to look for ways to ensure that the UN and the 172 states that are non-G-20 members are included at the "high table." Predictably, several non-G-20 states formed the Global Governance Group (3G); cries of illegitimacy and exclusion were widespread.[14] Mention of a possible secretariat for the G-20 (rather than the ad hoc organizational measures of changing host countries) sends shivers down the UN's institutional spine.

Many if not all global challenges require global norms, policies, institutions, and compliance. As such, the universality of the UN and the resulting legitimacy of its decisions remain enduring political strengths. "The G-20 can blow past the structure of sovereign equality in a crisis (thankfully)," Bruce Jones argued, "but if it operates against that system over time, it will sow the seeds of instability in other elements of the international system."[15] The most pressing question for ECOSOC is, can G-20 deliberations help it and the UN perform better and reform faster?

In the midst of the 2008–09 financial and economic meltdown, the G-20 shifted away from being a photo opportunity for finance ministers and became serious. Decisions in spring 2009 not only resulted in the infusion of substantial funds into the IMF but also gave life there and at the World Bank to long-sought governance reforms that provide more representation for developing countries.

These results benefited all 193 UN member states. Complaints about the G-20 process are hollow if the outcome is a more stable global economic order in which all countries and even ECOSOC can pursue other objectives. Indeed, the one-state, one-vote interpretation of UN Charter Article 2 is merely one way to frame the sovereign equality of states and desirable routes to enhanced global governance. With 80 percent of the world's population and 90 percent of the world's gross domestic product (GDP), the argument that the G-20 lacks legitimacy is far-fetched. The G-7 lacked legitimacy; the G-20 does not.

If the G-20 were to develop a stance on institutional reform, no international organization could easily resist. Multilateral agreements within the UN will increasingly be based on minilateral consensus reached first among a subset of key states. A unified G-20 stance on climate change or pandemics, for example, could jump-start subsequent negotiations and help garner wider consensus quickly. For years the global South along with Germany and Japan have moaned in unison that the Security Council and other intergovernmental organizations represent the past and not the present. However, the G-20 and other "groups" could help infuse ECOSOC and the UN more broadly with political dynamics that are representative of contemporary global power to the benefit of all.

Realizing that ideas matter

ECOSOC as a whole, as well as the development organizations reporting to it, should integrate an oft-ignored reality into deliberations and priority setting: ideas and concepts are a main driving force in human progress and arguably the most important contribution of the UN over the last six and a half decades. This conclusion emanates from research by the independent UN Intellectual History Project, the directors of which (Richard Jolly, Louis Emmerij, and I) summarized their findings from 17 books and an oral history in their 2009 *UN Ideas That Changed the World*.[16]

The system that ECOSOC oversees should provide more intellectual leadership about the fundamentally changed nature of crucial contemporary problems and their solutions; it should seek to bridge the deepening gap between scientific knowledge and political decision-making. Because policy research and ideas matter, the world organization should enhance its ability to produce or nurture world-class public intellectuals, scholars, thinkers, planners, and practitioners. UN officials are typically considered second-class citizens in comparison with counterparts from the Washington-based international financial institutions. This notion partially reflects the resources devoted to research in these institutions as well as their respective cultures, media attention, dissemination outlets, and the use of the research in decision-making.

Reality is different. Nine persons with substantial experience within the UN and its policy discussions have won the Nobel Prize in economic sciences—Jan Tinbergen, Wassily Leontief, Gunnar Myrdal, James Meade, W. Arthur Lewis, Theodore W. Schultz, Lawrence R. Klein, Richard Stone, and Amartya Sen—whereas only one from the World Bank—Joseph Stiglitz—has done so, and he resigned from his post at the Bank in protest and is now deeply associated with UN policy work. This list is in addition to individual Nobel Peace Prize winners who worked for years as staff members of the United Nations: Ralph Bunche, Dag Hammarskjold, Kofi Annan, Mohammed ElBaradei, and Martti Ahtisaari. In total, some 15 organizations, diplomats or statesmen associated with the UN have also won a Nobel Peace Prize. No other organization comes even close to being such a center of excellence, a fact missed by many politicians, the media, and a global public looking for answers to global predicaments.

In order to have ideas and the people who produce them taken more seriously, a number of priority steps should be taken to improve research, analysis, and policy work. ECOSOC might well put on its agenda: facilitate staff exchanges from universities and think tanks for original and synthetic research; create space within the UN system for truly independent research and analysis; increase interaction and exchanges between the analytical staff of the Bretton Woods institutions and the UN economic and social departments and offices; ensure more effective outreach and media promotion activities so that the economic and social research produced by the UN reaches more audiences and has more impact on the decisions of economic and finance ministers around the world; and transform recruitment, appointment, promotion, and organization of responsibilities as an integral part of a new human resources strategy to exert intellectual leadership.

Despite a rich tradition of contributions from various UN agencies and organizations, the system's full potential for policy research and analysis has scarcely been tapped.[17] Cross-agency collaboration is too rare; research staff in different parts of the world organization reporting to ECOSOC seldom venture beyond the walls of their departmental silos. Regular, mandatory gatherings for sharing research and ideas could reduce parochialism. ECOSOC should establish a research council to expand opportunities for information-sharing and collaboration, and reduce the chances of redundancy and the pursuit of different projects at cross-purposes.

The UN should seek as many alliances as possible with centers of expertise and excellence—in academia, policy think tanks, government policy units, and corporate research centers. Human resources policy should also do more to foster an atmosphere that encourages creative thinking, penetrating analysis, and policy-focused research of a high intellectual and critical caliber. The model of the Inter-governmental Panel on Climate Change could well be replicated for other issues. The intellectual firepower of staff members is essential, which will depend on improvements and better professional procedures in recruitment, appointment, and promotion. These nuts-and-bolts issues of operational alliances and staffing affect directly the quality of policy outputs from all of the organizations reporting to ECOSOC.

By definition, if any organization pursues a bold and forward-looking policy agenda, it cannot please all 193 member states all of the time. Calling into question conventional or politically correct wisdom requires longer-term funding. Encouraging free thinking and exploration of ideas and approaches is vital but not cheap. Ideally donors should provide multi-year funding for research and analysis, with no strings attached, through assessed contributions, but voluntary funding is more likely. In any case, conversations about the system-wide need for such policy autonomy should be on ECOSOC's agenda.

Without first-rate people and adequate funding, messages typically are watered down to satisfy the lowest common intergovernmental denominator. Yet we have learned since 1990 from the howls often greeting the annual Human Development Report that intellectual independence can be tolerated.[18] This experience suggests that researchers can be liberated from the need to clear with boards or donors and check analyses for bureaucratic and governmental sensitivities before publication. Protecting "islands" or "safety zones" will be required because serious and independent analysis can take place not only away from daily tasks but also without fearing the loss of income or publication because one or more administrators and governments are irked. The tolerance for controversy should be far higher; academic freedom should not be an alien concept for researchers from organizations reporting to ECOSOC from within secretariats working on twenty-first-century intellectual and policy challenges.

Conclusion

Commissions, high-level panels, task forces, and summits come and go. Fundamental reform and transformation of the UN system will not result from incremental thinking and tinkering. When I argue that the next generation of international organizations is not out of reach, colleagues think that I have been inhaling as well as smoking. The inertia and interests to be overcome in ECOSOC are especially formidable. Indeed, Sir Robert Jackson undoubtedly turns over in his grave with some regularity because he began his 1969 evaluation of the UN development system by writing that "the machine as a whole has become unmanageable in the strictest sense of the word. As a result, it is becoming slower and more unwieldy like some prehistoric monster."[19] That lumbering dinosaur is now 40 years older and not adapted to the climate of the twenty-first century.

It is hard to be sanguine about implementing the suggested changes in ECOSOC's operations: closing down the North-South theater; pursuing consolidation; emphasizing comparative advantage not defensiveness; and realizing that ideas matter. Without them, however, the lack of coherence damages credibility and gives rise to further public cynicism. Institutional fragmentation and competition lead not only to wasteful overlap and redundancy but also to issues falling between agencies. In continuing the unfinished journey to better global governance,[20] individuals and states can be as strong as the institutions that they create. There are plenty of things wrong, but many can be fixed.

Notes

1 This chapter reproduces parts of "ECOSOC Is Dead, Long Live ECOSOC," which the Friedrich Ebert Stiftung commissioned for a retreat by member states and published in *Perspectives.*

2 Commission on Global Governance, *Our Global Neighbourhood* (Oxford: Oxford University Press, 1995).

3 High-level Panel on Threats, Challenges and Change, *A More Secure World: Our Shared Responsibility* (New York: UN, 2004).

4 Mark Malloch-Brown, "Can the UN Be Reformed?" *Global Governance* 14, no. 1 (2008): 1–12.

5 Thomas G. Weiss, "Moving Beyond North-South Theatre," *Third World Quarterly* 30, no. 2 (2009): 271–84.

6 Conor Cruise O'Brien, *United Nations: Sacred Drama* (London: Hutchinson & Company, 1968).

7 For overviews of the three illustrations, see: Richard Price, "Reversing the Gun Sights: Transnational Civil Society Targets Land Mines," *International Organization* 52, no. 3 (1998): 613–44; Richard J. Goldstone and Adam M. Smith, *International Judicial Institutions* (London: Routledge, 2009); and Thomas G. Weiss, *Humanitarian Intervention: Ideas in Action*, 2nd edn (Cambridge: Polity Press, 2012).

8 John Gerard Ruggie, "global_governance.net: The Global Compact as Learning Network," *Global Governance* 7, no. 4 (2001): 371–78.

9 Bertrand Ramcharan, *The UN Human Rights Council* (London: Routledge, 2011).

10 United Nations, *Delivering as One* (New York: UN, 2006).

11 Thomas G. Weiss, "Humanitarian Shell Games: Whither UN Reform?" *Security Dialogue* 29, 1 (1998): 9–23.

12 See Future of the United Nations Development System, "A Global Perception Survey," April 2010, available at www.surveymonkey.com/s/JLVM53D; and also "Fact Book on the UN Development System," November 2010, available at www.fundsproject.org/?p=270.

13 Andrew Cooper and Ramesh Thakur, *The G-20* (London: Routledge, 2012 forthcoming).

14 Global Governance Group, "Letter dated 11 March 2010 from the Permanent Representative of Singapore to the United Nations addressed to the Secretary-General," document A/64/706.

15 Bruce Jones, "Making Multilateralism Work: How the G-20 Can Help the United Nations," Stanley Foundation Policy Analysis Brief, April 2010, 7.

16 Richard Jolly, Louis Emmerij, and Thomas G. Weiss, *UN Ideas That Changed the World* (Bloomington: Indiana University Press, 2009). For more details, see www.unhistory.org.

17 See Thomas G. Weiss, Tapio Kanninen, and Michael Busch, *Sustainable Global Governance for the 21st Century: The United Nations Confronts Economic and Environmental Crisis amidst Changing Geopolitics* (Berlin: Friedrich Ebert Stiftung, 2009), Occasional Paper 40.

18 Craig N. Murphy, *The UN Development Programme: A Better Way?* (Cambridge: Cambridge University Press, 2006).

19 United Nations, *A Capacity Study of the United Nations Development System* (Geneva: UN, 1969), volume I, document DP/5, iii.

20 Thomas G. Weiss and Ramesh Thakur, *Global Governance and the UN: An Unfinished Journey* (Bloomington: Indiana University Press, 2010).

Part II
Focus on Africa

7 Lessons to be learned from the challenges to achieving the MDGs in Africa

Craig N. Murphy

This chapter grew out of research on the relative likelihood that the different Millennium Development Goals (MDGs) would be achieved throughout the African continent by the 2015 target date. In the course of that research, I became aware that my own initial skepticism about the usefulness of the whole MDG system as a mechanism for reducing poverty had waned since the goals were promulgated more than a decade ago. As a result, the first part of the chapter is devoted to explaining those grounds for skepticism, which I shared with many other observers, and the reasons why my own doubts about the MDGs have been somewhat resolved. The second section of the chapter prognosticates about performance vis-à-vis the differences in Africa goals by the 2015 target date. It is followed by a discussion of the reasons some goals will not be achieved. The chapter's fourth section turns to a set of 10 recommendations for the continued reduction of poverty in Africa, as measured by the current MDGs, beginning with what may seem the most politically feasible recommendations, and continuing to the most difficult to achieve. Rather than ending on the somewhat depressing note that the most critical of the recommendations are the least likely to be accepted, the chapter ends with a critique of some of the assumptions that my own field, international political economy (IPE), has long made about the sources of major change in international social policy. If this critique is correct, then the later recommendations, while still politically unlikely, may prove to be less critically important.

Waning skepticism about the MDGs

When the MDGs were first announced at the 2000 summit and throughout the first half of the following decade I remained skeptical of the entire political program of which they are a part. While working on a critical history of the UN development system,[1] I learned from

Secretary-General Kofi Annan's close collaborator, Mark Malloch-Brown (who was the World Bank Vice-President in charge of public relations when the MDGs were formulated, head of the UN Development Programme (UNDP) at the time of the summit, and then Deputy Secretary-General) that he (and, presumably, the Secretary-General) believed that the MDGs could play the same role, with global poverty in the twenty-first century, that the "shopping basket ... of the basics of life"[2] developed by Seebohm Rowntree to quantify poverty in Yorkshire played in the massive reduction of poverty throughout Britain in the twentieth century. That seemed a plausible goal, but Rowntree's studies only played an enabling role in a long and complicated battle in which the Pensions Acts, the Beveridge Report, the 1944 Education Act, the National Health Service, and the emergence of the post-war "collectivist" consensus played much more decisive roles.[3] Moreover, I knew that there was good reason to believe that even the statistical work encouraged by the MDG program would have some unfortunate opportunity costs because it would crowd out other, more creative, useful, and politically significant statistical programs focused on poverty in Africa and other developing regions.

To understand how that was likely to happen, it is important to remember that in many of the poorest countries, and in many of the poorest regions of some countries that are quite a bit wealthier, the creation of sophisticated measures of poverty and the careful analysis of poverty and inequality is still a luxury, not a political necessity. It is something more often supported by international development assistance than by local budgets. Since the early 1990s, one of the major global sources of such assistance has been the UN Development Programme's (UNDP) Human Development Office. The sponsors of the annual global *Human Development Report* also sponsor national and local teams that undertake more specific studies of particular developing countries, regions and cities within them, and sometimes even studies of neighborhoods within cities. These reports characteristically focus on measurements of social life in addition to those that have been developed by the central UNDP office in New York.[4]

The processes of developing and reporting on such additional indicators have two major advantages over attempts (like the MDG process) to apply the same set of global indicators to the entire world. First, the local human development reports (HDRs) are apt to give a much more accurate picture of poverty and inequality because they concentrate on measures that are significant within the actual local economy: for example, control of livestock is a much more accurate measure of wealth in many parts of rural Africa than is any, somewhat suspect, measure of purchasing power parity (PPP) income. Second, the local reports give us more of a picture of how poverty is understood by the poor themselves because the processes used to create the local HDRs always involve some degree of direct interaction with the communities to which they apply. At the very least, the reports' authors will consult with non-governmental organizations (NGOs) that purport to represent significant parts of the communities involved and are judged to be relatively representative by UNDP officials who work in the country.

Amartya Sen has written eloquently about how Mahbub ul Haq's Human Development Office created a research program that, over the years, through its openness and participatory nature, is likely to give us a clearer picture of the impediments to development while at the same time directly empowering and increasing the capacity of those disadvantaged who have been engaged by the process, which are, after all, the real goals of "human development."[5] The MDGs, with their broad scope that emphasizes a wide range of impediments to the development of human capacity certainly come out of that same research program, but they, and the entire process for monitoring and assessing progress toward them has none of the epistemological openness—especially the constant awareness that the wrong thing may be being measured—or the participatory nature of the local HDRs. Moreover, because UNDP has been given the central role in providing those assessments without being given new resources to do them, it would not be surprising if the work needed to serve the top-down purpose of MDG assessment might come at the expense of the support for local HDRs.

There is evidence consistent with the argument that this has happened. The graph below (Figure 7.1[6]) shows the number of HDRs published each year, only one of which is the global report. The number of local

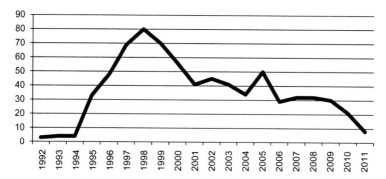

Figure 7.1 HDRs published
Source: UNDP Human Development Reports database

reports fell off dramatically with the announcement of the MDGs and has remained at around 30 per year since then, less than half the average number published each year from 1995 to 2000. Of course, these data do not tell us whether the drop-off in the number of reports was a consequence of the Programme's new responsibility for monitoring the MDGs, or of some other causes. Moreover, since 2008, UNDP has published 60 national and six regional reports on progress toward the MDGs, reports that are similar to the HDRs, albeit with a somewhat narrower scope.[7]

Even so, the relatively comprehensive and sometimes quite insightful national reports on progress toward the MDGs that UNDP has recently sponsored are not the primary mechanism that the MDG process uses to monitor policies directed toward achieving the goals. That process is, at its core, the system of Poverty Reduction Strategy Papers (PRSPs) that the International Monetary Fund (IMF) and World Bank require of their developing country members.[8] The PRSP system is more a top-down process of surveillance imposed on the governments of the developing world by the major aid donors who dominate the Bretton Woods institutions than it is an attempt to share experience and best practice across the developing world. The system has been criticized as a Foucauldian form of disciplining that forces Third World governments to embrace neoliberal globalization while taking national responsibility for the increased poverty and inequality that often comes along with it.[9] Yet there is also evidence that the writing of national PRSPs can sometimes become a process of significant, productive contestation over the direction of national policy[10] and in a relatively democratic country such as Ghana, the PRSP can serve as an effective indicative planning instrument for a legitimate and responsive government.[11]

Perhaps the most important thing about the political and policy processes surrounding the MDGs is the way in which they have become the center of a network of local and transnational social movements committed to the abolition of poverty and willing to name and shame those actors at all levels who help perpetuate the problem by their words, their deeds, or their inaction. The elimination of poverty has, as a result, in a very short time become a "super norm" embraced by a wide coalition of governments, non-governmental bodies, social movements, and international organizations.[12] Only a generation ago, in the era of disappointment that set in after the failure of the First Development Decade, it was quite commonplace to assume that global poverty was intractable and that, therefore, you could still be wise and compassionate even if you ignored the problem. That, today, is no longer the case and much of the responsibility for that change goes to the MDG project.

The hortatory acceptance of this new norm may have its greatest potential for good in Africa where poverty, as measured by the MDG indicators, is unusually widespread and persistent. For that reason alone, Africa's experience of the MDGs is of particular significance. If the MDGs have not made a difference in Africa, it would be unsurprising if the global commitment to end poverty were to wane dramatically.

The MDG targets in Africa

Some of the 2015 MDG targets will be met in some countries in Africa,[13] but looking at the continent as a whole, none of the goals will be met by then. Here is what is almost certain to happen, starting with the better news and going to the worse:

- Africa will come a long way toward meeting the primary education (MDG 2) and gender parity (MDG 3) goals, perhaps getting 90 percent of the way toward some of the specific targets.
- The most important of the African environmental targets for the world (for example, those concerned with species depletion) differ from those that are, today, the most important for Africans themselves: the ones concerned with a clean local environment (MDG 7), especially access to clean water, where the continent will end up about 70 percent of the way toward the target.
- More disappointing will be the record relative to the poverty (MDG 1) targets, where the number of people in absolute poverty will be reduced by less than one-quarter instead of the goal of one-half, perhaps 40 percent of the way toward the target.
- The record vis-à-vis the health-related goals—reducing child mortality (MDG 4) and the impact of infectious disease (MDG 6) and improving maternal health—will be mixed, but the almost non-existent decrease that we will see in maternal mortality is indicative of the larger story.
- Finally, given the lack of coherence of, and the lack of information about the quantitative targets for MDG 8, the development partnership goal—the only one that refers to the responsibilities of the developed world—is difficult to assess. Nonetheless, it will probably be the case that the average African will be responsible for more debt to the developed world in 2015 than her counterpart was in 2000, while the barriers to entering developed country markets that she will face will be the same or greater.

This is a bleak assessment. Nevertheless, two factors, both of them related to statistics, may brighten the dark picture outlined above.

The first has to do with the simple availability of data. This summary assessment, or anyone else's, can easily be challenged or critiqued by anyone with access to the internet. This one is based on a critical assessment and straightforward projections of data that are readily available online in the 2010 joint African Union (AU), UN Economic Commission for Africa (ECA), African Development Bank (ADB), and UNDP assessment,[14] the UNDP-sponsored reports of individual countries,[15] the African PRSPs,[16] and the raw data used in all these reports as presented by UNDP and other UN agencies.[17]

These data, in this form, allow a fundamentally new kind of global engagement with problems of poverty *in* all parts of the world, *from* all parts of the world. In *World's in Transition: Evolving Governance Across a Stressed Planet*, Joseph A. Camilleri and Jim Falk call this kind of ability for people in all parts of the world to reflect on the specificity of issues within any part of the world "holoreflexivity," and they celebrate it as an emergent human cognitive ability that may eventually make tractable the seemingly impossible global problems of climate change, financial turmoil, and global inequalities.[18] That may seem far-fetched, but there is at least some evidence from the MDG process of what Camilleri and Falk anticipate. If nothing else, the global process has led some international organizations and advocacy groups in the wealthier countries to help many of Africa's most overstretched governments to begin to collect data on some of the MDG issues, especially the health issues, that they have never before monitored.[19] As Camilleri and Falk emphasize—reiterating the kind of argument that Mark Malloch-Brown makes when referring to the work of Seebohm Rowntree—it is impossible to make rational policy on any level without having the information about what needs to be changed.

The second statistical issue may be of even greater salience in Africa; it has to do with the way in which the MDGs are constructed, for example, demanding the reduction of poverty by 50 percent in 15 years, rather than, say, having a goal of reducing the absolute number of people in poverty. Many more people would be brought out of poverty by a reduction of poverty in a typical African state by 40 percent, than by a much larger percentage reduction in a similarly populous middle-income state in Southeast Asia or South America. Similarly, the MDG designers chose a starting date (1990), which assured that Africa's pre-MDG decade of stagnation counted against its achievement of the goals, while China's go-go economy of the 1990s would count in its favor. Focusing on these kinds of measures obscures astonishing progress that has occurred in some of Africa's poorest countries—rates of improvement in some aspects of social welfare that are greater than in many other parts of the world, even than in China's and India's rapidly growing economies the success of which will account for most of the global gains, as measured by the MDGs. This has become a common critique of the MDGs as applied to Africa,[20] but it remains one that needs to be emphasized. The fact that Africa will "miss the MDG targets" does not mean that Africans or African governments have "failed."

Outline of an analysis of causes

Nevertheless, it is worth reflecting on the African experience since 2000 in order to identify those reasons why the MDGs will not be met that are more than just statistical artifacts.

The immediate impediments to Africa's achievement of the education and gender parity goals are a lack of commitment on the part of some African governments (for example, some are simply not willing to give up a school financing system that relies on families to pay school fees and to buy uniforms, books, and supplies), but there is also a question of government capacity to oversee and manage a complex national educational system, let alone to direct the system toward new social goals.

The problems associated with maintaining a clean environment are more complex. Government capacity is even more sorely tried when trying to maintain and allocate a scarce resource like water. Moreover, it is not just a question of locating and maintaining control of the resource so that it can be used sustainably: most African countries lack the physical infrastructure to store and distribute water with minimal waste. Finally, almost all the environmental issues in Africa are linked to two factors that are largely outside of government control: population growth (especially the growth that will continue throughout the penultimate phase of the demographic transition, after fertility rates have declined, but before the population pyramid has stabilized) and climate change.

The sources of Africa's relative poverty have been the subject of so much debate that it may seem foolish to assert that we have any consensual knowledge about poverty's causes. Nonetheless, it is certainly the case that redistribution *within* Africa would be insufficient to solve the problem; therefore, a lack of growth must be a central cause. Africa's slow growth is undoubtedly connected to the very small scale and scope of most African enterprises, a condition that has much less to do with the preferences of African producers than it does with the constraints that those producers face. Most African producers only have access to very small trading areas: local infrastructure—especially the road system—simply does not connect them to enough consumers. On top of which, many markets have been fractured or put off-limits by protracted violent conflicts (which, of course, have other negative consequences for growth), let alone by the barriers created by Africa's political division into more than four dozen former colonial states, each of which was originally designed to serve a purpose other than the welfare of its subjects.

The sources of Africa's health crises include all that has gone before, and a great deal more. The continent's relative poverty and the factors that prevent the development there of modern industries of vast scope and scale are the major impediments of the use of the most up-to-date, costly medicines by the victims of infectious diseases including, but not limited to, HIV/AIDS (the prevalence of which is a significant factor in the continent's appalling rates of maternal mortality). Nevertheless, the proximate causes of many of the continent's acute health problems are less the lack of access to modern medicines than they are the lack of access to medical care of any kind. Poor infrastructure (bad roads) and conflict are part of the story. The continent's fractured medical systems mean that many births are not attended by doctors, nurses, or trained midwives; therefore, mothers and infants die. The continent's medical systems, in turn, have been harmed by a lack of government commitment (often initiated by the neoliberal policies of lenders during the Washington Consensus era). Moreover, everywhere in Africa, trained medical personnel are regularly siphoned from the continent, pulled by the higher wages and greater social stability in the developed world.

The major causes of the imperfect achievement of the development partnership goal may be too complex, and too poorly studied, to delineate, but it is still possible to go beyond saying that there are some powerful vested interests in the wealthy countries that oppose specific reforms of the system of international development cooperation. The problem, for example, is not one of moral parochialism, of an inability to see the world's poor as like oneself. Ethicist Richard Shapcott makes a strong case that all of the complex, internally consistent Western traditions of ethics (including the most conservative) accept that:

- global poverty is a significant moral problem that all have a duty to address;
- that further obligations "extend from harms which may have arisen in specific causal relationships both historically and in the past"; and
- that all have "a duty to significantly reform the current international order which extends from the harm that it does to the poorest."[21]

While it is hardly dispositive, Bono explains his success at convincing conservatives such as Jesse Helms and George W. Bush to embrace generous African initiatives, as a consequence of his direct, coherent appeal to ethics.[22] It follows that perhaps one reason for the failure of MDG 8 has been the failure to raise the question not only frequently and persistently, but also framed within the ethical discourses that the leaders of developed countries accept. Doing so may make it possible to create for MDG 8 the kind of specific, measurable indicators of developed country performance that have been created for the performance of the African policy-makers who are held responsible for the other seven goals.

Ten recommendations

These follow from the analysis outlined above:

- Citizens throughout Africa and external actors with influence over specific African governments should work to increase the commitment of laggard governments to the anti-poverty agenda. It would be helpful if we could be more precise about how to achieve this goal; for example, if we could rely on the predictions of selectorate theory[23] to tell us how civil society organizations and aid donors might undermine anti-poor, autocratic governments. Unfortunately, the real correlations among political system characteristics, anti-poverty policies, and actual outcomes are not as straightforward as we might hope. More deeply historical, socially embedded analysis is needed to understand how social contracts that reach the poorest groups have sometimes been created.[24]
- Intergovernmental, bilateral, and non-governmental organizations should help lagging African governments develop the capacity to staff and manage national education systems that serve all citizens. Unfortunately, perhaps, evidence suggests that the key innovation that has assured near-universal education in some countries is the provision of truly free schooling.[25] Some of the poorest governments simply may not have the resources to do that at the same time that they attempt to maintain critical infrastructure.[26]
- Intergovernmental, bilateral, and non-governmental organizations should help African governments improve and build basic infrastructure, especially roads and water systems. Even World Bank economists have recognized the problem, and suggested economically sustainable solutions.[27] It is time to implement them. Now, not in 2015 when the MDGs have not been met.
- To gain all the benefits of improved infrastructure, the move toward African economic integration must be revitalized, urgently. This is

one thing on which today's followers of Kwame Nkrumah and of
P.T. Bauer (for example, the "anti-Bono," Dambisa Moyo[28]) agree.

- Roads and economic integration agreements will not be effective if
the kinds of violent conflicts that have wracked the continent continue.
The reports of the Simon Fraser University-based Human Security
Project[29] demonstrate that the conflict prevention work of the UN,
sitting African leaders, and independent groups like the Elders has
been very effective. Such work needs to be continued and enhanced
by the strong support of opinion leaders throughout the world.

- Conflict prevention needs to be facilitated by reconciliation in those
protracted social conflicts that remain across the continent. Reconciliation is much more than the management of conflict, even when
such management involves seemingly "radical" measures like the
creation of new states (as in Eritrea and South Sudan). As John Paul
Lederach has argued in many places,[30] the overwhelming empirical
lesson across traditions of peace research is that the emergence of
stable peace from a situation of "asymmetric" or "unbalanced" social
conflict requires truth, justice, and forgiveness. For governments (and
their domestic and international allies) to turn away from the larger
problem of reconciliation as soon as the violent stage of a conflict
has ended is very tempting, but it is foolhardy.

- Even with a focus on conflict prevention and reconciliation, it is important to remember that militias do not kill people—it is the bullets in
their guns that do. That is why many African governments, and even
more African civil society organizations (especially associations of
war victims) champion the current effort to create an arms trade
treaty[31] and similar efforts to control the global flow of the weapons
that are most often used in today's wars. If governments of arms-
producing countries are really serious about ending poverty in Africa,
they should support those efforts, too.

- Similarly, international actors need to help African governments
rebuild national medical systems destroyed by violent conflict, the
years of economic stagnation, and the pull of higher salaries and
better working conditions outside Africa. The real material costs that
would be involved here may be an order of magnitude larger than
what is needed to support the educational systems in the poorest
African countries. Again, as with trying to increase the anti-poverty
commitments of African governments, this is a problem for which
the existing social science literature provides little sure guidance; it
is a field in which a great deal of research is needed.

- Sometimes, when we do not have sure guidance from policy research,
experiments can both help resolve the problem and help us learn

more about it. Part of the problem in Africa is the loss of trained medical workers to more prosperous countries. The governments of those countries, who are the primary financiers of medical training in their own countries, should experiment with requiring all doctors and nurses to work for two years in underserved parts of Africa as a condition of receiving medical training.

- Finally, continuing the focus on things that should be done by those outside of Africa, we need real, monitorable targets for MDG 8.

As mentioned in the first section of this chapter, Mark Malloch-Brown often talks about the MDGs as the equivalent, at a global level, of Seebohm Rowntree's basket of goods that defined what was needed to live a decent life in industrial York a century ago. Of course, it proved impossible to give everyone in Britain that minimum level without creating a national system of redistribution from the wealthiest to the poorest. When we look at why Africa will not meet the MDGs, we can find no reason to believe that what was once true for Great Britain will not also be true for the world. That, in fact, may be what achieving MDG 8 really means.

Unfortunately, though, the above list of recommendations is ordered from those that would be the easiest to achieve, to those that would be the most difficult; those that are the most difficult are those that would require the most of people outside of Africa who are not poor.

Is it really that difficult?

Let me conclude by cautioning that the assessment I have made here may be colored by the dominant historical narrative in my own field, IPE. In 1999 one of the founders of the field, Susan Strange, condemned what she called "the Westfailure system" for our recurrent financial crises, failure to confront global environmental problems, and persistence (in fact, the rapid growth) of global inequality and poverty.[32] Yet, while Strange argued that she was attacking a system, the immediate object of her ire was the irresponsibility of the governments of the great powers (perhaps particularly that of the United States), the organizations that she understood as having the greatest influence over the prospects for fundamental change in this so-called "system." In this, Strange followed the general argument current in IPE across its various, supposedly warring, "paradigms" (even though Strange was, in fact, the least likely of the founders of IPE to overemphasize state power; she always drew attention to the roles of corporate power and the power of ideas).

To a large extent, the argument began with Charles Kindleberger, the oldest of the founding figures in the field, someone who actually remembered the Ur-moment when the problems that bothered IPE's founders emerged, the moment when everything started to go wrong: the Great Depression. Kindleberger's lesson was that the Depression had been deepened and lengthened by the failure of the United States to take responsibility for the world economy, in particular by refusing to act as a lender of last resort, something that only it could do.[33] IPE scholars rapidly extended Kindleberger's argument about the specific role that the United States could have played in maintaining the global financial order (and finally did play after World War II) to a much broader set of arguments about the need for "hegemonic stability" to maintain global welfare along all dimensions. In the versions of the resulting history produced by most of the field's American leaders, the problems of the 1970s onward all had something to do with the United States no longer being able to play the benign "hegemonic" role it played in the economy that linked the rich capitalist countries and the dependent Third World. In Susan Strange's more critical, British version, the problem was the disappointing way in which the United States increasingly used its power only to serve its narrow interests. Nonetheless, the larger story was still the same.

Even John G. Ruggie relied on US power to help explain the postwar agreement among industrialized capitalist nations to provide global support for the development of the welfare state—the social transformation in which Rowntree's statistical goal-setting played its role[34] and other scholars (myself included) saw a similar Ruggie-like pattern of US power *plus* global normative and institutional change as the explanation of the regime of "decolonization and development" that brought most of the dependent Third World into the US hegemonic system after the war. Ruggie, of course, is the rare IPE scholar who is also a significant political actor, someone who joined Kofi Annan's team and helped spearhead the process of institutional reform that was Annan's major goal, the process of which the MDGs were a part.

There is a way in which that process also goes back to Kindleberger—specifically, to Kindleberger's early recognition that the postwar national and continental industrial economies of mass production and mass consumption were going to be transformed into an economy of global commodity chains linked by transnational corporations and that there would be a need for global regulation, a Global Agreement on Investment, to assure (among other things) that the welfare state was maintained, global inequality did not grow, and companies were given no incentive to destroy the environment.[35] Of course, major powers blocked the creation of multinational regulations toward those ends and one major part of Annan's, Malloch-Brown's, and Ruggie's reform agenda was to find alternative means to achieve the same end. The variables that Ruggie considered alongside the power of major states—that is to say, global normative and institutional change—were, from the beginning, at the center of their plan.

Arguably, they always should have been there in the IPE analysis. Perhaps the only essential thing that US power provided in the "Golden Years" of the postwar economic order (the 1950s and 1960s) was a lender of last resort. The triumph of the welfare state (and, in the United States, civil rights) was an outcome of domestic struggles, including the ethical transformation—the sense of being one community—that came with the shared experience of sacrifice during World War II. Likewise, decolonization and the creation of the development system were not the gift of the world's powerful states—albeit the United States and the Soviet Union were sometime supporters of both; these transformations came from the success of anti-colonial movements and the new sense of what was right that also grew from the experience of shared sacrifice during the war.[36]

Annan regularly framed his reform agenda in the terms of the moral consensus that existed among the wartime allies (the original "United Nations"), Roosevelt's "Four Freedoms"—the freedoms of speech and religion and the freedoms from want and fear. Prem Shankar Jha concludes his *Twilight of the Nation State: Globalisation, Chaos, and War* by outlining this vision, praising Annan's deep commitment to the rule of law, and suggesting that transformative social change has always depended on broad, complex, ethically inspired movements that may sometimes have included the currently powerful, but have always depended on many, many others.[37] That is a view that students of IPE need to consider. It is one that may make us think differently, not about the prospects for meeting the MDG targets in 2015, but about the possibility of the eventual success of the movement united by the global anti-poverty norm.

Notes

1 Craig N. Murphy, *The UN Development Programme: A Better Way?* (Cambridge: Cambridge University Press, 2006).
2 Jonathan Bradshaw of the University of York quoted in Julian Knight, "The Changing Face of Poverty," BBC News, 26 July 2005, news.bbc.co.uk/2/hi/business/4070112.stm.
3 The reference is to Samuel H. Beer, *British Politics in the Collectivist Age* (New York: Knopf, 1966).
4 See Murphy, *The UN Development Programme*, 250–57.
5 Amartya Sen, "A Decade of Human Development," *Journal of Human Development* 1, no. 1 (2000): 17.

6 Found at UNDP, *Human Development Reports 1990–2011*, hdr.undp.org/en/reports.

7 UNDP, "MDGs: Tracking Country Progress," www.undp.org/mdg/countries.shtml.

8 They are relatively public documents available on a regularly updated IMF website, Poverty Reduction Strategy Papers, www.imf.org/external/np/prsp/prsp.aspx.

9 See Celine Tan, *Governance through Development: Poverty Reduction Strategies, International Law, and the Disciplining of Third World States* (London: Routledge, 2011); and Jonathan Joseph, "Poverty Reduction and the New Global Governmentality," *Alternatives* 35, no. 1 (2010): 29–51.

10 See Niam Gaynor, "The Global Development Project Contested: The Local Politics of the PRSP Process in Malawi," *Globalizations* 8, no. 1 (2011): 17–30; and Kate Meagher, "The Anti-Governance Machine: Ownership and Accountability in National Development," paper prepared for the conference, "Beyond Accra: Practical Implications of Ownership and Accountability in National Development Strategies," London School of Economics, 22–24 April 2009.

11 See Murphy, *The UN Development Program*, 310–12.

12 David Hulme and Sakiko Fukuda-Parr, "International Norm Dynamics and 'the End of Poverty': Understanding the Millennium Development Goals," Brooks World Poverty Institute Paper 96, University of Manchester, June 2009, explains the emergence by demonstrating the similarity between the process of its promulgation and acceptance with a model developed to explain the emergence of other global social norms, such as the abolition of slavery.

13 The broad statements in this section are true both of "Africa" as the whole continent, the member countries of the African Union, as well as, more specifically, the "Africa" of UNDP's African regional bureau, a group of countries that is equivalent to what is often referred to as sub-Saharan Africa.

14 AU, UN-ECA, ADP, and UNDP, *Assessing Progress in Africa toward the Millennium Development Goals*, www.undp.org/africa/documents/mdg/full-report.pdf.

15 UNDP, *Human Development Reports 1990–2011*, hdr.undp.org/en/reports.

16 Available on a regularly updated IMF website, Poverty Reduction Strategy Papers, www.imf.org/external/np/prsp/prsp.aspx.

17 The best single gateway to all these reports is UNDP, "MDGs: How do we track MDG progress," www.undp.org/mdg/progress.shtml; and the official UN system-wide data site is UN Statistics Division, MDG indicators, mdgs.un.org/unsd/mdg/default.aspx.

18 Joseph A. Camilleri and Jim Falk, *World's in Transition: Evolving Governance Across a Stressed Planet* (Cheltenham: Edward Elgar, 2009).

19 John W. McArthur, Jeffrey D. Sachs, and Guido Schmidt-Traub, "Response to Amir Attaran," *PLoS Medicine* 1, 11 (November 2005): 1190–92.

20 William Easterly sounded the clarion about the MDGs' bias against Africa in "How the Millennium Development Goals are Unfair to Africa," *World Development* 37, no. 1 (2009): 26–35.

21 Richard Shapcott, *International Ethics: A Critical Introduction* (Polity Press, 2010), 224–25.

22 Public Broadcasting System, *Frontline*, "The Age of AIDS," interview with Bono, 30 May 2006, www.pbs.org/wgbh/pages/frontline/aids/interviews/bono.html.

23 See Bruce Bueno de Mesquita, Alastair Smith, Randolph M. Siverson, and James D. Morrow, *The Logic of Political Survival* (Cambridge, MA: MIT Press, 2003). Bueno de Mesquita and Smith have worked out some implications for using international assistance to encourage policy reform in "Foreign Aid and Policy Concessions," *Journal of Conflict Resolution* 51, no. 2 (2007): 251–84.

24 Sam Hickey, "The Politics of Protecting the Poorest," *Political Geography* 28, no. 8 (2009): 473–83.

25 Lalage Brown, "Lessons for the Future," in *Maintaining Universal Primary Education: Lessons from Commonwealth Africa* (London: Commonwealth Secretariat, 2009), 124–40.

26 Edith Omwami and Edmond Keller, "Public Funding and Budgetary Challenges to Providing Universal Access to Primary Education in Sub-Saharan Africa," *International Review of Education* 56, no. 1 (2010): 5–31.

27 For example, Piet Buys et al., "Road Network Upgrading and Overland Trade in Sub-Saharan Africa," *Journal of African Economics* 19, no. 3 (2010): 399–432.

28 Deborah Solomon, "Questions for Dambisa Moyo: The Anti-Bono," *The New York Times Magazine*, 19 February 2009, www.nytimes.com/2009/02/22/magazine/22wwln-q4-t.html; Dambisa Moyo, *Dead Aid: Why Aid is Not Working and How there is a Better Way for Africa* (New York: Farrar, Strauss, and Giroux, 2009), 124.

29 Human Security Report Project, www.humansecuritygateway.com.

30 For example, John Paul Lederach, *Building Peace: Sustainable Reconciliation in Divided Societies* (Washington, DC: US Institute for Peace, 1997); and Lederach and R. Scott Appleby, "Strategic Peacebuilding: An Overview," in *Strategies of Peace: Transforming Conflict in a Violent World*, ed. Daniel Philpott and Gerald F. Powers (Oxford: Oxford University Press, 2010), 19–44.

31 A survey that places the effort in a larger context can be found in Denise Garcia, "The Arms Trade Treaty," in her *Disarmament Diplomacy and Human Security: Regimes, Norms, and Moral Progress* (London: Routledge, 2011), 36–102.

32 Susan Strange, "Susan Strange, 'The Westfailure System'," *Review of International Studies* 25, no. 3 (1999): 345–54.

33 Charles P. Kindleberger, *The World in Depression 1929–1939* (Berkeley: University of California Press, 1973).

34 John G. Ruggie, "International Regimes, Transactions, and Change: Embedded Liberalism in the Postwar Economic Order," *International Organization* 36, no. 2 (1982): 379–415.

35 Charles P. Kindleberger and Paul M. Goldberg, "Toward a GATT for Investment: A Proposal for the Supervision of the International Corporation," and Kindleberger, "A GATT for International Direct Investment: Further Reflections," in *Multinational Excursions* (Cambridge, MA: MIT Press, 1984), 202–31, 247–65.

36 Dan Plesch, *America, Hitler, and the UN* (London: I.B. Tauris, 2011), is a wonderfully detailed treatment of the sources of the global normative unity in the late 1940s.

37 Prem Shankar Jha, *The Twilight of the Nation-State: Globalisation, Chaos, and War* (London: Pluto Press, 2006), 359–61.

8 Africa and the MDGs

Challenges and priorities

Admos Chimhowu and David Hulme

This chapter identifies the main challenges facing MDG achievement in sub-Saharan African countries and presents a set of conclusions about how progress towards the MDGs might be accelerated. It also examines "what" should come after the MDGs. At the outset it must be made clear that this is not simply about external actors (the UN, World Bank, aid donors, among others) doing better, nor is it simply about internal actors (African governments and Africans) delivering better outcomes. Both sides of the development equation need to change what they do and improve their mutual interactions for Africa to flourish. While African governments may need to take on more responsibility for improving the welfare of their citizens, aid donors and international agencies will need to operate with more humility. Before we focus on the challenges, we examine what has been achieved so far.

An MDG score card for Africa

With just three years to go to 2015 only nine of the 48 countries in sub-Saharan Africa (for which data are available) seem likely to meet the main target of halving poverty.[1] On the surface this sounds like abysmal failure but these figures fail to capture the rapid progress that many of the countries have made in the different target areas. Although the proportion of people living in poverty has declined[2] from 58 percent in 1990 to 51 percent in 2008,[3] sub-Saharan Africa as a region will likely miss the target for MDG 1. In fact, the actual number of Africans living in poverty will have increased.[4] Table 8.1 presents the main highlights of a score card based on some selected indicators.

So far, the best record of achievement is the 18 percentage point gain in education between 1999 and 2009 in universal primary education, with some outstanding gains being made by countries such as Mozambique, Niger, Mali and Gambia which all recorded more than 25 percentage

Table 8.1 MDG score card—highlights for Africa

MDG progress so far	The outstanding MDG target
• Decline in number of households living in poverty from 58 percent in 1990 to 52 percent in 2008	• Likely to hit 36 percent by 2015 against the target of 29 percent
• Primary school enrolment raised from 58 to 76 percent between 1999/2000 and 2008/09	• Target of 100 percent unlikely to be reached by 2015
• Maternal mortality reduced from 870 deaths per 100,000 in 1990 to 640 per 100,000 in 2008	• Reduction by two-thirds benchmark almost certainly will not be met
• Increased proportion of women in parliament, from 13 percent in 2000 to 20 percent in 2011	• Gender parity unlikely to be reached by 2015
• Under-fives mortality reduced from 180 per 1,000 to 127 per 1,000 between 1990 and 2009	• Reduction by two-thirds benchmark unlikely to be met
• Decline in HIV incidence rate per year per 100 people aged 15–49 from nearly 6 per 1,000 to 4 per 1,000 between 2001 and 2009	• Unlikely to have halted the spread by 2015
• Population with access to safe drinking water increased from 56 to 65 percent between 1990 and 2008	• Unlikely to halve number of people without access to safe drinking water

Source: Score card highlights compiled from UN, *Millennium Development Goals Report* (UN, 2011), www.un.org/millenniumgoals/pdf/(2011_E)%20MDG %20Report%202011_Book%20LR.pdf

point gains in this target area. Similarly, some countries, like Uganda and Ghana, have already achieved their main target of halving the number of people living in poverty while countries like Angola and Burkina Faso emerging from civil wars have made remarkable progress. Quite clearly generalizing on Africa's achievements of the MDGs is problematic as often regional and internal variations within countries make this task less credible (for example, Namibia is shown as having met its child malnutrition target yet we know that many of the non-white Namibians living in rural areas and in inner-city slums are well below target). In contrast, Ghana reports already achieving this benchmark and this is supported by experiences on the ground.

Despite this significant progress and problems of generalizing on MDG achievement there is general consensus that poverty remains a (perhaps *the*) major policy challenge for Africa post 2015. Current evidence suggests that the *global* target for MDG 1 (halving poverty by 2015) is likely to be achieved thanks mostly to rapid gains in China and India, but less so Africa where the extreme poverty rate is expected to fall only to below 36 percent (compared to the target of 29 percent) by 2015.[5] What the targets do not highlight, however, is that there will still be another half of the "original 1990 benchmark poor" living in poverty on the continent because of increased population. Recent revisions suggest that the global figure may be as many as 900 million people, many of whom will be Africans.[6] Probably one-third of the people who will remain in poverty will have lived in poverty for most, if not all their lives. Estimates suggest that between 30 and 40 percent of up to 443 million people living in chronic poverty are in sub-Saharan Africa.[7] Clearly, present and future progress in poverty reduction after the MDGs have come and gone will depend to a large extent on what happens to this core group living in sub-Saharan Africa. They are caught in "poverty traps" that have not responded as well to the MDGs effort and this, in part, can explain why Africa will not meet its poverty target by 2015. Comparing sub-Saharan Africa to other developing countries also shows the region lagging behind in several core areas of performance, as Figure 8.1 shows.

It is clear from Figure 8.1 that although by 2007 three of the eight goals had already been met by all developing countries, sub-Saharan Africa looks very unlikely to meet these goals unless some new momentum is found to accelerate the rate of achievement. However, the question

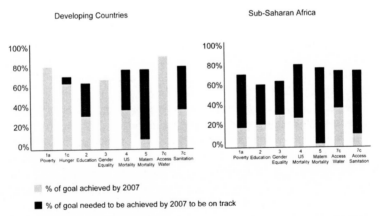

Figure 8.1 Comparing MDG progress between sub-Saharan Africa and other developing countries

Source: blogs.worldbank.org/africacan/africa-and-the-millennium-development-goals that has to be asked is whether Africa's development is all about the MDGs. Like many things in life, the MDGs have been a blessing and a curse. They have been a blessing in focusing attention on the moral unacceptability of extreme poverty on a mass scale in an affluent world. How can 1 billion people be hungry and under-nourished when another 1 billion eat too much food? How can it be that a child can die for one dollar's-worth of medicine when an ice-cream (for a child in the United Kingdom) costs the equivalent of three dollars? By forcing an international comparison, the MDGs raise the difficult questions that force action. However, the MDGs have also been a curse through exaggerating the role of foreign aid in the processes of national development and poverty reduction, in creating the impression that Africa is "missing the targets" and that somehow Africa is "different" from all other parts of the world. Further, have the MDGs stopped the policy elites in Africa from thinking "outside the box" and coming up with home-grown plans that make a better fit to their development contexts and aspirations? This is a question that we seek to return to later, but now, the focus is on trying to understand and explain Africa's performance challenges.

Challenges facing the achievement of the MDGs in Africa

While much of the discussion generated by the MDGs has focused on aid volumes, the starting point for poverty reduction has to be at the national level. It is true that most DAC countries shifted their respective aid budgets towards the social sectors for much of the 1990s and 2000s at the expense of the productive sectors, but it was not inevitable that much of Africa relied on handouts to spur their development. Only Africans can lead and will lead the continent towards economic and social progress. From across the world, the historical record shows clearly that sustained poverty reduction is closely related to national strategies that promote employment, generating growth and broad-based human development. The exact nature of these strategies varies with context and timing, but evidence from the "rapid improvers club" consisting of Brazil, India, China, and Bangladesh suggests that central to this are effective national institutions and "good enough governance."

From this perspective one of the greatest, if not *the* greatest, challenges facing Africa is the failure of its governments to formulate and implement strategies for inclusive growth. This means growing national wealth in conditions where the benefits are equitably shared by the majority, not a few selected and well connected political and bureaucratic elites. At times this may be a technical failure, resulting from inadequate analysis or weak public management, but in many cases it derives from deeper political processes that mean pro-poor growth and/or human development are not genuine policy goals. In too many countries African elites (and sometimes middle classes) have treated national development as a rhetorical project while systematically focusing on increasing their own and their followers' share of national income and assets and, in some cases, subverting popular will to stay in power.

Achieving the MDGs (or other national goals—we should not get hung up on the MDGs, but they are a good enough starting point) has been something for African leaders to pontificate about at UN and African Union (AU) meetings, but not a priority activity for domestic public policy. The "form-filling" rituals that accompany tracking of the MDG targets are often meaningless to a majority of Africans for whom social progress is but an historical metaphor of days gone by. They have experienced the mal-governance excesses and seen their quality of life decline while select bureaucratic and political elites extract all types of rents and "entitlements" from them. In the worst cases these elites have been predatory (as with Mugabe in Zimbabwe and increasingly Mutharika in Malawi) and have actively created poverty to maintain and increase their personal wealth. While this can be simplistically presented as being a leadership (or "big man") problem, in truth bad governance needs the support of other elites and social groups and is often abetted by foreign actors (governments, businesses and others).[8] There is no doubt that many African states need better leaders—driven by a desire to improve their citizens' lives—but, more widely, improving the quality of governance in Africa has to be a priority for MDG achievement and national progress.

Related to the problems of governance in Africa is the fact that many African states are fragile and/or affected by chronic conflict. This is a particular problem for the MDGs as one of their underpinning assumptions is that there is a "stable state" in place and that its "performance" can be improved (by additional resources, better policy choice and technical upgrading of institutions). When this is not the case—as in Somalia, northern Uganda, Zimbabwe, the Democratic Republic of the Congo (DRC) and others—then the idea of better policy and better service delivery has little purchase on the most powerful actors (authoritarian patriarchs, militias, secessionist movements, war economy "tycoons," drug barons and the like).

These problems of poor governance, state fragility and violent conflict produce other problems. Skilled manpower relocates to foreign countries so private-sector development and public management weaken and, more broadly, many important institutions follow a downward spiral.

More significantly, such countries lose their valuable consumer class which often helps to drive effective demand for goods and services. While it is possible that the migration cycle can create "brain circulation," it goes without saying that so far there has been little if any "brain gain" for Africa. Public "tax effort" is low (it is hard to tax very poor people and corrupt elites are able to avoid taxation) so that increasing public needs are matched by decreasing public resources. In too many countries, universities and institutions essential to skills formation, knowledge creation and accountability, have become shells of their former selves. Non-governmental organizations (NGOs) often become the main brokers of skills and knowledge but they are dependent on short-term aid contracts and often on expatriates. Foreign direct investment steers clear and domestic elites siphon off their capital to Swiss (and other) bank accounts.

In such circumstances aid becomes important. While aid has many problems, and is often used ineffectually, it is not the "cause" of Africa's poverty, as popular but flawed airport paperbacks (by authors such as Dambisa Moyo)[9] claim. Aid does *work* when it is aligned to national priorities and contexts (and when it comes along the lines suggested in the Paris Declaration), but aid is only a stop gap measure. It can help circulate resources essential to kick start development but will not substitute for home-grown development efforts. Aid is only effective if local policy elites know what they need it for and can direct it to the areas of need rather than donor dictates. New mechanisms like Direct Budget Support (DBS) showcase innovative ways of delivering and utilizing aid as long as they do not create dependency, in cases such as Malawi, Sierra Leone and Liberia. In situations like this, aid dependency can subvert local democratic processes as donors become a major unelected stakeholder.

While Africa's challenges are severe (or, indeed, very severe) one must not fall foul of Afro-pessimism nor lose sight of the ways in which Africans at the individual, family, business and community levels innovate to find ways to overcome the difficulties of everyday economic and social life. In such contexts they struggle but they also do their jobs, make a profit, help friends and neighbors, and smile (and sing, dance and tell jokes). The agency to achieve the MDGs is latent at the grass roots of African society, in its businesses and its social support networks—it just needs the opportunity to move forward.

This takes us to the external challenges facing the achievement of the MDGs in Africa. At its very best, external support can only assist African institutions and Africans to achieve national development and poverty eradication. Poverty eradication is not a gift that rich countries (such as the United Kingdom or United States), or rich people (such as Bill Gates and Warren Buffett), or celebrities (like Bono and Bob Geldof) can give Africa. The main challenge for external actors, and particularly for the governments of the rich and emerging worlds,[10] is to stop lying—they need to say what they will do and then do it. They need to:

- Stop being insincere about having a development round in the World Trade Organization (WTO) (the so-called Doha Development Agenda),[11] while continuing to protect and subsidize their domestic agricultural industries.
- Refrain from pretending to give African countries easier access to technologies and lower costs for accessing intellectual property while at the same time using the same instruments to prevent developing countries from accessing productive and, in some situations, life-saving intellectual property such as essential drugs.
- Stop pretending to be concerned about the effects of climate change on poor Africans (at the 16 plus summits on climate change—most recently at Copenhagen and Cancún) and yet fudging a global plan of action that would put words into action.
- Stop making promises about streamlining aid and using it more effectively (at New York, Gleneagles, Paris and Accra), while at the same time introducing new models like cash on delivery and results-based aid, which reverse the gains of some of these pledges.
- Stop pretending to be committed to a reform of the governance of the World Bank and International Monetary Fund (IMF) and/or bringing the membership of the UN Security Council into the twenty-first century while keeping the BRIC countries out of the core structures of global economic and political governance.

Being credible and living up to promises will be difficult as it has been the "business as usual" for almost 50 years for many rich countries to say one thing and then do another. The recent recession and austerity measures adopted by the rich North do not help matters; however, it is not as difficult as the next step—to start doing some of the things that have been promised.

Some of the challenges facing Africa are geographical and dealing with these will go well beyond the 2015 deadline of the MDGs and, indeed, well beyond 2025. While the African natural environment may present challenges in terms of agricultural productivity and health risks,[12] there are two non-debatable problems that it faces. First, the majority of its poor people are based in rural areas where populations are often dispersed: providing services to dispersed rural populations is a big challenge and is usually very costly (but, note that this challenge is gradually lessening as more Africans move to urban areas and mobile telecommunications reach remote areas and unit costs reduce). Second, the territorial boundaries of many African states were drawn up by colonial authorities and have commonly created "societies" that do not feel connected to their "state." While some re-specifications may be possible (as with Eritrea and South Sudan), redrawing Africa's borders, or shifting to sub-national units that federate into a supra-national union, is the work of centuries.

The ten most pressing recommendations for achieving the MDGs in Africa

To achieve the MDGs in Africa we need to turn the MDG concept on its head. Rather than framing the meta-goal as global poverty reduction, we need to get back to the frame of national development. It is precisely this approach that we took in formulating the Johannesburg Statement on the Millennium Development Goals (see Appendix 2). Africans have to be in the driving seat with support coming from the international system—not the other way around. The image of poverty eradication as something that the UN or the rich world can deliver to Africa's poor has to be dismissed. The UN MDG summits have focused too much on foreign aid and technical assistance and raised false hopes, many of which have remained a mirage. The World Bank and IMF's Poverty Reduction Strategy Papers (PRSPs) have focused too much on getting the approval of people based in Washington, DC— rather than national leaders, political parties and/or wider civil societies in Africa. PRSPs are barely mentioned in Africa's national parliaments or assemblies as they belong to the external world and are separated from domestic political debates. They have become a barren ritual agreed to, or often crafted, at the behest of the multilateral institutions of global governance, but not embedded in political processes and public debates in Africa.

In addition, it would be foolish to focus African governments on basing their contemporary plans on a sprint towards the 2015 MDG "finishing line." Plans have to pursue short-term and long-term goals and strengthen institutions. While the UN system (including the IMF and World Bank) and aid donors and civil society in the rich world may be interested in how close "we" get to the MDGs, African governments also have to be thinking beyond 2015. So, what would this mean?

- Thinking about both economic policy and social policy and thus refocusing energies on the productive sector. The MDGs were born out of the narratives that emerged from the Copenhagen Social Development Summit of 1995 and always had a deliberate focus on the social sector. In historical terms, rapid and impressive progress has been made in the social sector especially health and education. However, it is quite clear that tackling the problems of those living in chronic poverty will require a focus on the macro-economy and the productive sectors, particularly agriculture, where a majority of these people eke out a living. The formulation of the Comprehensive Africa Agriculture Development Programme (CAADP)[13] is already an indication of serious pan-African intent and needs to be followed through at national level. The framework for this has already been outlined through the Maputo Declaration of 2004 and just needs serious focus at the national level.
- Individual African countries should be encouraged to set national goals and targets for poverty reduction (or they could choose other concepts—reducing inequality, promoting social welfare). The MDGs might be a starting point for these goals but technical analyses of the domestic situation and historical record would inform these processes. These goals might be for 2015, or 2020 or 2025—it is up to the country. Foreign advisors may advise, but not direct, these processes in countries with low technical capacity.
- African governments should review their experience with PRSPs over the last 10 years and re-formulate their approach to development planning. While they would be free to continue with PRSPs, many may opt for national development strategies with goals beyond poverty reduction that they genuinely "own." Recent experiences in Uganda and Ghana (which have introduced five-year national development plans—NDPs) provide potential guidelines for the post-PSRP generation of development strategies.
- African governments need to have a bigger voice in the determining of medium-term expenditure frameworks (MTEFs) and the IMF needs to recognize that less monetarist frameworks may deliver more poverty reduction (and ultimately growth) than their orthodox model (how can you have domestic policy ownership when the key document belongs to the IMF?). Associated civil society campaigns to stop the IMF's "Promoting Illiteracy in Africa Programme" and its "Enhanced African Child Mortality Programme" will be needed to help push the IMF away from its orthodoxy.
- To help African governments move forward in setting national goals and designing plans and budgets and improving implementation,

efforts must be made to create or re-launch pan-African technical assistance and political dialogue. This could mean re-energizing the New Partnership for African Development (NEPAD) or starting a new initiative with a new generation of African leaders. As the MDGs era draws to a close there is a need for African governments to revisit NEPAD (which already sounds like yesterday's news). African governments should not wait for someone to reformulate a successor to the MDGs but they should start now to re-imagine African development and ensure that their views count in influencing how the world approaches development challenges after the MDGs.

• Apart from generating their own ideas, African governments can learn from others. Knowledge about how to reduce poverty now circulates much more effectively than ever before thanks to the effects of technology and the emergence of non-state actors (like BRAC[14]) working at a transnational scale. African governments should be encouraged to examine the international evidence and facilitate adaptation of ideas for local use. Specifically, they should take a closer look at the impacts of social protection programs (and particularly social assistance schemes) and may consider the role of social protection in their national plans. Effective social protection programs are contributing to poverty reduction across Latin America, Asia and Southern Africa but are only lightly established in West, East and Central Africa (with the exception of Ethiopia). The pan-African Livingstone Process must be re-energized and national poverty eradication efforts must incorporate social protection. There are major roles here for South-South cooperation alongside foreign aid and conventional technical assistance.

• The UN needs to focus on the re-framing of its poverty reduction activity after 2015. It might well find that an approach that seeks to promote an international "anti-poverty" social norm is more productive than a results-based management, top down planning approach (planning is still essentially a national activity in the twenty-first century). If African governments, and rich world governments, are to take poverty reduction seriously they need active civil societies telling them that extreme poverty is morally unacceptable—perhaps even branding it along the same lines as slavery is today.

• Do not let the financial woes of the rich world lead to higher aid volatility—we know aid volatility makes aid ineffective so stick to present commitments. Overseas development assistance (ODA) levels are still well short of the target 0.7 percent of the gross domestic products (GDPs) of the major Organisation for Economic Co-operation and Development (OECD) Development Assistance Committee

(DAC) countries, and this target adjusts downwards in real terms when rich countries are in recession.

- As Africa becomes a major player in global commodity production (especially minerals and hydrocarbons) Extractive Industries Transparency Initiative (EITI)-type programs should be actively encouraged as a means of reducing the leakage of natural resource gains and confronting Africans and foreign investors who are illegally siphoning off national wealth.

- Any future MDG-type international goals should report in ways that highlight African achievements and not just shortfalls. As Easterly[15] has shown, the technical construction of the MDGs sets Africa up to fail.

Conclusions

The MDGs have produced a profound paradox: while Africa seems certain to be reported as having failed to achieve the MDGs, the continent will have experienced its historically most rapid improvement in economic and social conditions over the period 2000–15. The global goals have been framed in a way that will record Africa's significant achievements as a failure. Whatever comes after the MDGs in terms of global goals must be technically framed in a way that does not misrepresent Africa.

In addition, the process that creates "whatever comes after the MDGs" must create goals that are genuinely owned by African governments and Africans, rather than aid donors and international agencies. For many African governments this will be taking on more responsibility for setting goals, planning, implementing and tracking development strategies. For aid donors and international agencies it will mean operating with more humility.

As the colonial era closed 60 years ago, the prospects for Africa were seen as bright compared to those of the countries of East and Southeast Asia. That scenario turned out to be inaccurate. We must hope that the Afro-pessimism that informs much of the debate about contemporary Africa proves to be as inaccurate as the colonial scenarios about Asia. Things have been getting better in Africa since 2000 and efforts must focus on accelerating this progress. To achieve this will require improved leadership and governance in African countries but also the main actors outside of Africa will need to move away from "business as usual." The arrival of Chinese investment and aid may already be helping to reshape the thinking of OECD countries and donors so that they will listen more to what Africans think about their regional and national priorities and strategies.

Notes

1 UN, *Millennium Development Goals Report* (UN, 2011).
2 We have often wondered if this decline is mainly due to the high death rate among those living in poverty.
3 See UN, *Millennium Development Goals Report* (UN, 2011).
4 Largely due to high population growth rates.
5 UN, *Millennium Development Goals Report* (UN, 2011).
6 See UN, *Rethinking Poverty: A Report on the World Social Situation* (UN, 2010).
7 Based on Chronic Poverty Research Centre, *Chronic Poverty Report 2004–2005* (Manchester: CPRC, University of Manchester, 2005), 9; and *Chronic Poverty Report 2008–2009* (Manchester: CPRC, University of Manchester, 2008), 16.
8 While the contemporary problems of African governance appear to be "here and now" an analysis of their roots usually goes back into colonial (and sometimes pre-colonial) history and reveals the lingering impacts of colonial strategies on the evolution of African governments and civil societies.
9 Dambisa Moyo, *Dead Aid: Why Aid is Not Working and How There is Another Way for Africa* (New York: Farrar, Straus and Giroux, 2009).
10 The main emerging powers are usually seen as the BRIC countries (Brazil, Russia, India and China). However, other countries, such as Turkey and South Africa, are becoming active in terms of international discussions about aid, trade negotiations and so on.
11 See the sister volume to this book: James Scott and Rorden Wilkinson, eds., *Trade, Poverty, Development: Getting Beyond the Doha Deadlock* (London: Routledge, 2012).
12 John L. Gallup and Jeffrey D. Sachs, "The Economic Burden of Malaria," *American Journal of Tropical Medicine and Hygiene* 64, no. 1 (2001): 85–96.
13 See www.nepad-caadp.net/pdf/Highlighting%20the%20successes%20280611%20v3%200%20web.pdf.
14 See Ian Smillie, *Freedom from Want: The Remarkable Success Story of BRAC, the Global Grassroots Organization That's Winning the Fight Against Poverty* (Sterling, VA: Kumarian Press, 2009).
15 See William Easterly, "How the Millennium Development Goals are Unfair to Africa," *World Development* 37, no. 1 (2009): 26–35.

9 Challenges to the achievement of the MDGs in Africa

Frances Stewart

Among countries in sub-Saharan Africa, some are "on target" to meet the Millennium Development Goals (MDGs), and others are far from the target. This chapter reviews experience and considers some outstanding barriers limiting the attainment of the existing MDGs in Africa. Major obstacles to the achievement of the MDGs include gross failure of economic growth due to a range of factors, including civil wars, extremely bad management and/or a very unfavorable international environment. A further potential hazard comes from climatic fluctuations which can devastate livelihoods and undermine food availability. In addition, the distinct possibility of prolonged food shortage at a world level would constitute a severe adverse influence.

Moreover, experience with the MDGs since they were agreed in 2000 has revealed both advantages and disadvantages associated with the approach that they take. In some respects the MDGs represent a huge global achievement—especially that global agreement was reached on the critical objective of reducing world poverty; moreover, the goals have become a very useful advocacy instrument both internationally (for example, in arguing for more aid, aid for sectors that would contribute to the goals, and a reduction in royalty payments for essential medicines), and nationally, providing a way for local populations, non-governmental organizations (NGOs) and donors to put pressure on governments to direct their efforts towards the MDG goals, where achievements are lagging. However, where the goals have already exceeded the objective nationally, the approach can induce complacency and a relaxation of effort, despite the fact that achieving the goals can be consistent with the continued existence of considerable deprivations. A further problem with the goals is that if translated into national objectives, they involve very different levels of ambition according to the starting point, as will be discussed further below.

There are also some important defects in the specific set of agreed goals. One is that they make no reference to the economy and consequently may encourage diversion of resources from economic infrastructure to social expenditure, despite the fact that it is the economy that underpins the sustained achievement of the goals. Another major issue is that countries can be on track to meet the MDGs and yet suffer increasing inequality, as well as social problems such as rising criminality and similar ills. These considerations mean that satisfactory development involves much more than the mechanical achievement of the MDGs. Yet the MDG approach encourages a focus on the specified goals, to the neglect of other objectives. These considerations need to be incorporated into any post-2015 goal formulation, as will be discussed below.

African performance on the MDGs to date

In order to assess challenges to the achievement of the MDGs, it is necessary to have some idea of progress to date. Yet it is complicated to make a fair assessment of progress on the MDGs for a variety of reasons:

- Targets involving halving particular variables (such as the poverty rate of child mortality) are more difficult to achieve the larger the variable initially; thus halving poverty involves a far more dramatic decrease in poverty for a country with an initial poverty rate of 50 percent than for one which starts with a poverty rate of just 10 percent. Should a country with an initial 50 percent poverty rate which reduces this to 30 percent be regarded as "failing" the goal of halving poverty, while one which reduces the poverty rate by much less (for example, from 10 percent to 4 percent) be regarded as having succeeded?
- Ironically if a country has already achieved a target (such as in gender equality of education) further progress is not possible.
- For some countries reliable data, or indeed *any* data, are lacking.
- Finally, it is difficult to make a fair assessment because the results vary according to the method of assessment.

Figure 9.1 shows performance on MDGs across the particular goals, using UN Development Programme (UNDP) data, which divides performance into "achieved," achievement that is "very likely" or "possible," and "off track." The last means that a country will almost certainly fail to achieve the target. The best achievements are on primary education, with 20 countries on track, and only four total failures; the worst are in maternal health with 18 countries not on track and only six on track. Other weak performances are with respect to child mortality, gender equality and extreme poverty. Even the one success—education—must be qualified as many observers have noted the very poor quality of the

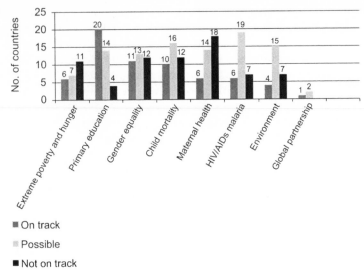

Figure 9.1 Number of countries meeting the MDGs
Source: UNDP, MDG Monitor

education and have suggested that future goals should include quality indicators.

When it comes to comparing country performance (Figure 9.2), it appears that particularly successful countries are Ethiopia, Gabon, Mauritius and Rwanda, all of which have met, or are likely to meet, six of the goals. Failures seem to be Chad, Ghana, Democratic Republic of the Congo (DRC), Lesotho, Swaziland and Togo, defining failure as off track exceeding the number of goals achieved or likely by at least three. The "failure" list includes some unexpected countries, in particular Ghana, usually classified as a success case.

An alternative assessment is provided by an ODI Report.[1] Their top 20 achievers globally on all goals include the following sub-Saharan African countries in terms of absolute progress: Mali, Ethiopia, Gambia, Malawi, Uganda, Mauritania, Ghana, Burkina Faso and Togo; and Benin, Malawi and Gambia in terms of relative progress. They do not provide a "bottom 20," but their data on relative progress for the bottom 10 are shown in Table 9.1. These lists, of course, suffer because the probable "worst" cases do not have data so do not appear (for example, Somalia and Zimbabwe).

Among the "failure" countries, weak economic growth seems to have been important—Djibouti, Côte d'Ivoire and Guinea-Bissau all

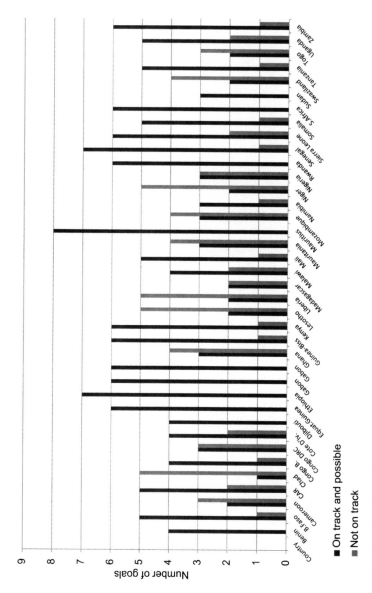

Figure 9.2 Number of goals met by country

Table 9.1 Countries appearing as ranked among bottom 10 globally in terms of absolute progress

MDG 1 (proportion of population below $1.25)	MDG 2 (net enrolment ratio primary education)	MDG4 (under-five mortality rate)
Djibouti*	Congo*	Kenya
Côte d'Ivoire*	Cape Verde	Congo*
Guinea-Bissau*	South Africa†	Cameroon†
	Lesotho	Chad*
		Zambia
		Central African Repub.*
		Gabon
		Sâo Tomé

Source: ODI, *Millennium Development Goals: Report Card. Measuring Progress Across Goals* (London: Overseas Development Institute, 2010)
Note: * have suffered civil war recently; † suffered political upheaval during period.

experienced negative growth from 1990 to 2005. Some did a little better (South Africa, Lesotho, Chad), but still had negative growth in per capita terms. Only Sâo Tomé had positive per capita growth in this list. Serious growth failure clearly disposes to MDG failure, even though one or two countries, such as Madagascar, had negative growth but do not appear on the failure list. Among the four countries we picked out above as particular successes, Ethiopia, Mauritius and Rwanda had reasonably good growth (above the sub-Saharan African average), but Gabon (which has a relatively high average per capita income) had negative growth. It does not follow from this that having good growth is sufficient for success—clearly other policies are needed. Mozambique, for example, had a growth rate well above average (at 3.8 percent per annum, 1990–2005), yet is only on track (or possible) for three MDGs and off track for four.

A review of the major features of countries that experienced least progress in human development over a 40-year period lends support to the view that growth failure over a prolonged period is universally significant as a source of weakness in progress on the human dimensions, even though high growth is not sufficient to guarantee success.[2] All the weakest countries in terms of progress in human development during 1970–2007, as measured by changes in the Human Development Index (HDI), had experienced very slow or even negative economic growth, often associated with recurrent civil war. Selecting the three weakest performers in terms of progress in HDI during 1970–2007 in three categories of countries—those starting in the low, medium and high HDI categories—all three in the low category were from Africa (Uganda, DRC and Central African Republic (CAR)—data for Zimbabwe were lacking), while Zambia qualified as the weakest in the middle HDI category. Exceptionally weak economic growth was a feature of all these African poor performers. In addition, they also showed particularly low secondary school enrolments. However, like the analysis of MDGs, the human development (HD) story shows that growth alone is not sufficient: by no means all high growers achieved success in HD progress—indeed the *Human Development Report* for 2010 found very little correlation between growth in incomes and growth in the non-income component of the HDI. Lessons from analyses of progress in human development are clearly relevant to MDG achievements since the countries successful in HD were also successful in poverty reduction, while among the weak HD performers, poverty (both income poverty and a Human Poverty Index (HPI),[3] a measure of wider dimensions) was higher and was reduced at a below-average rate. In addition, of course, the HDI includes measures of progress on education and life expectancy.

Avoiding economic failure is important because the economy provides the resources from which tax revenue is generated and social services financed and the employment and output that provide the incomes which permit poverty to fall and human development to improve. Yet policies directed towards promoting the share of social services and improving income distribution allow countries to succeed without exceptional growth rates, although very weak growth seems to be an almost insuperable handicap. Equally, of course, it is possible to experience very high growth but to distribute it badly and end up with poor performance on poverty reduction and social indicators.

Clearly, there are many factors besides economic growth which determine progress on the MDGs, including resource allocation (to social sectors especially) and income distribution. For the future, however, this analysis suggests that one critical obstacle to success on the MDGs among African countries may be growth failure.

Avoiding economic growth failures

Analysis of the past suggests three factors that predispose to serious growth failure: violent conflict; gross mismanagement of the economy; and highly adverse terms of trade. Conflict was undoubtedly a major factor behind weak growth in many of the countries that failed on MDGs, and also the weak performers on human development over the 40-year period. Research has shown that civil war generally reduces economic growth and affects human indicators adversely, unless it is on the periphery of the country.[4] Serious violent conflict occurred in all the cases that were particular failures on MDG 1, and among all the human development failures, with the exception of Zambia, while Zambia suffered especially from worsening international terms of trade and high rates of HIV/AIDs.

Avoiding violent conflict

A first essential condition for success in the MDGs, then, is to avoid violent conflict which has directly adverse consequences for health and poverty as well as by undermining growth. Both case studies and econometric evidence show that conflict reduces economic growth. For example, one study found that 13 out of 14 countries suffering the worst conflicts between 1975 and 1995 experienced a negative impact on their growth, although with considerable variability in magnitude.[5] Estimates suggest that incomes were halved in Sierra Leone over their 11-year war, and by 80 percent in Liberia.[6] Regression analysis suggests an annual loss of gross domestic product (GDP) of 2 to 2.4 percent per annum during war and in the years immediately following.[7] Both case study and cross-country econometric evidence shows that wars with more widespread geographic coverage have a more negative impact.

There are many hypotheses about the conditions that predispose to violent conflict. A history of past conflict and low per capita incomes are correlates, as well as the presence of high value natural resources and a large youth population (though there is more controversy about the latter two factors).[8] Some have argued that environmental pressures are a cause.[9] Many of these factors represent conditions that countries inherit and can do little about in the short run; however, they are risk factors and by no means always lead to conflict, suggesting that where present it is particularly important to manage the situation carefully to avoid precipitating conflict. My own work has focused on the presence of horizontal inequalities (HIs) as a cause of conflict. These are inequalities between identity groups, groups divided by religion/ethnicity/race/region or some overlapping combination.

HIs encompass economic, social, political and cultural status dimensions: economic HIs include inequalities in ownership of assets and of incomes and employment opportunities. Social HIs include access to a range of services—education, health and housing—and inequalities in achievements in health and educational outcomes. Political HIs consist of inequalities in the group distribution of political opportunities and power, including control over the presidency, the cabinet, parliamentary assemblies, the army, police and regional and local governments.

Finally, cultural status HIs refer to differences in recognition and (*de facto*) hierarchical status of different groups' cultural norms, customs and practices.

Research shows that where there are inequalities in access to social and economic resources between salient groups (which may be divided by religion, ethnicity, race or region or some combination), the risk of conflict rises; it is particularly high where the socio-economic inequalities are accompanied by political and cultural status inequalities *in the same direction* (that is, with the same groups deprived on each dimension). Although HIs in any dimension can provide an incentive for political mobilization, group leaders may be primarily motivated to lead rebellion by political inequalities (such as political exclusion), as can be seen, for example, in the recent case of Kenya, while the mass of people may be more readily mobilized to fight because of the existence of severe socio-economic and/or cultural status inequalities.

Empirical investigation suggests that the effect of HIs on the probability of conflict occurrence is quite high: according to Østby,[10] who explored conflicts across countries for the years 1986–2003, the probability of conflict increases threefold when comparing the expected conflict onset at mean values of all the explanatory variables to a situation where the extent of horizontal inequality of assets among ethnic groups is at the 95th percentile. In the case of the interregional HIs, the probability of conflict increases two and a half times, as HIs rise from mean value to the 95th percentile value. Similar evidence is found by Cederman *et al.*,[11] Barrows (for African countries only),[12] Mancini (for districts within Indonesia),[13] and Murshed and Gates (for regions in Nepal).[14] Cederman *et al.* and Lindemann[15] show that political HIs themselves predispose to conflict, while Cederman *et al.* and Østby show that the risk rises where socio-economic HIs are accompanied by political exclusion.

Thus if conflict is to be avoided, it is important to avoid excessive HIs—and to introduce policies to reduce them where they exist. A range of policies contribute to reducing such inequalities, including policies that target resources towards particular groups directly, such as quotas, and ones that have the same effect achieved indirectly through their design (like comprehensive services or progressive taxation). Similarly, inclusive political systems can be secured by formal consociational arrangements; by particular constitutional design, like federalism and proportional representation; or by informal convention. Variants of all these approaches have been adopted in different African countries. The best approach is likely to differ according to the circumstances of the country, but it needs to be emphasized that it is important to make the reduction of HIs a conscious objective of policy, and to undertake appropriate policy reforms and monitoring of outcomes. A reduction of HIs is not the automatic result of market reforms or of multiparty democracy—indeed, both can be associated with widening inequalities. Achievement of the MDGs themselves can be associated with worsening HIs unless a conscious policy is adopted to avoid this. For example, in Ghana initially poverty reduction was largely focused on the South, where it was easier to achieve, while poverty in the North—much poorer than the South—showed little change with the result of worsening the South-North HI. Similar developments have occurred in Uganda. In a similar way, while achievement of the employment MDG is likely to make conflict less probable by reducing the number of unemployed youth, it may not do so if employment expansion is biased across salient groups.

International conditions

African growth is highly dependent on international conditions—above all the terms of trade for commodity-dependent countries—and flows of aid. Over the past decade, the terms of trade have been broadly favorable to African commodities after years of stagnation, and this above all explains the improved growth performance compared with the previous 20 years (see Figure 9.3). In addition, aid flows were substantially higher in the 2000s than in previous decades and to date have not been

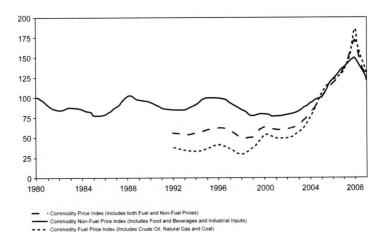

— · Commodity Price Index (Includes both Fuel and Non-Fuel Prices)
—— Commodity Non-Fuel Price Index (Includes Food and Beverages and Industrial Inputs)
- - - Commodity Fuel Price Index (Includes Crude Oil, Natural Gas and Coal)

Figure 9.3 The commodity terms of trade, 1980–2009
Source: Spatafora and Tytell 2009

affected by the financial crisis (Figure 9.4). Even the downturn associated with the 2008 crisis left the commodity terms of trade well above the average of the previous two decades (Figure 9.3). Spatafora and Tytell found that "median output growth is nearly 2 percentage points per annum higher during booms than during busts," partially challenging the "resource curse" view.[16] A continuation of favorable terms of trade and aid flows is important for success on the MDGs. Sustained improvement in terms of trade may be threatened by the global economic crisis of 2009+, but the continued resilience of Chinese and Indian growth, despite some slow down, may support continued favorable terms of trade; on aid, there are pressures for reductions in the aid flows of many donors, although heavy Chinese investment may offset this, while the Chinese focus on economic infrastructural investment is likely to be favorable to growth.

The heavy hand of the International Monetary Fund (IMF) in the 1980s was in part responsible for the worsening in human conditions in Africa over that decade. The reduced presence of the IMF in the 2000s, as well as international agreement on the MDGs, has improved the conditions for MDG progress. This and China's presence as a source of finance reduces the likelihood of international financial institutions (IFIs) again becoming a major source of cutbacks. The MDGs strong focus on social goals, however, diverted investments away from economic infrastructure. As Figure 9.5 shows, in 1991 aid to the social sectors and to economic sectors accounted for about 18 percent of total aid, but since then aid to the social sectors has soared and now accounts for almost 45 percent of the total, while aid to the economic sectors fell until 2005, when it was just 10 percent of the total. It subsequently

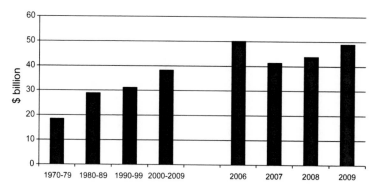

Figure 9.4 Net overseas development assistance to Africa, 1970–2009
Source: OECD, DAC statistics

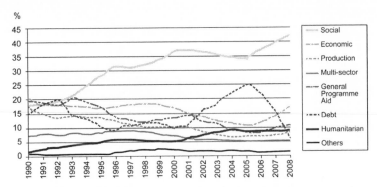

Figure 9.5 Overseas development assistance to Africa by sector
Source: OECD, DAC statistics

rose, but only to its 1991 share of 18 percent. Not all this change can be attributed to the MDGs, since the rising share of the social sectors preceded the agreement on the goals, but the MDGs undoubtedly contributed to the trend. Underinvestment in economic infrastructure is a serious problem which affects the goals themselves, albeit indirectly, via the employment, productivity and income earning opportunities that it supports, which contribute to the income poverty goal and to tax revenue to support social sector expenditure.

Other policies relevant to MDG achievements

Although there is no simple recipe for success, sufficient expenditure on the social sectors to allow the extension of basic education and health services to all, and the generation of income-earning opportunities to include the whole population of working age are established as important ingredients for sustained achievements on human development.[17] Cash transfers can also be important. For example, in South Africa, grants supporting the poor together amount to 3.5 percent of GDP. The child support grant there has been shown to be progressive covering 70 percent of children in the lowest decile households compared with around 3 percent in the top decile. It is estimated that the child grants halved the poverty impact of the financial crisis in 2007–09.[18] Female education and empowerment are also critical ingredients improving health and nutrition outcomes. None of these policies are very costly—all are doable so long as the economy does not suffer dramatic collapse, and so long as there is political will to support such policies.

New threats

While the current situation is broadly auspicious for African achievement of the MDGs, there are important new threats on the horizon connected with climate change and possible food shortages. Climate change is likely to cause (and already is causing) droughts, floods and desertification, reducing farming potential. Moreover, world food shortages loom, not only because of climate change but because of global rises in population and incomes and insufficient investment and development and use of technology in agriculture. Urban consumers in Africa (accounting for a growing proportion of the poor) may suffer a radical reduction in their real incomes as food prices rise. Rural/subsistence farmers may gain from food price rises in so far as they have surplus to sell, but may find their productivity adversely affected by the climatic situation. For both groups a concerted attempt to sustain food production—by investments in agriculture and agricultural technologies—is essential if the MDGs are to be realized. Moreover, the economic crisis in advanced economies is likely to have serious knock-on effects on African economies, through depressed markets leading to some worsening in the commodity terms of trade and reduced flows of aid compared with the pre-2007 situation.

Moving forward: should the MDGs be changed?

The MDGs were beneficial in moving attention away from exclusively Washington consensus-style policies, which focused on advancing market mechanisms in the economy and neglected social sectors and poverty, while they contributed to a reversal of the devastating cuts in social expenditure of the 1980s. They may also have contributed to raising aid and changing its distribution. However, the MDGs have been widely criticized from several perspectives.

Certain criticisms emerge from the analysis above. First, not enough attention was given to the economic aspects of development which are essential for sustained success on the social side. Second, there was a failure to consider the distributional implications of the goals, both among groups and individuals. Rising inequalities are consistent with achievement of the MDGs and yet can have a very damaging impact on the social fabric. Inclusive growth should be the objective, which means growth in which poor individuals (for example, the bottom fifth of the population) and poor groups participate at least proportionately. We should note that this is not the same as "pro-poor growth," which is commonly interpreted as growth in which there is some trickle down to poor individuals (no mention is normally made of groups). Such growth can be consistent with worsening vertical and horizontal income distribution. Distributional considerations also need to be incorporated into the other MDGs: for example, an improvement in average infant mortality is consistent with worsening health inequalities. One way of incorporating distributional concerns here would be to define the goal in terms of reducing infant mortality for the tenth or so of the population with the worst initial indicators. Cambodia adopted specific pro-poor performance targets in relation to the allocation of funds to hospitals and in contracts with NGOs to operate primary health services, with a marked positive impact on health coverage of the poor.[19] Both these aspects need to be incorporated into any revised (or post-2015) set of goals.

Another common criticism of the goals is that while specific goals were agreed for developing countries, Goal 8, which represented the developed country component, was presented in vague terms. Goals need to be included in the obligations of developed countries for aid flows, intellectual property rights, and trade access, which are of fundamental importance for the economic and social development of African countries.

A further issue, raised above, is that the burden of any goal for a specific country depends on how it is formulated. If it is defined as a given percentage improvement in some positive aspect—for example, percentage at school—then it is easier to achieve, the lower the starting point; however, if it is interpreted as a given percentage improvement in a negative aspect (such as percentage reduction in children not at school), then it is more difficult to achieve, the worse the initial situation. When first formulated, the MDGs were global, not country, goals, so this issue did not arise, but in practice they are commonly interpreted as country goals, yet no efforts were made to adapt the targets to a country's starting point. One way of overcoming this problem is to tailor the targets to particular initial conditions. This can be consistent with a single set of global goals.

Other problems arise in relation to the use of *any* set of goals as policy guidance. Goals exclude as well as include, and inevitably the items excluded get neglected by those who take the goals seriously. For the MDGs, neglect of the economy, just noted, is an example. Another is distribution of incomes and resources. Further, quantitative goals often ignore quality considerations, as they have in the MDG for education, for example. Thus the goals need to be revised periodically to ensure that important issues are not neglected. Yet the more goals are included, the less meaningful they become. As goals proliferate, prioritization among them becomes especially important. The MDGs are not prioritized at all, yet prioritizing is often essential since, even with a limited number of goals, countries cannot always focus on all of them simultaneously. Prioritization has to be decided at a country level, where the needs and possibilities are most apparent.

Global goals are not designed to respond to the particular needs of particular countries. In the past there has been an automatic translation from the global goals to country goals. Yet this does not allow for differences in initial achievements across goals, as well as across countries; for the special problems a country faces; and for local decision-making on priorities. There is a potential conflict here. If each country is left free to determine its own goals, in the light of its own situation and preferences, how much meaning is left for the global goals? Yet most people concerned with human development and poverty reduction would agree that local participation in choices about priorities is essential, and that local conditions must inform policy.

The big question, then, is whether these problems are so great that we would be better off without such global goals, or whether the advantages of the goals, in reorienting focus and raising resources, can be realized while leaving countries to define their own priorities, avoiding making the MDGs a straitjacket.

For post-2015, what is needed is first agreement on the pressing problems that have emerged and consequent priorities for post-2015. To achieve a global consensus on this would require a long debate, which should be conducted on the basis of participatory discussions across the world. From a personal perspective I suggest that protection of the environment is a clear imperative, which must be central to any post-2015 goals; second, distribution of resources among individuals and groups must be incorporated into any goals; third, economic development for all low-income countries must be included (but *not* necessarily for middle-income countries); fourth, progress needs to be speeded up on the outstanding failure areas, in particular maternal and child mortality in Africa. This is urgent and should precede 2015.

Finally, the MDGs have been criticized because they do not include consideration of process and do not propose changes in the development discourse.[20] My own view is that it would be a mistake to attempt to revise the goals to include process and discourse. This is not because process is unimportant, nor because I think that the present development discourse is satisfactory. It is because, first, there is no unique "best" process, and countries should be free to adopt a variety of approaches, including experimenting with new ones—as they have in the past; and second, a global arena leading to a global agreement which considers development discourse is likely to lead to a vacuous and anodyne statement with little real content. The MDGs represent a nudge towards progress in

172   *Frances Stewart*

specific areas, not an entirely new approach to development—and they
cannot be expected to be more than this.

Notes

1 ODI, Millennium Development Goals: Report Card. Measuring Progress
  Across Goals (London: Overseas Development Institute, 2010).
2 Gustav Ranis and Frances Stewart, "Success and Failure in Human
  Development, 1970–2007," Human Development Research Papers (2010).
3 The newly developed Multidimensional Poverty Index (MPI) (see UNDP,
  *Human Development Report: The Real Wealth of Nations: Pathways to Human
  Development* (New York: Palgrave, 2010)) is preferable to the HPI from a
  methodological perspective but data are not available over this period.
4 Anke Hoeffler and Marta Reynal-Querol, *Measuring the Costs of Conflict*
  (Oxford: Centre for the Study of African Economies, 2003); Frances Stewart, Valpy Fitzgerald and Associates, eds., *War and Underdevelopment: The
  Economic and Social Consequences of Conflict*, Vol. 1 (Oxford: Oxford
  University Press, 2001).
5 Frances Stewart, Cindy Huang and Michael Wang, "Internal Wars: An
  Empirical Overview of the Economic and Social Consequences," in *War
  and Underdevelopment*, ed. Stewart, Fitzgerald and Associates.
6 UNDP, *Human Development Report: The Real Wealth of Nations*.
7 Paul Collier, "On the Economic Consequences of Civil War," *Oxford Economic
  Papers* 51, no. 1 (1999): 168–83; Hoeffler and Reynal-Querol, *Measuring
  the Costs of Conflict*; Kosuke Imai and Jeremy Weinstein, "Measuring the
  Impact of Civil War," Center for International Development at Harvard
  University Working Papers 2000, Cambridge, Mass.
8 Juha Auvinen and E. Wayne Nafziger, "The Sources of Humanitarian
  Emergencies," *Journal of Conflict Resolution* 43, no. 3 (2001): 267–90; Paul
  Collier and Anke Hoeffler, "Greed and Grievance in Civil War" (Washington,
  DC: World Bank, 2000); James D. Fearon and David D. Laitin, "Ethnicity,
  Insurgency, and Civil War," *American Political Science Review* 97, no. 3
  (2003): 75–90; Macartan Humphreys, "Natural Resources, Conflict and
  Conflict Resolution: Uncovering the Mechanisms," *Journal of Conflict Reso-
  lution* 49, no. 4 (2005): 508–37; Henrik Urdal, "A Clash of Generations?
  Youth Bulges and Political Violence," *International Studies Quarterly* 50,
  no. 3 (2006): 607–30.
9 Thomas F. Homer-Dixon, "Environmental Scarcities and Violent Conflict:
  Evidence from Cases," *International Security* 19, no. 1 (1994): 5–40.
10 Gudrun Østby, "Polarization, Horizontal Inequalities and Violent Civil
  Conflict," *Journal of Peace Research* 45, no. 2 (2008): 143–62.
11 Lars-Erik Cederman, Kristian Skrede Gleditsch, and Nils B. Weidmann "Horizontal Inequalities and Ethno-nationalist Civil War: A Global Comparison,"
  American Political Science Review 105, no. 3 (2011): 478–95.
12 Walter L. Barrows, "Ethnic Diversity and Political Instability in Black
  Africa," *Comparative Political Studies* 9, no. 2 (1976): 139–70.
13 Luca Mancini, "Horizontal Inequalities and Communal Violence: Evidence
  from Indonesian Districts," Oxford: CRISE Working Paper number 22,
  2005.

14 S. Mansoob Murshed and Scott Gates, "Spatial-Horizontal Inequality and the Maoist Insurgency in Nepal," *Review of Development Economics* 9, no. 1 (2005): 121–34.

15 Stefan Lindemann, "Elite Bargains and the Politics of War and Peace in Uganda and Zambia," in *Politics* (London: London School of Economics, 2010).

16 N. Spatafora and I. Tytell, "Commodity Terms of Trade: The History of Booms and Busts," IMF Working Paper 09205 (September 2009).

17 Gustav Ranis and Frances Stewart, "Strategies for Success in Human Development," *Journal of Human Development* 1, no. 1 (2000): 49–70; Ranis and Stewart, "Success and Failure"; UNDP, *Human Development Report.*

18 UNICEF, *The Impact of the International Financial Crisis on Child Poverty in South Africa* (Pretoria: UNICEF (South Africa) and Financial Commission of South Africa, 2010).

19 Bruno Meessen, Wim Van Damme, Christine Kirunga Tashboya and Abdelmajid Tibouti, "Poverty and User Fees for Public Health Care in Low-income Countries: Lessons from Uganda and Cambodia," *The Lancet* 368, no. 9554 (2007): 2253–57; Davidson R. Gwatkin, "Making Health Systems More Equitable," *The Lancet* 364 (2004): 1273–80.

20 Phil Vernon and Deborrah Baksh, "Working with the Grain to Change the Grain: Moving Beyond the Millennium Development Goals" (London: InternationalAlert, 2010).

10   Global Development Goals and the international HIV response

A chance for renewal

Ilaria Regondi and Alan Whiteside

The deadline to meet the Millennium Development Goals (MDGs) is fast approaching. Little time remains between now and 2015, and our inability to meet many of the objectives set out in the year 2000 has now become clear. Although some fear that discussing post-2015 arrangements may derail the momentum to meet current goals,[1] such conversations are pressing and necessary. It took 10 years of political bargaining to devise and agree to the MDG framework; this consideration alone provides a distinct sense of urgency if any post-2015 agreement is to be achieved. Political capital has already been invested in this task, and the Johannesburg Global Poverty Summit of January 2011, along with the statement it produced, has certainly contributed to this thinking process.

In much of Southern and East Africa, the AIDS epidemic has been one of the biggest stumbling blocks to achieving the MDGs. Partly, this is because of the well-documented interconnectedness of the goals: our failure to achieve MDG 6 (to combat HIV/AIDS, malaria and other diseases) has limited progress on most other objectives, and vice versa. In addition, these linkages have brought into question both the effectiveness of the AIDS response, and the issue of "AIDS exceptionalism," on which Whiteside has written extensively.[2] As we look ahead, these are the sorts of questions that policy-makers will have to grapple with as they develop a new set of Global Development Goals (GDGs).

Negotiating a new set of goals

In some ways, it should be easier to come up with a new set of objectives than it was in the late 1990s. In large part thanks to the MDGs, we now have baseline data to guide our thinking and against which to set future standards; a number of institutions, both national and international, have developed their statistical capabilities and data collection skills. Tracking and reporting have become mainstream and regular feedback mechanisms have been put in place.[3] Having achieved it once, we also know that large-scale political agreement is possible and that massive funding can be successfully mobilized for development. Technical know-how is also on our side. Thanks to technological advances, it is now possible, from a practical point of view, to have a genuinely global roundtable discussion and include the voices of those whose interests the MDGs are supposed to serve.[4]

In other ways, of course, agreement will be more difficult. There may be resistance and unwillingness to commit to a new set of objectives given our current failure to achieve results. A sense of fatigue by developing country governments and by the international community could decrease enthusiasm and willingness to agree to a new set of goals. The credibility of any future enterprise may have been irrevocably tarnished, so national governments may find it difficult to justify—or find it an easy excuse to suspend—financial and political support for new international goals.

Negotiating the GDGs may also be complicated by the fact that the 1990s, a "benign era of relative stability, strong economic growth, and fairly buoyant aid budgets" is long gone.[5] The food, fuel and financial crises have had a lasting negative impact on the current socio-political context; they have had ripple effects on poverty, unemployment, food security, social protection and many other sectors. The more indirect impacts of these shocks to the international order will continue to be felt for the foreseeable future.[6] Any new development framework will therefore have to reflect this relatively hostile social and geo-political environment. The rise of G-20 members on the global arena;[7] the fact that 72 percent of the world's population, or close to 1 billion people, now live in cities;[8] environmental degradation; and structural unemployment: these are key elements of a changed world with which the new GDGs will have to contend. Many changes have also occurred within the health sector, a key part of the current MDG framework. International mobility and interconnectedness have globalized diseases; the burden of non-communicable diseases has escalated; and the nature of HIV has transformed from a fatal emergency into a chronic illness and "long-wave" event.[9]

Our conception of development and aid over the past 15 years has also dramatically changed. Severino and Ray argue that a "triple revolution" has occurred: the numbers of goals, players and instruments in the international development field have mushroomed,[10] thus complicating the constellation of challenges and opportunities for resolution. The current MDG framework has been said to reflect a classic donor-recipient relationship, rather than this multi-faceted and more complicated scenario. Any new agreement will have to factor in at least some of these considerations if it is to have any chance of surviving and being adhered to. In other words, this multi-polar, multi-dimensional worldview will undoubtedly complicate our attempt to create a single framework that encapsulates the international development "norm" as the current MDG framework manages to do.[11]

Linking the global HIV response to the post-2015 development agenda

From an HIV perspective, the establishment of new GDGs post-2015 should be considered an urgent priority. Much has been written about the reasons why and the ways in which the global HIV response is undergoing a crisis of funding and confidence. Meanwhile, the number of new HIV infections in the world still outpaces the scale-up of treatment. For every two people who access antiretroviral (ARV) therapy, five new infections occur.[12] While medical circumcision has been shown to reduce the chances of female-to-male transmission, protection is only partial and wide-scale roll-out will take time. The ultimate efficacy of microbicides is not yet known[13] and will also entail a time-lag, while the availability of vaccines is even further off. The idea of early ART-initiation and of using treatment for prevention has been widely proposed,[14] but more thought needs to be given to the implications of this policy, especially in resource-poor settings.

The lack of integration of HIV/AIDS interventions into national health systems, the donor-driven process of priority-setting, and the less-than-sustainable nature of its funding structures[15] are all issues that the HIV community (for lack of a better term) will have to deal with in the near future. In sum, the global HIV response has come under attack from all directions.

What better way to start afresh than to use the GDGs as an opportunity for the HIV response to address many of the criticisms that it has faced to date? The development of a new set of goals post-2015 provides the chance for it to make amends and reinvent itself. From our analysis of the potential options for a future GDG framework, undertaken with an HIV/AIDS lens, the most suitable outcome of this process includes three key elements:

- A reformed version of the current MDG framework, combining two of the most common scenarios currently on the table;
- Greater emphasis on interventions and policies than merely on indicators; and
- The integration of a "life-cycle" approach into the framework.

This chapter will discuss each of these three elements in detail and then outline a number of key considerations to help forge ahead with the revised framework. These considerations indicate that a new framework represents a golden opportunity to address widely perceived shortcomings of both the current MDGs framework and the global HIV response, while at the same time building on their key strengths and past achievements.

Reforming the current MDG framework

As suggested above, some thinking has already gone into the conceptualization of a post-2015 development framework. Andy Sumner and Meera Tiwari have mapped out three plausible scenarios.[16] The first stylized option—the "MDGs 2020/2025" scenario—involves adopting the current set of goals, with minimal changes, and setting a new deadline to meet them. This scenario would capitalize on the hard-won gains and compromises that the current goals represent, and renew pressure on wealthy countries to honor their commitments and stand by their financial pledges. This type of arrangement could easily be achieved in 2015 with little political compromise, so no time would be wasted between the expiry of one agreement (the MDGs) and the endorsement of another (the GDGs).

The second option, which Sumner and Tiwari have termed the "MDG-Plus" approach, involves an incremental expansion and modification of the current framework. It would entail a small set of three or four "core" universal goals, such as child education, health and nutrition, plus a small set of three or four new locally defined goals. The latter could go beyond the human development and short-term poverty reduction focus of the current framework, in order to emphasize the long-run transformation of societies. This approach would seize the opportunity to improve targets and indicators that are currently perceived as weak and add priorities that have previously been omitted.

The third, or "One World" approach, would be built around the neglected MDG 8 (to develop a global partnership for development), and would involve the design of a framework for the provision of global public goods and for addressing issues such as climate change, social protection and global governance. This scenario would be the most difficult to achieve, but if a consensus were reached, it would constitute a significant effort to address some of the most difficult challenges of our time. Sumner and Tiwari suggest that the third option would be ideal, but acknowledge that a combination of scenarios might be most feasible.

From a health and HIV perspective, we believe that a blend of the second and third option would be most sensible. This would also be in line with the spirit of the Johannesburg Statement (appended to this book), which recommends building on the MDGs, modifying some of the goals, and addressing new global concerns. A combination of approaches would be suitable for a number of reasons. The second scenario would allow us to retain targets that decrease vulnerability to HIV—such as poverty reduction and education—remove redundancies, and add key objectives relevant to the epidemic left out in the last round of negotiations. By adding locally defined goals, some of which would presumably relate to health systems broadly and to the HIV epidemic specifically, this scenario would help address what has been the relatively top-down, donor-driven nature of the HIV response. On the other hand, "One World" targets could include ambitious topics that can only be tackled on a global scale. Targeted research and development on issues of international health; the control and prevention of the cross-border spread of communicable diseases—including eradication and elimination programs; global surveillance activities; and the containment of antimicrobial resistance—as well as standardized data collection efforts: these are health-related global public goods[17] that should be part of the discussions and would also contribute to the fight against HIV.

Nevertheless, in light of the recent failures of the Doha round on trade agreements and the Copenhagen conference on climate change, reaching a consensus on these matters may be a chimera.[18] Caution should therefore be exercised when thinking about what could feasibly be agreed in the short amount of time that is left before 2015. Whatever precise shape the GDGs will take, we must ensure that we retain what we value about the current framework. The fact that it represents a common ground, a framework for international aid, a development norm, a yardstick against which to measure progress, and an advocacy tool for fundraising and raising awareness, is widely prized and should therefore be maintained.

We should also consider and retain the legitimacy that the MDGs have garnered around the world. Pollard *et al.*[19] conducted research into the perspectives of 104 representatives from civil society organizations in 36 developing countries, collecting both quantitative and qualitative data. Three-quarters of respondents thought that the MDGs were "a good thing." Regardless of reservations they expressed about the current framework, 87 percent of respondents wanted some sort of overarching, internationally agreed framework for development after 2015. Those aspects of the MDG framework that are valued by the people for whom it should theoretically cater, should guide our thinking in moving forward.

Creating a role for successful interventions and policies

One way to increase the effectiveness of the future GDGs could involve stakeholders investing energy in the design of indicators that commit them to specific interventions rather than abstract goals. This would entail a shift from the current focus on targets, such as a reduction in maternal mortality (an abstract goal), to say a 50 percent increase in skilled birth attendance (a concrete intervention). We believe that this approach would try to address the root causes of phenomena like maternal mortality, and focus on the means and not just the ends.

We present an example of a potential scenario relating to HIV and the health sector. Evidence suggests that immunization and medical circumcision are key tools in the arsenal of available interventions against polio and HIV, respectively. Countries affected by these diseases could then commit to specific interventions that are known to be effective in their prevention. For instance, Nigeria, Pakistan and Afghanistan could commit to vaccinating a certain percentage of children against polio. Countries like Swaziland, Botswana, Lesotho, and South Africa could agree to medically circumcise a certain percent of newborns and youth by 2030 as an HIV prevention measure. On both an international and domestic level, many of these countries have already planned to meet similar targets; including these objectives in future GDGs would increase pressure and accountability and help to mobilize resources towards the achievement of these objectives.

Lately, initiatives like the Copenhagen Consensus Center (CCC) have flourished. The CCC's mission is to conduct research and analysis into competing spending priorities in order to find the best and most cost-efficient solutions to key international challenges.[20] It adds value by working towards concrete answers for seemingly intractable problems like climate change and HIV/AIDS. For example, the Center has been discussing how best to spend an additional US$10 billion for AIDS in the next five years; its final conclusions are likely to be enlightening. Initiatives like this could help us draw up a list of priority interventions that we could focus on and guide our development of a post-2015 framework.

Let us assume that the "One World" scenario outlined above were to be adopted as part of a revised GDG framework. Interventions and policies, rather than abstract targets and indicators would be useful in two respects. First, once general objectives have been established (on global diseases, equity, and the like), interventions and policies to ensure service provision would help operationalize the goals and make them more concrete. Second, if specific service delivery targets could be linked to general, overarching goals such as climate change, the chances of reaching consensus on these issues—so far impossible—would be amplified.

As Moss recently put it, "health officials and their partners in donor agencies have much more scope to influence immunization rates than overall child mortality rates."[21] Rather than focusing on abstract end-goals like child mortality rates, we would be better off putting our energies into devising concrete interventions to which countries can commit. One objective could focus on health systems or policies that are generally beneficial for the health sector. Countries could set as a goal the achievement of universal health coverage, or a certain percentage of access to electricity in rural areas and urban informal settlements, or the institution of "sin taxes" on fatty foods and tobacco. We have plenty of evidence to back up the adoption of such policies, which have the added advantage of being easily tailored to country contexts.

This proposal, if seriously considered, could conceivably elicit some degree of controversy prior to agreement. Vandemoortele argues that "evidence-based" policy-making is just one more element in the vast portfolio of development jargon. Because it is easily manipulated, he claims, it is a euphemism "for misappropriating the policy debate in order to impose a certain worldview."[22] Others could accuse this proposal of fostering a "minimalist" conception of development.[23] Our support for a framework focused on tried and tested interventions stems from the belief that a "maximalist" view of development, although desirable, cannot easily be condensed into targets, nor realistically achieved. The need for pragmatism is paramount here and needs to be repeatedly emphasized.

Adopting a "life cycle" approach

Another innovative way of modifying the current framework is to integrate a "life cycle" approach into any future framework. This approach, as argued by Loewenson et al.,[24] provides a powerful lens for understanding human development in a comprehensive manner and is particularly suited to investing and achieving outcomes in the health sector, including HIV. On a practical level, adopting this approach would entail devising and slotting in the interventions and policies outlined above according to the stage of human life to which they belong. This would help address one of the key criticisms of the current MDG framework—that it offers a stilted vision of development and fragments issues (including HIV) into silos without capitalizing on potential synergies between different areas of development.

Waage et al.[25] explain that there are six stages of the life cycle: pregnancy, infancy, childhood, adolescence, adulthood, and old age. A number of interventions and service delivery targets that belong under each one of the stages can be identified. Under the pregnancy phase, for instance, our goal could be to provide access to antenatal care. Our target could entail providing a certain percentage of women in rural areas with access to a specific number of antenatal visits. If they test positive for HIV, treatment for the prevention of mother-to-child-transmission (PMTCT) will be administered in 100 percent of cases. In this way, HIV would be integrated into the provision of other health services and health systems would be strengthened as a result.

If instead we were to focus on maternal nutrition during the pregnancy stage, screening for micronutrient deficiencies during antenatal visits could be one of the objectives to which countries could agree. Indirectly, this would help HIV-positive mothers who need adequate nutrition to improve their adherence to ARVs. This kind of synergy would also capitalize on what Kim *et al.* call the "AIDS plus MDGs" approach, which entails building links between the global HIV response and the larger health and development agenda.[26] A similar exercise would have to be conducted for the remaining five life cycle stages and for interventions in other sectors. Although it would not be a simple endeavor, integrating a "life cycle" approach into the GDGs would finally address the issue of inter-generational equity. This is a crucial aspect of human development that the old framework has been accused of omitting.

Key considerations for moving forward

In broad strokes, we have outlined the three essential components of any post-2015 framework. The rest of the chapter describes the elements that are necessary to design a meaningful and effective global development compact. These elements can be gathered into two groups. The first set of four characteristics addresses commonly held criticisms of the MDGs, while the second group of three enhances and capitalizes on their most valued traits. In essence, we provide a series of suggestions for making progress on the future GDGs by addressing both the negative and positive aspects of the goals to date.

Four common criticisms of the MDGs are: their top-down nature; the lack of synergy between different goals; the reductionist conception of development that they represent; and their outdated reflection of the world. By contrast, the most valuable aspects of the MDGs are considered to be their parsimony; the fact that they are the product of hard-fought political bargaining; their ability to raise funds and awareness of international development problems; and their potential to address issues of inequality. Each of these features will be explored in detail below.

It is noteworthy that many of these criticisms and praises of the MDGs closely mirror those that are often directed at the global HIV response. It is for this reason that a new, revised, and better GDG framework would be a golden opportunity for the HIV response. The new agreement should be seen as a way for the international HIV community and for countries confronting the epidemic to find a way out of the political and financial difficulties conundrum in which they currently find themselves.

Building a framework from the bottom up

Textbooks of international development all emphasize the need for bottom-up decision-making. With regards to the GDGs, we know that we need to put in place processes that encourage responses from the ground up, as well as a number of feedback and accountability mechanisms. Our key suggestion for this to happen is to encourage each of the signatories to the next development framework to adopt and present a clear and formalized "localization" plan.[27] Given the context-specific nature of the HIV epidemic, this process is particularly important.

To some extent, we have already witnessed the adaptation of the current MDGs. A 2009 United Nations Development Programme (UNDP) study of 30 countries around the world suggests that 83 percent of countries had added, expanded and modified the MDG indicators and one-third of countries had added local goals.[28] Vision 2025 in Tanzania and Vision 2020 in Rwanda are examples of these processes of adaptation.[29] Nevertheless, more systematic ways of keeping track of localization efforts would address the criticism that the MDGs have been imposed on countries without consideration for local contexts. With input from developing country voices and members of civil society, a report could be compiled to incorporate the experiences of those countries that have successfully, unsuccessfully or creatively adapted or gone beyond the MDGs in the past. This could encourage and provide viable alternatives to countries and help operationalize the idea of "national ownership" of the GDG process. The wide-ranging global consultations that the Joint UN Programme on HIV/AIDS (UNAIDS) held with civil society prior to the UN High Level meeting on AIDS in June 2011 could offer some inspiration as a model.

There are a number of ways to monitor and review the progress in implementing local development strategies, which should be outlined in national localization plans. One option is to follow the model of UN Habitat's Global Urban Observatories, which bring together city officials, citizens and businesses to ask how well authorities are achieving results. Community-based monitoring systems and score cards, continuous improvement and benchmarking methods, as well as participatory impact assessments are other available options.[30] Others have suggested an international peer review mechanism to track national action, so that countries of similar development levels can help to hold each other accountable.

In sum, ensuring that clear plans exist for translating the MDGs in context-appropriate ways would have a number of benefits: it would increase the odds of achieving progress against end-goals; it would address the top-down nature of both the MDG framework and the HIV response; and it would augment the chances of fighting the HIV epidemic, for which tailored, country-specific responses are absolutely crucial.

Generating synergies between different objectives

Another common criticism of the current MDG framework is its failure to take advantage of the interconnected nature of many of its goals. As mentioned in the introductory section, since the HIV targets in sub-Saharan Africa will not be met, we know that most of the other MDG targets will not be attained either.[31] Since making progress on one goal will allow us to meet other goals, targets should not be tackled in isolation. In practice, however, how can this be achieved? One of our suggestions is for the future GDGs to encourage the use of combination interventions,[32] which are also a key part of UNAIDS' strategic vision for the epidemic going forward.[33] This would also be consistent with the idea, presented earlier, that the next development framework should focus on interventions rather than abstract indicators.

For example, within the field of HIV, "prevention packages"[34] that both commit to a proven biomedical intervention and try to change behavior would be favored over ones that only tackle one aspect of the epidemic. Medical circumcision for HIV prevention would be one such intervention. As for cross-sectoral initiatives, ones that promote education while trying to decrease vulnerability to HIV and encourage livelihoods promotion at the same time, for instance, would be welcomed. Other examples include microfinance programs that integrate HIV/AIDS awareness as a key component.[35]

Another distinct but related suggestion would be to combine the current MDGs. Rather than devote an entire goal to HIV (MDG 6), Vandemoortele also suggests merging the three health-related MDGs (4, 5 and 6) into one.[36] In sum, we need to encourage interventions that work towards meeting a number of goals rather than just one. This would not only highlight the links between different objectives, but would also lead to better outcomes.

Developing a holistic rather than reductionist development framework

Critics of the current framework have suggested that the MDGs offer a reductionist vision of development. The first goal, focused on reducing poverty by increasing income, views poverty through a narrow lens. A number of authors argue in favor of modifying our notion of development to reflect a more holistic conception of wellbeing, which they define as "the freedoms and capability to make choices and act effectively with respect to, for example, health, education, nutrition, employment, security, participation, voice, consumption and the claiming of rights."[37] We suggest that indicators and interventions of any future framework reflect this broader conception.

To assist with this process, it would be useful to look at the work of the Commission on the Measurement of Economic Performance and Social Progress (CMEPSP), led by Joseph Stiglitz, Amartya Sen and Jean Paul Fitoussi.[38] This Commission was created by French President Nicolas Sarkozy in 2008 to identify the limits of gross domestic product (GDP) as an indicator of economic performance and social progress, and assess the feasibility of alternative measurement tools. Essentially, the commission works towards the development of a statistical system that complements measures of market activity with measures centered on people's wellbeing, and that is able to capture the notion of sustainability in its economic, environmental and social dimensions. For instance, had country metrics incorporated assessments of sustainability (and indebtedness) prior to the global economic and financial crises, perhaps policymakers would have held more cautious views of their own economic performance.

Although by no means a panacea and in need of further elaboration, if such measures were successfully devised, they would provide a more comprehensive view of development—of which the UN, as a norm-setting institution, should be a pioneer. Among the key recommendations of the group is the idea that in our attempts to evaluate material wellbeing, we should be looking at income and consumption rather than just at production. We should also be emphasizing the household, rather than individual perspective, taking account of taxes paid to the government by the household, social benefits coming from government coffers and interest payments on household loans going to financial corporations. The household perspective is particularly relevant in the case of HIV, since households collectively bear the brunt of the epidemic both on a social and financial level. Efforts must also be made to measure people's quality of life by using both objective and subjective data,[39] as well as to measure the concept of sustainability, interpreted as variations of some underlying "stocks" of natural resources and of human, social and physical capital.[40] These considerations, although difficult to operationalize, would contribute to a more complete picture of development and would also expand the narrow and relatively isolationist lens through which the HIV response has looked to date.

Updating the framework to better reflect reality

The current MDG framework is a distinct product of the late 1990s. As a result, it necessarily fails to take into account a number of key factors that have become relevant for development since then. The first consideration relates to developments in technology. The GDGs must find a way to harness new technological advances and use social networks for development. Some argue that increasing connectivity should be one of the new goals, which would translate into targets on access to core infrastructure services such as water (included in the current framework), telecommunications (partially covered in MDG 8), power and transport (currently excluded).[41]

The second key element on which a GDG framework could build is the availability of new, cutting-edge research. What could distinguish the new agreement from the old is its ability to incorporate the latest research findings and innovations in, say, the healthcare sector. Findings relating to the efficacy of microbicides for HIV prevention or of new circumcision methods, which have surfaced in the past few years, could be developed into a recommended intervention or target, as suggested earlier in the chapter. The third relates to the fact that the MDGs have also been criticized for failing to pay adequate attention to the gender dimension of development. This is particularly relevant for goals relating to the HIV epidemic, given our awareness that the burden of HIV falls disproportionately on women. As outlined in the Johannesburg Statement, lack of sufficient progress on this[42] has affected our ability to meet many other goals, so a renewed attention to gender is paramount.

Let us now turn to the characteristics that are most valued about the current MDG framework and HIV response, in an effort to retain those elements moving forward.

Maintaining the parsimony of the current framework

One valuable aspect of the current MDGs, including MDG 6, is its pithiness and parsimony. Even if broader "One World" indicators are part of the next agreement, the way in which they are framed—using precise and measurable commitments/targets/indicators/interventions—should be maintained. The MDGs have political and popular power in part because of their clarity and concision.[43] Obviously, defining the content of the GDGs will require tough choices, but as Vandemoortele reminds us, "no matter the number of targets that are added, they can never adequately cover the many dimensions of human development,"[44] so we are better off settling on a few succinct measures of development on which we can agree, rather than trying to be comprehensive, and confusing as a result. This seems to be particularly important for our response to HIV. The risk is that, given the need for a comprehensive response to the epidemic, and given the multi-faceted and complex nature of the disease, we may wish to tackle every aspect of it, but this is neither possible nor advisable.

Remembering the importance of hard-fought political bargaining

The fact that the MDGs are the result of years of political compromise should guide us in two key ways. First, it should remind us that any agreement must have the strong backing and endorsement of the new G-20 powers, and particularly of the BRICS countries (Brazil, Russia, India, China, and South Africa). In the context of HIV, the collaboration and support of some of these countries is instrumental for an effective response to both sexually and drug-transmitted HIV. Given the changed socioeconomic context in which the GDGs will have to be negotiated, buy-in from countries that are rapidly developing and that can provide inspiration to other industrializing nations will be instrumental. Second, awareness of the difficulty of reaching past agreement should encourage us to put in place mechanisms, incentives and processes to support countries in meeting the goals to which they will commit. In this way, it may be more difficult to reach initial agreement, but there will be greater accountability and a higher chance that the objectives will actually be met. Particularly as attention—both political and financial—to fight HIV seems to be dwindling, built-in procedures to ensure long-term commitment and compliance are essential.

Harnessing the MDGs' ability to fundraise for development

One of the most recognized aspects of the MDG framework, as well of the global HIV response, has been its ability to mobilize capital and channel investment into development. At the time of the September

2000 UN Summit, total aid was around $60 billion per year. By 2005 the level had doubled to around $120 billion and has hovered around this level ever since. As Moss suggests, "a link between the MDGs and this spike in aid seems highly plausible."[45] The MDGs have helped catalyze a shift in overseas development assistance (ODA) from economic (or so-called productive) sectors to social sectors.[46] The health sector in general, and HIV in particular, have especially benefited from this transition. This ability to attract support for development must be retained in the next set of goals. Agreeing to a framework that focuses on concrete interventions, as suggested earlier, rather than abstract goals may facilitate this process.

Some have argued that the MDGs have helped change the concept of sustainability from one that is based exclusively on achieving domestic self-reliance to one that is complemented by sustained international support.[47] Nevertheless, to avoid adding fuel to the fire of donor dependency, the next round of GDG discussions could consider committing to the following arrangement: every country could be encouraged to set as a goal the adoption of some form of innovative and sustainable (domestic) financing mechanism in order to meet one or several of the GDGs. By way of example, countries with a high HIV prevalence but that are endowed with natural resources could commit to ring-fencing 5–10 percent of revenues to finance ARVs or other health-related goals.[48] This would contribute to the sustainability of financing for both development and HIV, as well as to greater country ownership of the development process.

Integrating equity issues into the new agreement

Equity is one of the most important dimensions of development. Although it would be difficult to reach an international agreement on issues of equality, feasible ways of integrating the subject in the new framework do exist. Unless countries willingly provide disaggregated data, progress in the current MDGs is based on national averages, which disguise local disparities. One way of holding countries accountable for their efforts to decrease inequality is suggested by Vandemoortele.[49] He argues that national statistics and the measures of progress towards MDG goals should be adjusted for intra-national disparities by using equity-adjusted weights. In this way, a reduction in maternal mortality among the poorest quintile could be given more importance than a reduction within the richest quintile. Data could be adjusted for disparities by weighing quintile-specific values in ways that accord more importance to progress for the lower quintiles than to similar progress for the upper quintiles. Given that HIV affects those who are economically and socially vulnerable the most, such adjustments would constitute an important step forward. In addition, countries could conceivably commit to a certain reduction in their Gini coefficients in an effort to reduce their levels of inequality. In order to avoid placing the most unequal countries (including G-20 powerhouses like Brazil and South Africa) at a disadvantage, rather than setting global standards in percentage terms, each country would independently determine how far they aim to reduce inequality from current levels.

Another potential idea could be to integrate targets on social protection into "One World Indicators." The MDG Summit held in New York in September 2010 acknowledged and accepted the concept of a Social Protection Floor (SPF) as a key tool to reduce poverty and inequality and as essential for achieving the MDGs.[50] As an example, a commitment to provide universal health coverage—suggested earlier as an intervention behind which countries could potentially rally—would definitely be considered part of national efforts to build a minimum level of social protection.

In sum, the elements outlined above suggest that the development of new GDGs offers the HIV community an invaluable opportunity: it represents the chance to improve its response to the epidemic; to address the challenges it has faced to date; and ultimately to achieve better outcomes.

Conclusion

The current MDG framework, and in all likelihood its offspring, the GDGs, may be stuck in an unfortunate series of dilemmas. First, by setting out goals that are too ambitious the international community may run the risk (again) of being unable to meet them; however, proposing goals that are too easy to achieve would lead to no real development. Second, because a holistic conception of development implies that the goals are linked to one another, failure to reach one goal means that others will not be met either, as past experience has demonstrated. Finally, we know that without addressing the underlying economic structures that drive the current socioeconomic context, we will only be able to make minor, superficial progress in human development in general, and in fighting HIV in particular. At the same time, it is so difficult to agree to wide-ranging changes in mechanisms and institutions at the global and national scale that waiting for progress on that end will result in even less advancement on the social front.

We are therefore caught in the middle of what we could consider one of the key conundrums of our time. For now, however, the MDGs and the future GDGs are our best short-term solutions to these difficult compromises. We must not forget that any target-setting exercise is bound to involve difficult trade-offs.[51] What is more, as this chapter has argued, for the HIV community the new GDGs represent an unprecedented opportunity. They offer a chance for real integration with other development goals and for a successful, comprehensive response to the epidemic from a multitude of angles. Until we find more satisfactory answers to our global problems, it is worth making the GDGs the best compromise that they can be. Pragmatism going forward will be essential. As Melamed and Scott highlight, "a post-2015 agreement does not need to encapsulate everything that is known about how to reduce poverty ... The quest should not be for the perfect agreement, but for the one that seems most likely to work."[52]

Notes

1 Andy Sumner and Meera Tiwari, "Global Poverty to 2015 and Beyond: What Has Been the Impact of the MDGs and What Are the Options for a Post-2015 Global Framework?" *Institute of Development Studies Working Paper 348* (2010).
2 Alan Whiteside, "Is Aids Exceptional?," in *Programmatic Response Working Group*, ed. Aids2031 (2010); Alan Whiteside and Julia Smith, "Exceptional Epidemics: Aids Still Deserves a Global Response," *Globalization and Health* 5, no. 15 (2009); Julia Smith and Alan Whiteside, "The History of Aids Exceptionalism," *Journal of the International AIDS Society* 13, no. 47 (2010).
3 Todd Moss, "What Next for the Millennium Development Goals?," *Global Policy* 1, no. 2 (2010).
4 Andy Sumner and Claire Melamed, "The MDGs and Beyond: Pro-Poor Policy in a Changing World," in *Institute of Development Studies Bulletin* (2010).
5 Sumner and Melamed, "The MDGs and Beyond," 5.
6 Alan Whiteside and Ilaria Regondi, "MDGs and HIV/AIDS: Policy Brief," in *Johannesburg Global Poverty Summit* (2011).
7 Sumner and Tiwari, "Global Poverty to 2015 and Beyond."
8 Claire Melamed and Lucy Scott, "After 2015: Progress and Challenges for Development," Overseas Development Institute (March 2011), www.odi.org.uk/resources/download/5671.pdf.
9 May Chazan, Michale Brklacich, and Alan Whiteside, "Rethinking the Conceptual Terrain of AIDS Scholarship: Lessons from Comparing 27 Years of AIDS and Climate Change Research," *Globalization and Health* 5, no. 12 (2009).
10 Jean-Michel Severino and Olivier Ray, "The End of ODA: Death and Rebirth of a Global Public Policy," *Center for Global Development Working Paper 167* (Washington, DC, 2009).
11 Sakiko Fukuda-Parr, "Are the MDGs Priority in Development Strategies and Aid Programmes? Only Few Are!," *IPC-IG Working Paper 48* (Brasilia: International Policy Centre for Inclusive Growth, 2008).
12 Julia Kim, Brian Lutz, Mandeep Dhaliwal and Jeffrey O'Malley, "The 'AIDS and MDGs' Approach: What Is It, Why Does It Matter, and How Do We Take It Forward?" *Third World Quarterly* 32, no. 1 (2011): 141–63.

13 Kim *et al.*, "The 'AIDS and MDGs' Approach."
14 Reuben M. Granich, Charles F. Gilks, Christopher Dye, Kevin M. De Cock and Brian G. Williams, "Universal Voluntary HIV Testing with Immediate Antiretroviral Therapy as a Strategy for Elimination of HIV Transmission: A Mathematical Model," *Lancet* 373, no. 9657 (2009): 48–57.
15 Princeton Lyman and Stephen Wittels, "No Good Deed Goes Unpunished: The Unintended Consequences of Washington's HIV/AIDS Programs," *Foreign Affairs* July/August (2010).
16 Sumner and Tiwari, "Global Poverty to 2015 and Beyond."
17 Richard Feachem and Jeffrey Sachs, eds., "Global Public Goods for Health," in *The Report of Working Group 2 of the Commission on Macroeconomics and Health* (Geneva: World Health Organization, 2002).
18 Jeff Waage *et al.*, "The Millennium Development Goals: A Cross-Sectoral Analysis and Principles for Goal Setting after 2015," *Lancet and London International Development Centre Commission* (2010).
19 Amy Pollard *et al.*, "What Should Come after the Millennium Development Goals? Voices from the South" (CAFOD/IDS, 2010).
20 Copenhagen Consensus Center, www.copenhagenconsensus.com.
21 Moss, "What Next," 219.
22 Jan Vandemoortele and E. Delamonica, "Taking the MDGs Beyond 2015: Hasten Slowly," *IDS Bulletin* 41 (2010): 62.
23 Waage *et al.*, "The Millennium Development Goals."
24 Rene Loewenson, Jacqui Hadingham, and Alan Whiteside, "Household Impacts of Aids: Using a Life Course Approach to Identify Effective, Poverty-Reducing Interventions for Prevention, Treatment and Care," *AIDS Care* 21, no. 8 (2009): 1032–41.
25 Waage *et al.*, "The Millennium Development Goals."
26 Kim *et al.*, "The 'AIDS and MDGs' Approach."
27 UN Development Programme, "Localizing the MDGs for Effective Integrated Local Development: An Overview of Practices and Lessons Learned" (New York: UNDP, 2007).
28 UN Development Programme, "Beyond the Midpoint: Accelerating Support for MDG Achievements" (New York: UNDP, 2009).
29 Waage *et al.*, "The Millennium Development Goals."
30 UN Development Programme, "Localizing the MDGs."
31 D.J. Fourie and R.E. Schoeman, "The Effects of HIV/AIDS on the Achievement of the Millennium Development Goals in Sub-Saharan Africa," *Journal of Public Administration* 45, no. 1 (2010): 236–360.
32 Kim *et al.*, "The 'AIDS and MDGs' Approach."
33 UNAIDS, "2011–15 Strategy: Getting to Zero" (UNAIDS, 2010).
34 Anne Kurth, Connie Celum, Jared M. Baetum, Sten H. Vermund and Judith N. Wasswerheit, "Combination HIV Prevention: Significance, Challenges, and Opportunities," *Current HIV/AIDS Reports* 8, no. 1 (2011).
35 Kim *et al.*, "The 'AIDS and MDGs' Approach."
36 Vandemoortele, "The MDG Conundrum."
37 Waage *et al.*, "The Millennium Development Goals."
38 Joseph Stiglitz, Amartya Sen, and Jean-Paul Fitoussi, "Report by the Commission on the Measurement of Economic Performance and Social Progress" (2009), www.stiglitz-sen-fitoussi.fr/documents/rapport_anglais.pdf.

39 Katharine Hagerman and Alan Whiteside, "Global Governance, HIV/AIDS and the MDGs: Where Are We Now and What Lessons Have Been Learnt for the Future?" (La Trobe University, 2011).

40 Stiglitz, Sen, and Fitoussi, "Report by the Commission on the Measurement of Economic Performance and Social Progress."

41 Richard Manning, "Using Indicators to Encourage Development: Learning Lessons from the Millennium Development Goals" (Copenhagen: Danish Institute for International Studies, 2009).

42 See the "Johannesburg Statement on the Millennium Development Goals," in Appendix 2.

43 Selim Jahan, "The MDGs Beyond 2015," *IDS Bulletin* (Brighton: IDS, 2010).

44 Vandemoortele, "The MDG Conundrum," 356.

45 Moss, "What Next," 218.

46 Sumner and Tiwari, "Global Poverty to 2015 and Beyond."

47 Gorik Ooms *et al.*, "Applying the Principles of Aids 'Exceptionality' to Global Health: Challenges for Global Health Governance," *Global Health Governance* 4, no. 1 (2011).

48 Whiteside and Regondi, "MDGs and HIV/AIDS."

49 Vandemoortele, "The MDG Conundrum."

50 Global Extension of Social Security (GESS), www.socialsecurityextension.org/gimi/gess/ShowWiki.do?wid=9.

51 Waage *et al.*, "The Millennium Development Goals."

52 Melamed and Scott, "After 2015," 4.

11 Combating poverty in Africa

2015 and beyond

Yusuf Bangura

Combating poverty has been an important global objective in the last decade. The elevation of social or human development in international development policy is perhaps one of the major contributions of the Millennium Development Goals (MDGs), in which governments commit to halve poverty and hunger by 2015. Development assistance is now strongly oriented towards poverty reduction and other MDG targets. This has led to a shift in aid allocation in favor of social services. The public expenditures of poor countries have also tended to reflect this shift, with increased spending on basic services used by the poor.

However, recent reviews of progress towards the MDGs suggest marked variation in outcomes across regions, with East Asia experiencing the sharpest fall and sub-Saharan Africa the least. Even though some African countries are on track to meet the MDG target of reducing poverty by half by 2015, most are likely to fall well short. Income inequality remains higher than in most other regions, while gender, ethnic and regional inequalities across a number of social indicators persist. Besides, the measure used by the international development community to track global poverty—US$1.25 a day—hides the real extent of deprivation in Africa and elsewhere. Countries may be declared as poverty-free or making progress in meeting the MDG target, when in fact many of their citizens may be mired in poverty along multiple dimensions.[1] It is also debatable whether current levels and patterns of growth can drive down poverty figures to levels that have been attained by industrialized and successful developmental states where poverty is now measured in relative, not absolute, terms.

This chapter examines Africa's development prospect and efforts at overcoming poverty beyond 2015. It seeks to throw light on how to transform African economies and societies in order to achieve significant and sustained dents into poverty. It focuses on four issues. The first underscores the importance of developing growth strategies that pay sufficient attention to productive capacities, employment generation and income levels. The second examines the need to rebuild and expand human capital through comprehensive social policies. The third discusses the political drivers for economic and social transformation. The fourth addresses issues that need to be taken into account in a post-2015 MDG agenda.

Employment-centered growth

Even though the MDGs are silent on the macroeconomic policy framework for achieving the targets, the Poverty Reduction and Strategy Papers (PRSPs) have largely been seen by donors as providing that framework. The PRSPs share a strong lineage with the structural adjustment policies of the 1980s. They emerged as a framework to channel resources freed up by debt relief to poverty reduction. Under the new arrangement, the International Monetary Fund's (IMF) instrument for providing loans to poor countries, the Poverty Reduction and Growth Facility (PRGF) was expected to support the PRSP goals of growth, poverty reduction and country ownership. In practice, however, the PRGF has remained narrowly focused on achieving fiscal stability and often predetermines the macroeconomic frameworks and low inflation targets of the PRSPs.[2] Although the inflation rates of many African countries were much lower by 2000–05, Gottschalk's study finds that almost all countries continued to set very low inflation targets in their PRSPs. Only a few countries' monetary policies had objectives other than price stability. Although the PRSPs' fiscal frameworks tend to be pro-poor because of the reorientation of aid policy towards basic services, they have not been pro-growth, especially in terms of infrastructure investment and capacity expansion in agriculture and industry.

Transforming African economies requires sustained growth and structural change that creates jobs and improved earnings. Without growth that delivers jobs, it will be even more difficult to achieve most of the MDGs. Employment represents an important route through which income growth can be widely shared. Growth with jobs can have strong multiplier effects on various MDG targets and over time result in major transformation of economies and societies. Following Africa's economic contraction of the 1980s and 1990s, growth picked up from 2000 through 2007, thanks to a boom in commodity prices and improvements in the world economy. This helped many countries, especially Ethiopia, Ghana, Mali and Senegal, to reduce poverty. However, even for these countries, poverty remains high and growth has not transformed their economies or delivered sufficient amounts of decent jobs. Indeed, except for mineral-rich economies like Equatorial Guinea, Angola and Mauritania, which have posted double digit growth rates, Africa's average growth rate (about 5.5 percent) has not reached the scale attained by emerging economies that helped put their economies on a trajectory of solid and rapid poverty reduction and structural change. Much of the growth is still dependent on good prices for commodities, weather and foreign aid.

It is crucial to understand how poverty was eliminated historically in now-developed countries. In the world's high-income countries, economic growth fuelled a shift from agriculture to industry and from industry to services, as well as a shift from self-employment to wage employment. As labor and capital left agriculture for more dynamic sectors, average productivity in the economy increased, leading to more demand for industrial goods and services. Productivity and earnings in agriculture also improved because urban industrial producers had to be fed by a declining agricultural workforce.[3] This kind of structural change was repeated in East Asia and is now being followed by China and South East Asian countries. These countries prioritized economic growth and established a strong state structure to influence investment decisions and the adoption of labor-absorbing industrial strategies. Credit, investments, entry and exit of firms in specific sectors, and pricing were coordinated to regulate competition and facilitate technological upgrading and industrial restructuring. They invested heavily in education, training and research, leading to a deepening of skills across sectors and income groups, and carried out land reform, which raised productivity and income levels in the rural sector. They combined selective import substitution and export-led growth through well-managed industrial policies.[4] Although the levels of skill formation, domestic savings, and state capacities are much lower in South East Asian countries than those in the East Asian developmental states, economic transformation in the former region is also unmistakable. In Malaysia, manufacturing employment expanded rapidly—from 7 percent in the 1960s to about 28 percent in 2000. Whereas 55 percent of Malaysians earned a living from agriculture in the 1960s, this share fell to 16 percent by 2000. Poverty fell from about 50 percent in 1970 to less than 6 percent in 2004.[5]

However, Africa has not been able to follow a similar course of structural change. Instead, industrialization in much of the continent has been stunted; productivity in agriculture and services has been low; and for countries with mineral wealth, economic growth is often associated with Dutch disease and specialization in a few products. As a result, labor markets have been segmented and unequal. There is widespread underemployment, and incomes in informal and agricultural activities remain low. Growth with jobs has been elusive because the links between agriculture and industry, which have always been tenuous even at independence when African governments had industrial and agricultural strategies, have become extremely weak. The development strategies of these countries were based on import substitution and, in some cases, the processing of agricultural products for export. Agriculture would provide foreign exchange, raw materials, food and labor for the industrial sector, which in turn would supply rural producers with production tools and, in the process, raise labor productivity and incomes. This strategy held much promise in Côte d'Ivoire between 1960 and 1980, when its manufacturing sector grew at a rate of 13 percent per annum, and manufacturing share of gross domestic product (GDP) rose from 4 percent to 17 percent.[6] Kenya's manufacturing sector also grew in the 1960s and 1970s, and accounted for about 14 percent of its GDP.[7] It was dominated by agro-processing industries, such as grain milling, sugarcane crushing, coffee and a small and medium-sized enterprise sector producing household goods, vehicle parts and farm implements.

However, linkages between industry and agriculture were weak even in Côte d'Ivoire and Kenya. A large proportion of the agricultural labor force remained in the subsistence sector, which accounted for the bulk of food production but received lower returns than the agricultural export sector and industry. Labor migration to the cities grew faster than industrial expansion, and agricultural labor productivity was low as industry failed to play its transformative and supportive role. Industry depended on massive importation of intermediate and capital goods, and was unable to supply the technological needs of agriculture. Agricultural exports, the terms of trade of which deteriorated in the 1980s, were not sufficient to pay for the large import bill and debts incurred to finance industrialization. Long-running economic crises and massive debts in the 1980s exposed most countries to the stabilization and liberalization policies of the international financial institutions and made matters worse. Urban people are now fed largely by imported food, which has made it difficult to expand domestic agriculture and improve the incomes of farmers. Countries also import most of their manufactured goods rather than expanding domestic production. Indeed, Africa is the only region of the world the citizens of which are largely clothed in second-hand goods, and which seems incapable of producing even basic household appliances.

What can be done? Employment-centered growth can be achieved through deliberate policies in a number of areas. These include industrial and agricultural policies that connect the agricultural sector more productively to industry and other sectors; investing in infrastructure as well as education to improve skills and the quality of employment;

and avoiding pro-cyclical or contractionary policies during periods of slow growth. The single most important ingredient in this package is strategic action in governing the economy. One of the unfortunate effects of 20 years of structural adjustment is the dismantling of key institutions, such as development banks, marketing boards and development planning ministries and expertise in favor of unfettered markets. Certainly, markets provide important information about global trends in consumption, distribution and production. However, achieving an optimal policy mix for sustained growth requires additional instruments. Markets are often inadequate in responding to large, complex and urgent challenges.[8]

A combination of state and market interventions is therefore required if African countries are to enjoy the kinds of growth and structural change that will deliver jobs. In this regard, governments should learn from the mistakes of the past in devising new strategic frameworks. In the 1960s and 1970s most African countries provided incentives to business but failed abysmally to enforce decisions about resource withdrawal when performance was poor. Incentives tended to be generalized and not targeted to any sector or group of firms identified as the growth sectors. There was no steering or strategic agency with the requisite technical expertise to guide economic transformation. Bureaucrats lacked the economic information needed by business to facilitate a healthy state-business relationship. Firms did not produce for export and were therefore not subjected to the discipline provided by international market competition. They often enjoyed huge rents, but refused to comply with agreed-upon targets. Building strategic and enforcement capacity is therefore vital in supporting state-business relations that will deliver agricultural and industrial transformation.

Universal social policies

Social policy is at the heart of the growth strategies of countries that have experienced far reaching structural change and sustained poverty reduction. Such countries pursued a number of welfare policies at fairly low levels of income that covered a large proportion of their populations. They were able to do this because of the developmental roles assigned to social policy, which was concerned not just with protection but also with economic growth or improving productive capacity. From this perspective, savings accumulated as social insurance funds, such as pensions or provident funds, can be used for infrastructure development and industrialization. Similarly, investment in human capital will not only improve the education and health of the population, but it will also raise the productivity of labor and help firms and employees to manage adjustments in labor markets during economic downturns. Social policies may also act as powerful stabilizers, since income-replacement schemes may help smooth economic cycles and avoid deflationary crises by stabilizing demand and domestic markets. Social policy can also legitimize the political order, enhance social cohesion and contribute to political stability.[9]

A large body of literature has shown that social policies can be decisive in lifting people out of poverty. For instance, poverty levels are drastically reduced in most Organisation for Economic Co-operation and Development (OECD) countries after social transfers have been made, with the most significant reductions in countries that have comprehensive social policies.[10] The International Labour Organization (ILO) estimates that non-pension cash transfers reduce the risk of poverty by more than 20 percent in most European Union (EU) countries; in Denmark, Finland, France, Hungary, the Netherlands and Sweden the reduction is even more than 50 percent.[11] The ILO also estimates that a basic social protection package (comprising pensions for the elderly and disabled, child benefits and essential healthcare) for low-income countries would cost between 2.2 percent and 5.7 percent of GDP in 2010. The cost of providing basic child benefits would be below 3 percent of GDP in most countries, and universal access to essential healthcare would cost between 1.5 percent and 5.5 percent of GDP.

Important complementarities often exist among different social services and systems of protection, which can be fully realized when they are provided on a large or universal scale. Universal access to healthcare, for example, is good for school enrolment and outcomes, which may not be constrained by illness. Similarly, universal access to education improves access to information about hygiene, nutrition and sanitation. Improved use of reproductive healthcare facilities is correlated with education.[12] Health and education services may reduce the cost of social protection, just as social protection schemes, such as cash transfers, may make it easier for the poor to access social services. Access to water, sanitation facilities and transportation can improve health outcomes and reduce the time spent collecting water or travelling.[13]

During the 1960s and 1970s social policies in Africa were an essential ingredient of economic development and nation-building.[14] Public expenditures on education and health grew rapidly in most countries. Primary and secondary school enrolment rose and infant mortality rates declined. In the 1980s, however, economic crises and trends towards commercialization led to severe cuts in social expenditures. The burden of financing shifted to consumers through user fees. Only a few countries, such as Mauritius and Botswana, refused to cut expenditures. In Kenya, government spending on basic services fell from 20 percent of total expenditure in 1980 to about 12 percent in 1997.[15] As a result, low-income groups tended to have access only to poor-quality services and could ill afford the fees required to access those of better quality.

An evaluation report in 1994 on the World Bank's role in human development in Africa found that the Bank's annual loans on education fell from $0.50 per person (in 1990 dollars) for the period 1972–81, to $0.32 per person during the period 1982–88.[16] The Bank's contribution as a percentage of the education budgets of a panel of 21 countries actually collapsed from 37.3 percent in 1975 to 0.9 percent in 1985.[17] Following criticisms from international organizations, such as UNICEF (the UN Children's Fund), civil society groups and social democratic governments, the Bank reviewed its expenditure reform policies in the late 1980s and early 1990s.

Popular pressures for improved services and shifts in aid allocations in favor of basic services have led in recent years to increased spending on social services. There has also been a proliferation of social assistance schemes, such as free healthcare for children, pensions for the elderly and income transfers for the poor. However, Africa spends only about 3.5 percent of its GDP on social protection, compared to 4.5 percent in low-income countries, 10.5 percent in middle-income countries and 20.6 percent in high-income countries.[18] Furthermore, there is a tendency to treat the poor and vulnerable as residual categories or groups that should be targeted in these new social schemes, thus separating poverty reduction from the dynamics of development.

African governments cannot avoid a universal approach to social policy if they take economic and social transformation seriously. First, long-running economic crises and structural adjustment have produced a system of social provision that is highly fragmented, exclusionary and dysfunctional for development. As a result, most people lack access to public services. When human capital is degraded, countries cannot compete or exploit international opportunities and move their economies forward. Second, even when services are available there is insufficient investment in personnel, infrastructure and materials, leading to poor outcomes. Third, weak state provisioning and commercialization have produced a dual system of health and education provision, consisting of a public sector that is under-resourced and neglected, and an unregulated private sector that may also be of poor quality.[19] Universalism may constitute a powerful tool in the rebuilding of solidarity, citizenship and national cohesion, especially in the context of Africa's ethnic fragmentation.

A social policy framework that will be transformative must be grounded in universal rights and linked to efforts at creating employment-centered growth. Indeed, the cost of social policy and the burden of universal coverage are reduced when the chosen development strategy delivers high levels of employment. For example, the industrialization strategy of East Asian countries generated low levels of unemployment. Together with the policy of life-long employment for many workers in key industries, this strategy helped raise the majority of their population out of poverty. Similarly, European countries with relatively universal social protection regimes, such as the Nordic countries, tend to incorporate more people in the tax net through active labor market policies that produce high levels of employment.[20] Attainment of full employment in the past helped to reduce the cost of funding these countries' universal social policies.

Politics of transformation

Transforming Africa for effective poverty reduction requires purposeful, growth-oriented and welfare-enhancing political systems, as well as competent bureaucracies. Good social outcomes require institutionalization of rights; embedding of political parties in broad social coalitions; construction of social pacts around key issues of growth, employment and welfare; and ensuring that the democratic regime is competitive. High levels of unionization can encourage groups to support policies that reconcile wage and welfare demands with the goals of profitability and growth.[21] In the Nordic countries, which were famous for their advanced welfare regimes, high levels of unionization and social pacts before their adoption of more liberal policies in the 1990s, unions supported policies of wage compression and equal pay for equal work across sectors, which spurred employers to raise labor productivity and avoid the option of cheap labor and segmentation.[22] Unions were able to restrain the short-term interests of their members because of their encompassing position in the economy: deals that arose from bargaining had wide worker coverage, and bargaining took place at the national, not industry, level.

The structure of labor markets in Africa's agrarian and informal economies can act as a constraint on unionization and on interest-group pressure for welfare development. However, despite the limited nature of the wage economy in much of Africa, unions were able to pressure governments and employers to act on the livelihoods of workers on numerous occasions before the adoption of stabilization policies in the 1980s. In alliance with other groups, they also managed to resist policies such as price increases on basic commodities and services that undermined the welfare of the poor.[23] However, unions' resistance to adjustment programs in the 1980s exposed them to attack from reforming governments and the international financial institutions, which argued that rural poverty was a product of discriminatory trade and pricing policies favored by an urban coalition that included the working class. Authoritarian measures were supported to free markets and release the grip of the so-called urban coalition on public policy.[24] While these measures weakened union power and undermined workers' livelihoods, they did not necessarily improve the incomes and power of farmers. Organizations of subaltern groups participated in the wave of democratization that swept through countries in the 1990s. However, their capacity to subsequently influence the direction of policy has been limited. Indeed, one of the stark anomalies of Africa's democratization is the loosening of links between political parties and broad social movements that defend the interests of the poor.

In Mauritius, one of Africa's oldest democracies, the peasantry collaborated with the growing agricultural labor force and urban trade unions to force the state to institutionalize social rights. These organizations played a role in the formation of the first nationalist party, the Mauritius Labour Party, which spearheaded social reforms. The deepening of democracy and extension of social rights eroded clientelistic relationships. Today, all the major parties, which alternate in government, consistently regard social rights as acquired rights by citizens. There is a universal basic pension, free primary and secondary education, and comprehensive free medical care.[25] A similar pattern of party-interest group ties and competitive politics in promoting welfare can also be found in Costa Rica and the Indian state Kerala. Although the growth rates of these welfare democracies did not reach the levels of the East Asian developmental states, they were respectable for much of the period of the 1960s–1990s (with growth in Mauritius reaching 6 percent; in Costa Rica, it averaged 5.3 percent in 1963–2000, and 7.6 percent in 1963–73). This ensured some economic transformation and funding of extensive social programs. Rural-urban alliances also facilitated the extension of welfare rights to all citizens.

In South Africa, democratic processes in which social movements and pacts play a role have also driven the expansion of social assistance, which has become the main vehicle for addressing poverty, although the growth strategy has failed to generate employment.[26] Despite periodic tensions, the social pact between the labor movement and the government has survived; when combined with electoral pressures, it has tended to push the government in a social democratic direction on social policy. An even more successful country with a history of high inequality is Brazil. Lula's government, which has been credited with the expansion of welfare rights in Brazil, represented the rise to power of the Workers' Party, with strong ties to the industrial working class and committed to the cause of redistribution and welfare policies. There has been substantial civic engagement with public authorities in many municipalities over budgetary issues, the most well known and successful being that in Porto Alegre. In Porto Alegre, which is run by the Workers' Party, participatory budgeting has led to considerable increases in the number of households with access to water and sewerage, and children in public schools; it has also led to the expansion of local government revenues. The main factors contributing to the success of the process include the willingness of mayors to delegate authority to citizens; the extent to which the rules of participation give genuine authority to residents to make decisions; and the ability of civil society organizations to cooperate in the program through a politics of contestation.[27]

Despite the delinking of political parties from social movements in much of Africa, it is important to note that electoral competitiveness has opened up possibilities for demanding accountability from leaders. For instance, taking advantage of a national election in 1993, the farmers' federation in Senegal, which had grown to more than 400,000 members, forced the country's president, who was worried about the rural vote, to discuss the government's agricultural policy. This resulted in an agreement to cut interest rates on agricultural loans, remove import taxes on agricultural inputs, issue a moratorium on farmers' debts, and institute dialogue between the farmers' organization and the agriculture ministry.[28] However, many African governments still enjoy huge parliamentary majorities and retain the capacity to immunize themselves from electoral defeat. Lack of electoral competitiveness and limited strength of social movements often make it difficult to sustain gains outside of electoral cycles.

2015 and beyond

In the few years that remain of the MDG process, there is a need to draw lessons from recent experiences about the most effective mechanisms for meeting the agreed-upon targets and that can help transform African economies and societies beyond the current MDGs. Surely the MDGs have mobilized resources around important goals, and progress has been significant in some areas—particularly in basic education. Net primary school enrolment in Africa rose from 58 percent in 1999 to 76 percent in 2008. In health, deaths of children under five have declined worldwide, although the progress in Africa is slower. Of the 36 countries in which under-five mortality rates still exceed 100 per 1,000, 34 are in Africa. Since 1990 the percentage of births attended by skilled personnel has improved overall, from 53 percent in 1990 to 63 percent in 2008, although in Africa more than half of all births are still unattended.

Increased access to antiretroviral drugs and improved knowledge about preventing the spread of HIV has meant that, worldwide, the numbers of new HIV infections and AIDS deaths have peaked; there has also been a sharp increase in the use of bed nets to protect people from malaria—this rose from 2 percent in 2000 to 22 percent in 2008.[29]

However, as this chapter has shown, a number of issues that are fundamental to development and sustained poverty reduction have not been addressed in the MDGs. These include productive employment; redistributive policies, especially in a context of growing inequalities; the constraints of conventional macroeconomic policies on growth; the political and social relations that structure power and exclusion; and the mechanisms required to achieve the MDG goals individually and exploiting the synergies between them. A post-2015 MDG agenda would require a focus on five key issues.

Productive employment

This chapter has argued that substantial poverty reduction requires a pattern of growth and structural change that generates productive employment and improves earnings. Employment policies must figure centrally in development strategies if such a pattern of growth is to occur. Recent experiences even in industrialized countries show that growth alone does not easily translate into jobs. It is indeed astonishing that the MDGs did not initially include employment. It took the intervention of the ILO to get global leaders to introduce employment into the MDGs.

However, employment was subsumed in the MDGs as a target under the goal of halving extreme poverty and hunger. Although the target, which calls on countries to "achieve full and productive employment and decent work for all" is laudable, it is not measurable and time bound. Annual reviews of progress have correctly focused on employment levels, vulnerable or informal employment, and the working poor. However, the links between these categories and the overarching target of full and decent employment remain unclear, making it difficult to hold governments to account. Besides, the fact that productive employment is only a target under the goal of reducing poverty and hunger reduces its visibility in advocacy and policymaking. A post-2015 MDG agenda needs to fix this problem.

Redistributive policies

Poverty is closely related to inequality. Indeed, it is the processes and institutions that connect people differently that make some poor and others rich. High levels of inequality may marginalize the poor even when economies grow and may create institutions that lock the poor into poverty traps. An increasing body of evidence shows that highly unequal societies need higher levels of growth than relatively equal ones to overcome poverty,[30] and that there is no trade-off between equity and growth. This implies that there is a strong need for specific policies and targets that promote greater equity in society. However, apart from a commitment to eliminate gender disparities in primary and secondary education, the MDGs do not explicitly focus on inequalities.

To compensate for this lapse, annual reviews of progress in meeting the MDGs have included references to various types of inequalities, including those based on gender, ethnicity, location and income or class position.[31] Gender, ethnic and regional inequalities intersect with vertical or class inequalities and produce multiple disadvantages for many people. Such disadvantages cannot be overturned if public policy is not sensitive to equality. Upholding the intrinsic value of equality is not a case for perfect equality, which can undermine effort, personal responsibility and freedom. However, a growing body of evidence posits that a Gini coefficient (a measure of inequality in which zero represents perfect equality and one represents total inequality) of more than 0.4 impacts negatively on economic and social wellbeing. Objectives of relative equality facilitate rapid poverty reduction, spread the benefits of growth more widely, and contribute to social cohesion. A post-2015 MDG agenda needs to confront this issue head on. It is not enough to refer to inequality and redistribution in annual reviews of MDGs when there are no specific goals and targets towards which countries can work.

Resource bargains

One reason for the limited vision of development in the MDGs is that they are largely driven by the donor community. Lack of attention to resource bargains and redistributive issues in the MDGs may be linked to the aid relationship. Since donors would provide most of the funds, governments do not need to strike bargains with taxpayers and confront the rich. The MDGs can be seen as a bargain that donors struck with poor countries for increased aid, which had experienced a downward trend in much of the 1980s and 1990s. Indeed, MDG 8 on financing strategies is largely about global partnerships or getting donors to deliver on aid, trade, investment, technology and medicines, and is completely silent on domestic resource mobilization. However, estimates by the MDG Gap Task Force Report show big gaps in meeting overseas development assistance (ODA) commitments, including those that are targeted to Africa.[32] It is increasingly clear that African countries cannot rely on aid alone if they are to launch on a trajectory of sustained growth and transformation. Domestic resource mobilization can improve policy space and ability to set agendas, as well as empower states to influence the orientation and strategies of business groups.

However, support for domestic resource mobilization does not guarantee that the desired amount of resources will be generated, let alone allocated to preferred programs, or that the burden of resource extraction will be distributed fairly among different population groups. Issues of contestation and bargaining are bound to influence the extent to which governments can succeed in extracting resources from their populace. Bargaining may involve acceptance by citizens of governments' tax and savings plans in exchange for services, social protection, employment guarantees and income support, making the politics of domestic resource mobilization inextricably interconnected with the politics of social development. Therefore, a post-2015 MDG agenda needs to include resource bargains in order to enhance endogenous development and accountability.

Universal services and social floor

The MDGs—which focus on alleviating hunger and poverty, promoting universal primary education, reducing maternal and child mortality, advancing gender equality, and easing the burden of major global diseases—are fundamentally about promoting social development. However, they do not provide a social policy framework for achieving the targets and exploiting the synergies between them. They have also been criticized as too limited in scope for a transformative agenda. For instance, the focus on education is on primary school enrolment, not on quality of instruction, school infrastructure, and retention of students; although secondary and tertiary education is tracked in annual MDG reviews, these two sectors are not included in the goals. Without complementary investment in post-primary education, the quality of primary education and availability of qualified teachers may decline.[33] Similarly, if curative healthcare is neglected, the poor are likely to be most disadvantaged because they are susceptible to non-infectious diseases but may lack access to private-sector treatment. Indeed, the separation of public and private sectors and reorientation of public spending towards primary services may undermine the redistributive benefits that are often associated with a unified system.[34]

Another vital omission in the MDGs is social protection. Evidence across the world suggests that social transfers drastically reduce poverty levels, with the most significant reductions in countries with universal systems of protection. Universalism is associated with solidarity, rights of various types, and collective responsibility for individual wellbeing. It fosters cohesion and is particularly important for cross-class alliance formation and nation-building, especially in multi-ethnic settings like those in Africa. The social protection floor championed by the ILO and embraced by the UN system in 2009 provides a useful start in thinking about a basic level of protection for all citizens in a post-MDG world.

Pro-poor politics

A post-2015 MDG agenda also needs to address the political dimension of economic transformation and poverty eradication. Although it is difficult to set targets on politics and institutions, advances can be made in this area if the will is there to incorporate these issues into the new agenda. One starting point will be to avoid the kinds of participatory politics that inform the PRSPs. This is because participation has been reduced to mere consultation in the PRSPs. Social groups often make their voices heard but lack power to effect real change. Many groups that participate in the process typically feel that real decisions on important policies, especially those on the macro-economy, lie elsewhere. Besides, participation tends to be limited to non-governmental organizations (NGOs), with limited involvement of associations of producer groups, such as those of workers, farmers or artisans.

Advances in welfare provision require that the democratic regime is made sufficiently competitive, which will allow citizens to change governments that pursue policies that are detrimental to their wellbeing. It also requires additional mechanisms of interest representation in the policy process if gains are not to be restricted to electoral cycles. How individuals organize into groups and affect public policy is important in understanding the politics of welfare development. Targets could be set on political rights; free, fair, credible and competitive elections; the types of links political parties and governments establish with citizen groups, especially those that are organized by, and/or represent, the poor; organizational capabilities of, and claims-making by, the poor; and representation of popular strata groups in key policymaking institutions and processes.

Conclusion

Transforming Africa for sustained poverty reduction requires strategies that transcend the MDGs. The MDGs have been useful in drawing attention to the terrible conditions of poverty in Africa and the rest of the world, and prompting leaders to take corrective measures. However, they do not go far enough in identifying the appropriate policies that poor countries need in order to get on a trajectory of growth and structural change. The MDGs seem to be walking on one, indeed very thin, social leg. They need to be grounded in both the "productive" and "social" sectors, exploit synergies between them, and be driven by the right type of politics. In other words, Africa needs a growth strategy that pays sufficient attention to productive capacities, employment generation and income levels. It also needs to generate domestic resources that can help to stimulate growth, encourage effective social contracts, and wean the continent from aid dependence and its attendant loss of autonomy in policymaking. The rebuilding and expansion of human capital in its various forms through universal social policies is vital in this regard. The appropriate type of politics for this enterprise encourages groups with strong ties to the poor to organize independently and establish links with, as well as hold to account, political actors who make decisions. Countries where governments are sensitive to redistribution have produced relatively egalitarian outcomes. Elections in which outcomes are uncertain can act as incentives for redistribution. However, without effective group organization and contestation, elections may not work for the poor. Indeed, the poor suffer when interest groups and social movements are weak and when the electoral system is not sufficiently competitive.

Notes

1 UNDESA, *Report on the World Social Situation: Rethinking Poverty* (New York: United Nations, 2010).
2 Ricardo Gottschalk, "The Effectiveness of IMF/World Bank-Funded Poverty Reduction Strategy Papers," in *Developmental Pathways to Poverty Reduction*, ed. Yusuf Bangura (Basingstoke: Palgrave Macmillan, forthcoming).
3 UNRISD, *Combating Poverty and Inequality: Structural Change, Social Policy and Politics* (Geneva: UNRISD, 2010).
4 Robert Wade, *Governing the Market: Economic Theory and the Role of Government in East Asian Development* (Princeton and Oxford: Princeton University Press, 2004); Ha-joon Chang, *Kicking Away the Ladder: Development Strategies in Historical Perspective* (London: Athens Press, 2003).
5 UNRISD, *Combating Poverty*; Khoo Boo Teik, *Policy Regimes and the Political Economy of Poverty Reduction in Malaysia* (Basingstoke: UNRISD/Palgrave Macmillan, forthcoming).
6 Aly Traoré, "Ivory Coast: Agriculture and Industrial Development," in *African Agriculture: Critical Choices*, ed. Hamid Ait Amara and Bernard Founou-Tchuigoa (The United Nations University/Third World Forum, 1990); Kouassy Oussou, Pegatienan Jacques and Bamba Ngaladjo, "Côte d'Ivoire: Policy Making and Implementation: Examples of Selective Trade

and Strategic Industrial Policies," in *The Politics of Trade and Industrial Policy in Africa: Forced Consensus?*, ed. Charles Soludo, Michael Ogbu and Ha-Joon Chang (Ottawa: Africa World Press and IDRC, 2004).

7 Gerrishon K. Ikiara, Joshua Olewe-Nyunya and Walter Odhiambo, "Kenya: Formulation and Implementation of Strategic Trade and Industrial Policies," in *The Politics of Trade*, ed. Soludo *et al.*

8 James Heintz, "Employment, Economic Development and Poverty Reduction: Critical Issues and Policy Challenges," background paper for UNRISD Report on Combating Poverty and Inequality (Geneva: UNRISD, 2009).

9 UNRISD, *Combating Poverty and Inequality*; Thandika Mkandawire, "Transformative Social Policy and Innovation in Developing Countries," *The European Journal of Development Research* 19, no. 1 (2007: 13–29).

10 John D. Stephens, "The Politics of Poverty Reduction in Developed Democracies: Lessons for Less Developed Countries," background paper for UNRISD Report on Combating Poverty and Inequality (Geneva: UNRISD, 2001).

11 United Nations Economic and Social Council, Commission for Social Development, Forty-ninth Session, 9–18 February 2011. Emerging Issues: Social Protection, 16 December 2010, New York: United Nations.

12 Santosh Mehrotra and Enrique Delamonica, *Eliminating Human Poverty: Macroeconomic and Social Policies for Equitable Growth* (London and New York: Zed Books, 2007).

13 UNRISD, *Combating Poverty and Inequality*.

14 Jimi Adesina, ed., *Social Policy in Sub-Saharan African Context: In Search of Inclusive Development* (Basingstoke: UNRISD/Palgrave Macmillan, 2007).

15 Winnie Mittulah, "Poverty and Social Service Provision in Kenya: Balancing Public and Private Provision," background paper for UNRISD Report on Combating Poverty and Inequality, 2008.

16 Ronald G. Ridker, *The World Bank's Role in Human Resource Development in Sub-Saharan Africa: Education, Training and Technical Assistance*, A World Bank Operations Evaluations Study (Washington, DC: World Bank, 1994), 44.

17 Ridker, *The World Bank's Role in Human Resource Development*, 103.

18 Yusuf Bangura, ed., *Democracy and Social Policy* (Basingstoke: UNRISD/Palgrave Macmillan, 2007).

19 Adesina, *Social Policy in Sub-Saharan African Context*.

20 Sven Steinmo, *Taxation and Democracy: Swedish, British, and American Approaches to Financing the Modern State* (New Haven and London: Yale University Press, 1993); Evelyn Huber and John D. Stephens, *Development and Crisis of the Welfare State: Parties and Policies in Global Markets* (Chicago, IL: The University of Chicago Press, 2001).

21 Torben Iversen, Jonus Pontusson and David W. Soskice, eds., *Unions, Employers, and Central Banks: Macroeconomic Coordination and Institutional Change in Social Market Economies* (Cambridge: Cambridge University Press, 2000).

22 Huber and Stephens, *Development and Crisis of the Welfare State*.

23 David Seddon and Leo Zeilig, "Class and Protest in Africa: New Waves," *Review of African Political Economy* 32, no. 103 (2005): 9–27; Bjorn Beckman and Lloyd Sachikonye, "Trade Unions and Party Politics: An Introduction" (Cape Town, SA: HSRC, 2010); Adebayo Olukoshi, ed., *The Politics of*

Opposition in Contemporary Africa (Uppsala: Nordiska Afrikainstitutet, 1998).

24 Bjorn Beckman, "Empowerment or Repression? The World Bank and the Politics of African Adjustment," in *Authoritarianism, Democracy and Adjustment*, ed. Peter Gibbon, Yusuf Bangura and Arve Ofstad (Uppsala: The Scandinavian Institute of African Studies, 1992); John Toye, "Interest group politics and the implementation of adjustment policies in Africa," in Gibbon *et al.*, *Authoritarianism, Democracy and Adjustment*.

25 Sheila Bunwaree, "The ballot box and social policy in Mauritius," in *Democracy and Social Policy*, ed. Bangura.

26 Jeremy Seekings and Nicoli Nattrass, *Policy, Politics and Poverty in South Africa* (Basingstoke: UNRISD/Palgrave Macmillan, forthcoming).

27 Brian Wampler, *Participatory Budgeting in Brazil: Contestation, Cooperation, and Accountability* (University Park, PA: The Pennsylvania State University Press, 2007).

28 Adam Sheingate, "Agrarian Social Pacts and Poverty Reduction," in *Developmental Pathways to Poverty Reduction*, ed. Bangura.

29 UNRISD, *Combating Poverty and Inequality*; United Nations, *The Millennium Development Goals Report 2010* (New York: United Nations, 2010); Africa Renewal, "Africa's Hard Road to the Millennium Development Goals," *Africa Renewal* (August 2010).

30 Augustin Fosu, "Growth, Inequality, and Poverty Reduction in Developing Countries: Recent Global Evidence," paper delivered at the UNDESA/ILO Expert Groups Meeting on Poverty Eradication, Geneva, Switzerland, 20–22 June 2011.

31 United Nations, *The Millennium Development Goals Report 2010*.

32 United Nations, *MDG Gap Task Force Report 2011* (New York: United Nations, 2011).

33 UNRISD, *Combating Poverty and Inequality*.

34 Maureen Mackintosh and Meri Koivosalo, eds., *Commercialization of Health Care: Global and Local Dynamics and Policy Responses* (Basingstoke: UNRISD/Palgrave Macmillan, 2005); UNRISD, *Combating Poverty and Inequality*.

12 Taking Africa beyond the MDGs
The role of higher education in development

H. Russel Botman

Africa is increasingly being identified as a success story, albeit a qualified one. Analysts have noted that "a new wave of optimism"[1] is sweeping across the continent and that the international discourse has shifted "from Afro-pessimism to Afro-optimism."[2] On the economic front, African growth has accelerated by an average of 5.7 percent since 2000, making it one of the world's fastest growing regions and one that is being promoted as a viable investment destination.[3] Politically, Africa also seems to be making good progress. Of the continent's 54 countries, 20 are now considered full-fledged electoral democracies and only Somalia and Swaziland have not held competitive elections to date.[4] Yet Africa continues to face major challenges. The continent scores poorly on the Human Development Index (HDI) of the United Nations Development Program (UNDP), which measures life expectancy, education and gross domestic product (GDP). Of the world's 42 least developed countries, 35 are African.[5]

In terms of corrective action, Africans themselves seem to be in agreement about what the priority should be. According to the most recent World Values Survey,[6] 63 percent of African respondents identified poverty as "the most serious problem in the world." We should be able to take heart from the fact that eradicating extreme poverty and hunger is the first of the eight Millennium Development Goals (MDGs)[7] of the UN, but unfortunately it seems that despite some successes, as we have seen throughout this book, many countries in sub-Saharan Africa will neither be meeting this goal, nor the other MDGs by the target date of 2015.[8] Good intentions have not yet been translated into the required results.

In an attempt to remedy this situation, it is important to identify the obstacles in Africa's way, and the opportunities open to the continent. As 2015 approaches, it is crucial to set out a long-term agenda now— one that can take us into the future, beyond the MDGs.

The inaugural Global Poverty Summit (GPS) held in Johannesburg in January 2011, laid a solid foundation for this. In the Johannesburg Statement on the Millennium Development Goals[9] issued at the end of the Summit, participants identified the need for "a new policy framework for national development and global poverty reduction beyond 2015." The scope of the Summit went beyond Africa, but the situation on the continent did feature significantly in proceedings. I served on the Summit's MDG Task Force, and this chapter stems from my input in this regard.

My main point is that higher education should get more attention, because it generates, transfers and applies the knowledge required for development to take place. I unpack this argument with reference to, amongst others, a recent study by Cloete, Bailey, Pillay, Bunting and Maassen.[10] In the main, they weigh in with Castells,[11] who defined a role for the university as "engine of development" in the "information society" and its accompanying "knowledge economy." I support my contention by looking at university research and practical interventions addressing some of the challenges facing Africa. This falls into two categories, which I term physical and intellectual resources. In each case I look at two examples. Under physical resources, to be considered are the issues of which route of development to take and how to turn subsistence farming into profitable and sustainable agribusinesses. Under intellectual resources, I look at improving the standing of scholarship in Africa, and also the issue of the continent's academic interaction with the so-called developed world. I conclude by looking at key areas that would need attention for Africa to be taken beyond the MDGs.

Higher education's contribution to development

In the second half of the twentieth century there was a strong push for developing countries to place significant emphasis on primary and secondary education. At the same time, there was an assumption that higher education in Africa was of lesser importance; a luxury for the privileged few with private benefit that cannot be extrapolated to society as a whole.[12]

How did this come about? Cloete *et al.*[13] trace the debate about the significance of higher education for development in Africa through several stages—from "development university" to "luxury ancillary" to "engine of development." It seems that the MDGs got stuck in the second phase, in which universities were "delinked" from development. Now, as we look ahead beyond 2015, we have the opportunity to correct this mistake. We should seize the moment and consolidate the revitalization of higher education in Africa—not for the sake of universities *per se*, but in the interest of future generations of Africans, the people whom the continent's universities serve in the first instance.

According to Cloete *et al.*, the story unfolds as follows. In the first two decades after African states gained their independence from colonial rule—starting with Ghana in 1957—universities on the continent were expected to be key contributors to the human resource needs of the countries where they were situated. The next marker was the 1972 Accra declaration by delegates attending a workshop of the Association of African Universities (AAU). They decided that all universities should be "development universities." The participants went as far as saying that it was the responsibility of governments to steer universities in this direction. This did not go down well with African academics more comfortable with the Western model of the university as an independent institution governed by its own community of scholars. Many governments and academics became skeptical of the university's role in national development. Cloete *et al.* conclude that "[t]his led to the notion that higher education was a 'luxury ancillary'—nice to have, but not necessary"[14].

The World Bank decided that development efforts in Africa should be refocused to concentrate on primary education, which resulted in a dramatic decrease of 82 percent in per capita public spending on higher education in Africa between 1980 and the first decade of the twenty-first century.[15] Cloete *et al.* point out that "the World Bank strategy in Africa had the effect of delinking universities from development."[16] This might explain why higher education is not included in the MDGs. The only reference to education is MDG 2, which is to "achieve universal primary education," as well as in the associated target 2A, which is to "[e]nsure that, by 2015, children everywhere, boys and girls alike, will be able to complete a full course of primary schooling."[17]

Schooling—at both primary and secondary level—is very important, but it would be a mistake to continue ignoring tertiary education in pursuit of development. Let me explain why by using the example of a child born in 2000, the year that leaders adopted the MDGs. For the sake of this example, I will look at the position of a child from the most vulnerable group—the African girl child. Such a child would have benefited from the MDG-inspired drive towards universal primary education. Several countries, such as Uganda and South Africa, have in recent years made primary education for all children not only compulsory but also free. She might also have benefited from the subsequent additional support for secondary education that came through in a number of countries. If so, she would now be entering high school, and by 2015 she would be starting to think seriously about her future. Imagine that our case study has both the potential and interest to pursue a university education. What would happen if she were to finish school with excellent marks, only to be stopped in her tracks by severely limited opportunities due to a lack of funding for higher education? All the investment that had brought her to the point of readiness for the next step would have been wasted—because someone had decided that higher education was more of a private good than a public good.

What a good thing, then, that in the 1990s and 2000s arguments started to be made for the revitalization of the African university and for re-linking universities to development. Cloete *et al.* point out that "[t]he World Bank itself, influenced by Castells' path-breaking paper, *The University System: Engine of development in the new world economy*, started embracing the role of higher education in the knowledge economy, and for development in the developing world."[18] Castells (in Cloete *et al.*) describes the "engine of development" role for higher education as follows:

> In the current condition of the global knowledge economy, knowledge production and technological innovation become the most important productive forces. So, without at least some level of a national research system, which is comprised of universities, the private sector, public research centres and external funding, no country, even the smallest country, can really participate in the global knowledge economy.[19]

I would like to link this to my understanding that there are two fundamental dimensions of development within which the university has a role: human development and socioeconomic development. The first is about human dignity. It has to do with access to such requirements as health services and education. It also relates to basic freedoms and rights consistent with democracy. Universities can promote these and other aspects of human development through fulfilling their core functions—the discovery of knowledge (research), the transfer of knowledge (teaching and learning), and the application of knowledge (community interaction). The second area of development within which the university has a role to play is socioeconomic development. This is all about innovation through knowledge production. The social dimension is about the spaces between people, but what is social also relates to the economic.

Knowledge links human development and socioeconomic development. The knowledge factor triangulates the role of universities in development. Little wonder, then, that Castells assigns an engine-of-development role to the university.

Cloete *et al.* report that the idea of development is increasingly being informed by the notions of "human capital," "research," "innovation" and "technological development," and that "[h]igher education institutions are seen by many as playing a key role in delivering the knowledge requirements for development."[20] The Conference of Executive Heads of the Association of Commonwealth Universities confirmed as much when they met in South Africa in April 2010 to discuss "Universities and the Millennium Development Goals." Delegates resolved that higher education had a vital role to play in advancing the MDGs and future development goals "by producing the skills, data and networks through which developing countries are able to express and address their own needs."[21]

Higher education produces graduates for the public good, imparts knowledge and produces professionals who directly and indirectly impact on macroeconomic institutions, the information and telecommunication infrastructure, the national system for innovation and the quality of human resources. Graduate attributes go beyond technical knowledge. It includes qualities that prepare students to be agents for social good. On the level of values, universities can instill in their students an understanding of and respect for human diversity, heterogeneity and interdependence, which is becoming ever more important in the context of the societal conflicts thrown up by globalization. The World Bank has recognized this, saying that, "[a]s knowledge becomes more important, so does higher education ... The quality of knowledge generated within higher education institutions, and its availability to the wider economy, is becoming increasingly critical to national competitiveness."[22]

Looking at 2015 and beyond, we cannot continue dashing the hopes of millions of young people in Africa who are "all dressed up" for university "with nowhere to go." We need to provide them and their respective communities with real hope that takes them beyond 2015 and beyond the MDGs. Next, I turn to a case study of a university paying particular attention to its role in development—that of my own institution, Stellenbosch University (SU).

The case of Stellenbosch University

SU is situated in Stellenbosch, 50km east of Cape Town, South Africa. It is one of 23 public universities in the country, which have a combined head count of 521,000 students in higher education contact tuition. Stellenbosch has approximately 28,000 students (of whom more than one-third are at postgraduate level), 10 faculties, four campuses, and approximately 900 academic staff members.

In the year 2000 an important policy statement, the University's *Strategic Framework for the Turn of the Century and Beyond*,[23] signaled a new direction. In it, "[t]he University acknowledges its contribution to the injustices of the past ... and commits itself to appropriate redress and development initiatives." This was a reference to South Africa's apartheid history, which had affected all universities and other institutions, whether public or private.

When I was appointed Rector and Vice-Chancellor in 2007, I dedicated my term of office to the tangible realization of this commitment. In my installation address,[24] I pointed out that the University faced the challenge of "relevance." I proposed that we develop a "pedagogy of hope" at Stellenbosch. This was inspired by, amongst others, the work of the Brazilian educator, Paulo Freire (1921–97). It was his *Pedagogy of the Oppressed*[25] and *Pedagogy of Hope: Reliving Pedagogy of the Oppressed*[26] that had led to a global emphasis on a "critical pedagogy" within education, conveying the idea that education should play a role in changing the world for the better. In particular, he had argued that education should stimulate critical thinking and a critical consciousness. People should be empowered so that they may free themselves from oppression, poverty, injustice and the difficult task of living peacefully with former oppressors in a new situation. I felt that by infusing our work as a university with this kind of hope, we would be able to become not only "significantly different" from our past, but also "significantly better" for the future—in terms of our excellence and commitment to the people of our country and continent.

My colleagues and I looked at local, regional and international development agendas, including the UN's MDGs. We ended up distilling five themes to guide our core academic functions as a university. These themes are to fight endemic poverty and related conditions; promote human dignity and health; consolidate democracy and human rights; deepen peace and security; and balance a sustainable environment with a competitive industry.

The next step was to galvanize academic and support staff around these themes. The University community responded with enthusiasm, and proposals based on existing expertise and programs streamed in. A committee sifted through them, and by 2008 we had a solid batch of 21 strategic, hope-generating initiatives. The list has since grown to nearly 40 initiatives under the HOPE Project,[27] which was publicly launched on 21 July 2010.

In a policy document adopted by its Senate and Council, *Hope as guiding concept for Stellenbosch University*, SU states that it "is committed to creating hope in and from Africa by means of excellent scholarly practice."[28] This idea is expanded upon as follows:

The University endeavours to create the conditions that will ignite the imagination of scientists to solve problems in creative ways through basic and applied research and through multi-, inter- and trans-disciplinary academic activities. The three core academic functions of the University, namely scientific research, learning and teaching and expertise-based community interaction are integrated and used in the service of both the private and the public good.[29]

This shows that Stellenbosch is acting as an "engine of development," focusing on both human development and socioeconomic development. Next, I look at research and community interaction practically illustrating this approach.

Physical resources

Swilling[30] maintains that the fact that Africa trails on nearly every MDG indicator is at odds with the new wave of optimism sweeping across Africa as good economic growth is sustained. As I noted at the outset, Africa is considered to be one of the world's fastest growing regions. Cornelissen[31] attributes this to the expansion of the industries in the global commodity sector and the concomitant rise in commodity exports by many African countries. She adds that growth in such sectors as telecommunications, finance and tourism points to significant diversification in Africa's economic bases. As a result, the continent's contribution to global output—even if much lower than that of the world's advanced economies—is increasing.

However, as Swilling indicated at a meeting of the International Panel for Sustainable Resource Management of the UN Environment Programme (UNEP) in Stellenbosch in November 2010, Africa cannot escape the resource depletion challenges that face the rest of the world. Real wealth accumulation per capita will not keep up with population growth unless economic growth rates are decoupled from resource depletion rates, and resource rents are reinvested in human capital development.[32]

Which development route?

Earlier on, I referred to the low placement of African countries on the UNDP's HDI. More-developed countries are regularly placed much higher up, but at the expense of having a large ecological footprint. Swilling argues that if Africa invests in a growth path that is as resource and energy intensive as that followed by the countries of the North, the key conditions for development on which the continent is dependent for the eradication of poverty might end up being undermined.

Africa's growth is related to the worldwide boom in commodities, Swilling points out. The continent relies heavily on the export of primary natural resources. As part of the trade liberalization agenda pushed by the International Monetary Fund (IMF), African governments were encouraged to lift protective tariffs across the board contrary to the development strategies pursued by the successful Asian tigers. Swilling warns that resource extraction and export at prices that are too low undermine investments in development infrastructures and human capital.

This leads to the conclusion that if Africa continues to export primary resources at discounted prices, it will effectively get ever poorer, which will result in it struggling to build up the financial resources required to invest in the kind of human capital and physical infrastructures it needs to succeed in poverty eradication. "The alternative is to invest in human capabilities, technological innovations, infrastructures and renewable natural resources that set up African economies for a long-term sustainable future,"[33] Swilling maintains. His call for larger investment in Africa in both "human capital" and "technological innovations" meshes well with seeing the university as an engine of development. The next example illustrates how this works in practice.

From subsistence farming to agribusiness

According to Van Huyssteen,[34] Africa largely has an agricultural economy, with the majority of the population practicing subsistence farming or making a basic living from farming. He argues that small-scale agriculture is likely to remain a key source of income of rural communities in most African countries for the foreseeable future. However, agriculture does not only have a rural impact. Van Huyssteen points to rural-urban social and economic linkages and migrations, which means that rural poverty and wealth influences urban poverty and wealth. This leads him to argue that income growth through rural entrepreneurship in agribusinesses is central to achieving the MDGs in Africa, which is also urbanizing like the rest of the world.

Van Huyssteen believes that "the potential of agriculture as a formidable instrument for sustainable economic development in African countries is unequivocal." He bases his view on estimates that the continent holds 60 percent of the world's uncultivated land, which provides the potential for yields in Africa to grow by more than threefold in value from US$280 billion currently, to $880 billion in 2030. Van Huyssteen argues that one of the things holding African agriculture back is the use of outdated technologies and practices. He says that there is an urgent need for existing practices to be re-examined and supplemented with new technologies in order to enable African farmers to produce world-class products in a sustainable manner. He proposes that agriculture needs to be approached as a knowledge-based entrepreneurial activity. This is where universities come in. As an "engine of development" they produce the knowledge that can lead to innovative approaches to development. In applied programs they can use that knowledge to promote both human development and socioeconomic development. An example of university input in this regard is the organization, Agribusiness in Sustainable Natural African Plant Products (ASNAPP). Based in the Department of Agronomy at SU's Faculty of AgriSciences, ASNAPP is aimed at enhancing economic opportunities in rural communities.

The ASNAPP program, established in 1999, is currently operational in South Africa, Ghana, Zambia, Senegal, Rwanda and Liberia, with satellite projects in Angola, Malawi and Mozambique. It develops Africa's natural products and horticulture sectors by promoting income-generating activities for resource-limited entrepreneurs. It focuses on such crop clusters as herbal teas, herbs and spices, essential and pressed oils, medicinal and cosmetic plants, as well as crops produced in intensive production systems, for example specialty vegetables, mushrooms and fruit. The key area identified for market development is organic production.

Van Huyssteen explains that in order to guide resource-limited producers through the commercialization process, ASNAPP community projects usually start with low entry-cost activities, followed by the introduction and implementation of more sophisticated technologies. By acting as an informal trade exchange, ASNAPP encourages commercial enterprises to work directly with rural African producers as a supply source of choice.

One of the initiatives of ASNAPP is the Livingstone Project in Zambia. It benefits vulnerable community members, including the disabled, orphans and widows and those receiving palliative care. The Sun International hotel group is the major buyer of farmers' produce. Having started in 2006, the Livingstone Project recorded its first $1 million in sales by the end of 2010.

According to Van Huyssteen, ASNAPP shows that "[t]here is now reason for optimism that smallholder farming can become a sustainable economic activity in Africa, and a means to overcome some of the continent's biggest challenges." What the project also shows is that the role of the university, as engine of development, is key to both human and socioeconomic development. How capable are universities of fulfilling their developmental role, though? This is the question I turn to next.

Intellectual resources

Africa has over decades been experiencing a debilitating brain drain. We continue to lose some of our brightest minds as highly skilled people pursue opportunities for further study or work in developed countries. This has contributed to Africa's low output of scientific research, which amounts to only 0.7 percent of the global total.[35] Effectively, Africa is not coming up with enough home-grown solutions of the right kind— innovative and environmentally friendly—to its own developmental challenges.

Research

According to Pauw and Van Zyl,[36] part of the reason for Africa's low research output is that many African scientists, including those in the African diaspora, publish under their affiliation to institutions in developed countries. In so doing, they receive greater visibility, recognition and financial benefit. However, this also means that these publications are not recognized as African contributions to world scientific output. They point out that to be included in the world's largest commercial bibliographic databases, journals need to satisfy a set of formal criteria that developing countries often fail to meet. The result is that many articles published in Africa and other developing regions are not being recorded. Moreover, articles that are not included in these databases are difficult to find and cite.

Pauw and Van Zyl maintain that research in parts of Africa where salaries are low and research facilities are weak does not encourage publishing in journals because there are often more lucrative opportunities for the dissemination of research results. African researchers are often contracted to produce research results on topics that concern agencies, non-governmental organizations (NGOs) or private companies. This so-called "consultancy culture" was criticized by Mamdani[37] for relegating research to "finding answers to problems defined by a client," rather than "formulating a problem."

Pauw and Van Zyl make two suggestions for strengthening and growing the quality and quantity of African research output—one concerning greater research collaboration, the other centered on incentives for research. They point to a 2011 Royal Society report on worldwide scientific collaboration, which emphasizes that collaboration is becoming an important indicator of competitiveness because it enhances the quality of research, improves its efficiency and effectiveness, and is increasingly necessary as the scale of both budgets and research challenges grow. Pauw and Van Zyl maintain that Africa-based researchers traditionally have very limited contact with their colleagues in other African countries. Probably as a consequence of colonization, higher education institutions maintained contact with their former colonial powers after independence but were slow to build ties with other institutions on the continent.

This leads them to recommend that the traditional mode of North-South collaboration needs to be expanded to South-South and South-South-North collaboration. They say this makes sense because of shared contexts and developmental challenges, and it would also pool the limited human resources of the South. For this to happen, according to Pauw and Van Zyl, there would need to be institutional backing in the form of well-administered university-exchange agreements that support potential areas of collaboration and provide seed funding for joint research and teaching. Research managers who understand the complexities of research networks would also be essential, as would national programs that allocate research spending to support transnational higher education collaboration in Africa.

They list various examples of collaboration. For instance, South Africa's department of science and technology has concluded bilateral science agreements with Kenya, Mozambique and Namibia, and in some cases both parties have contributed funding towards research collaboration. Institutionally, there are jointly administered university degree programs such as the African Economic Research Consortium, the Partnership for Africa's Next Generation of Academics (more about PANGeA in the next section, on partnerships), the Regional University Forum for Capacity Building in Agriculture, and a mobility initiative among six African universities on climate change adaptation and resource efficiency called TRECCAfrica.

Pauw and Van Zyl point out that for these networks to engage more fluidly across Africa, harmonizing Africa's accreditation systems is essential. The AAU and the Association for the Development of Education in Africa has initiated this process, and it formed a central theme of the AAU's Conference of Rectors, Vice-Chancellors and Presidents of African Universities held in Stellenbosch in 2011.

I expand on partnerships below, but first turn to the second strategy for strengthening and growing the quality and quantity of African research output suggested by Pauw and Van Zyl. It involves new incentives to create strong alternatives to the "consultancy culture" among African researchers. They argue that governments and universities should offer bonuses to researchers who publish in international accredited and national peer-reviewed journals. The current South African national research subsidy model is highlighted as an example of such post-performance research funding. Pauw and Van Zyl maintain that increasing the scholarly output of African academics will require increases in library resources, internet connectivity, research equipment and facilities, as well as more funding for further research, research collaboration and conference participation. I concur with their assessment that governments should be encouraged to invest in transnational collaboration initiatives, in access to global research outputs and in open source publishing. In the next section I expand on one of these aspects—transnational collaboration initiatives.

Partnerships

Universities have a key role to play in goal number eight of the MDGs: developing a global partnership for development. Groenewald[38] argues that a real partnership entails an association to pursue a common goal, where members all contribute inputs and share both the risks and benefits of the endeavor. This implies an element of trust among the partners, without which the partnership would cease to function effectively. He points out that many international partnership-like associations exist in higher education. There is, however, "an informal yet well-understood academic pecking order in terms of which especially institutions in developing countries would boast of their partnerships with well-known or high ranking institutions in the North," Groenewald maintains. "[I]n the real world of uneven exchange relationships, scholarships, grants, academic opportunity, honors and credits flow mostly from Northern partners to institutions in the South, who are increasingly in a position of dependency."

Groenewald argues that it is hard for some to imagine a way out of this vicious circle because the world of higher education is obsessed with rankings, based on indicator systems that favor research intensity or peer rankings of research standing, with little or no attention to teaching and learning effectiveness, student experience, graduate competencies, employability, employer satisfaction, outreach or engagement. A global partnership for development could break this cycle, but only if it is "constituted in fundamentally different ways to prevent a simple reproduction of the status quo." He proposes that African institutions become the "lead agents" in the formation of such partnerships. "This requires a fundamental mind shift on both sides of the North-South divide, namely acceptance of the idea that Africans can take the lead; that they too are valued contributors—not only recipients—in partnerships; and that they can harness their assets and capabilities in pursuit of a common goal."

An example is PANGeA, a collaborative partnership referred to above. It was formally constituted in 2010 on the annual African University Day, 12 November. Following negotiations going back to 2006, six African universities banded together in a collaborative network. They are the universities of Botswana, Dar es Salaam, Makerere, Malawi, Nairobi and Stellenbosch. Groenewald points out "[i]n this partnership, African institutions of higher education join together to become the lead institutions in the execution of an integrated strategy to develop research capacity, to develop and offer supervision for the pursuit of doctoral studies and advanced research programs focused on Africa, and eventually to offer joint doctoral degrees."

The first cohort of 31 full-time doctoral students—22 from African countries other than South Africa—enrolled in the PANGeA-linked Graduate School, of which Groenewald is the project leader, in January 2010. A year later 26 students were awarded full-time doctoral scholarships, of whom 22 were from other African countries than South Africa. Students and staff are supported by the African Doctoral Academy, which provides training in supervision, research methodology and management to create a pool of supervisors and co-supervisors distributed over partner campuses to enable and encourage student and staff mobility in the context of collaborative research programs focused on Africa's development challenges. The question of how universities should best be empowered is dealt with next.

Paving the way

Cloete *et al.*[39] pose three requirements for universities to be able to play an effective role in development. The first is that there must be a "broad pact" in a particular country between the government, universities and socioeconomic actors about the nature of the role of universities in development. In their study of eight African countries,[40] Cloete *et al.* found that there was a lack of clarity and agreement in this regard. However, they did find an increasing awareness, particularly at government level, of the importance of universities in the global context of the knowledge economy.

The second requirement is that the "academic core" of universities must be strong. In this regard, Cloete *et al.* found that research production at the eight African universities they sampled was not strong enough to enable them to build on their traditional undergraduate teaching roles and make a sustainable, comprehensive contribution to development via new knowledge production. This links up with what Pauw and Van Zyl had to say about research at African universities. Major stumbling blocks include inadequate funds for staff to engage in research, and inadequate incentive regimes to support knowledge production.

The third requirement listed by Cloete *et al.* is that countries need "knowledge policy coordination" and strong "connections between key stakeholders." In none of the sampled countries did they find this to be the case.

Using the above outline, the task for those wishing to promote development in Africa by focusing on higher education is clear: get the various role players to agree, strengthen the academic core of universities and promote partnerships.

Conclusion

Research emanating from universities shows that in order to deal with its challenges related to physical resources, Africa needs to decouple economic growth rates from resource depletion rates, and reinvest resource rents in human capital development. The continent also needs to build green economies by investing in technological innovations, infrastructures and renewable natural resources. Agriculture needs to be approached as a knowledge-based entrepreneurial activity. All of this should set African economies up for a future that is resource-efficient and low-carbon—and therefore sustainable.

We have seen that casting the African university in the role of engine of development is quite appropriate. In fact, without more emphasis on higher education the continent is unlikely to meet the challenges posed by the information age and its knowledge economy. However, universities in Africa are not nearly as strong as they need to be, nor are there enough of them. In order to mitigate the African brain drain, higher education participation rates should be increased, and more academics and professionals should be produced by universities. Higher education should also be used to produce graduates who can be agents for social change by instilling in them an understanding of and respect for human dignity.

The research output of African universities should be increased—coordinated in such a way that it is focused on the developmental challenges of Africa. For Africa to truly benefit from global partnerships in higher education, African institutions must become the lead agents in such partnerships.

Developmental programs—be they the worldwide MDGs, country-specific programs, or local and regional institutional initiatives—can be summarized in terms of their impact on three key areas: people, institutions and the environment. Government structures and civil society bodies, including public universities, play an enabling role. They lay the foundation on which efforts to promote both human development and socioeconomic development can be pursued. By continually posing the demand of relevance to institutions, one can ensure that they become and remain purposeful, involved in the actual needs of society.

Notes

1 Mark Swilling, "Africa 2050—Growth, Resource Productivity and Decoupling," policy brief for the 7th meeting of the International Panel for Sustainable Resource Management of the United Nations Environment Programme (UNEP), Stellenbosch, South Africa, November 2010, www.learndev.org/dl/BtSM2011/Africa%20Policy%20Brief.pdf.
2 Scarlett Cornelissen, *The Start of History? The Promises and Limitations of Emerging Vectors in Africa's Political Economy* (Stellenbosch, South Africa: Stellenbosch University Language Centre, 2011).
3 Cornelissen, *The Start of History?*
4 Larry Diamond and Marc F. Plattner, eds., *Democratization in Africa: Progress and Retreat* (Baltimore: The Johns Hopkins University Press and the National Endowment for Democracy, 2010).
5 UNDP, *The Real Wealth of Nations: Pathways to Human Development, Human Development Report 2010* (New York: Palgrave Macmillan, 2010).
6 www.worldvaluessurvey.org.
7 www.un.org/millenniumgoals.
8 See UN Department of Economic and Social Affairs, *The Millennium Development Goals Report 2010*, June 2010, www.un.org/millenniumgoals/pdf/MDG%20Report%202010%20En%20r15%20-low%20res%2020100615%20-.pdf.
9 media.povertydialogue.org/2011/01/Statement-on-the-Millennium-Development-Goals-final1.pdf, also appended to this book.
10 Nico Cloete, Tracy Bailey, Pundy Pillay, Ian Bunting, and Peter Maassen, *Universities and Economic Development in Africa* (Wynberg, South Africa: Centre for Higher Education Transformation, 2011).
11 See Manuel Castells, *The University System: Engine of Development in the New World Economy* (Washington, DC: World Bank, 1991); and "Universities as Dynamic Systems of Contradictory Functions," in *Challenges of Globalisation: South African Debates with Manuel Castells*, ed. Johan Muller, Nico Cloete and Shireen Badat (Cape Town, South Africa: Maskew Miller Longman, 2002).
12 H. Russel Botman, Arnold van Zyl, Ayesha Fakie and Christoff Pauw, "A Pedagogy of Hope: Stellenbosch University's Vision for Higher Education and Sustainable Development," in *12th General Conference of the Association of African Universities: Selected Papers*, ed. Pascal Hoba and Vera Doku (Accra: Association of African Universities, 2009), 11–24.
13 Cloete *et al.*, *Universities and Economic Development in Africa*, 4–5.
14 Cloete *et al.*, *Universities and Economic Development in Africa*, 5.
15 World Bank, *Accelerating Catch-up: Tertiary Education for Growth in Sub-Saharan Africa* (Washington, DC: World Bank), xxvii.
16 Cloete *et al.*, *Universities and Economic Development in Africa*, 3.

224   H. Russel Botman

17 www.un.org/millenniumgoals; see also Appendix 1.
18 Cloete *et al.*, *Universities and Economic Development in Africa*, 4.
19 Cloete *et al.*, *Universities and Economic Development in Africa*, 5.
20 Cloete *et al.*, *Universities and Economic Development in Africa*, 1.
21 See capetown2010.acu.ac.uk.
22 Task Force on Higher Education and Society, *Higher Education in Developing Countries: Peril and Promise* (Washington, DC: World Bank, 2000), 3; and World Bank, *Constructing Knowledge Societies: New Challenges for Tertiary Education* (Washington, DC: World Bank, 2002).
23 www.sun.ac.za/university/stratplan/statengels.doc.
24 www.sun.ac.za/university/Management/rektor/docs/russel%20installation%20speech.pdf.
25 Paulo Freire, *Pedagogy of the Oppressed* (London: Penguin, 1996 [1970]).
26 Paulo Freire, *Pedagogy of Hope: Reliving Pedagogy of the Oppressed* (London: Continuum, 2004 [1992]).
27 www.thehopeproject.co.za.
28 www.sun.ac.za/NEWS/dokumente/algemeen/Hoopmotief.pdf.
29 www.sun.ac.za/NEWS/dokumente/algemeen/Hoopmotief.pdf.
30 Swilling, "Africa 2050."
31 Cornelissen, *The Start of History?*
32 Swilling, "Africa 2050."
33 Swilling, "Africa 2050," 9.
34 Leopoldt van Huyssteen, "Innovation in Small-Scale Farming in African Communities," position paper for Colloquium on Systemic Entrepreneurship, Coventry University, UK, July 2011.
35 Williams E. Nwagwu and Allam Ahmed, "Building open access in Africa," *International Journal of Technology Management* 45, no.1/2 (2009): 82–101.
36 Christoff Pauw and Arnold van Zyl, "Africa: Collaborate to integrate," *Mail & Guardian*, 9 September 2011.
37 Mahmood Mamdani, "Africa's post-colonial scourge," *Mail & Guardian*, 27 May 2011.
38 Johann Groenewald, "Universities and the Millennium Development Goals: Rethinking partnerships in Africa," background paper prepared for the signing of the PANGeA Memorandum of Understanding, Stellenbosch University, South Africa, November 2010.
39 Cloete *et al.*, *Universities and Economic Development in Africa*.
40 Botswana, Ghana, Kenya, Mauritius, Mozambique, South Africa, Tanzania and Uganda.

Appendix 1
The Millennium Development Goals

Goal 1: Eradicate extreme hunger and poverty

Target 1.A: Halve, between 1990 and 2015, the proportion of people whose income is less than one dollar a day.

Target 1.B: Achieve full and productive employment and decent work for all, including women and young people.

Target 1.C: Halve, between 1990 and 2015, the proportion of people who suffer from hunger.

Goal 2: Achieve universal primary education

Target 2.A: Ensure that, by 2015, children everywhere, boys and girls alike, will be able to complete a full course of primary schooling.

Goal 3: Promote gender equality and empower women

Target 3.A: Eliminate gender disparity in primary and secondary education, preferably by 2005, and in all levels of education no later than 2015.

Goal 4: Reduce child mortality

Target 4.A: Reduce by two-thirds, between 1990 and 2015, the under-five mortality rate.

Goal 5: Improve maternal health

Target 5.A: Reduce by three-quarters, between 1990 and 2015, the maternal mortality ratio.

Target 5.B: Achieve, by 2015, universal access to reproductive health.

Goal 6: Combat HIV/AIDS, malaria and other diseases

Target 6.A: Have halted by 2015 and begun to reverse the spread of HIV/AIDS.

Target 6.B: Achieve, by 2010, universal access to treatment for HIV/AIDS for all those who need it.

Target 6.C: Have halted by 2015 and begun to reverse the incidence of malaria and other major diseases.

Goal 7: Ensure environmental sustainability

Target 7.A: Integrate the principles of sustainable development into country policies and programmes and reverse the loss of environmental resources.

Target 7.B: Reduce biodiversity loss, achieving, by 2010, a significant reduction in the rate of loss.

Target 7.C: Halve, by 2015, the proportion of people without sustainable access to safe drinking water and basic sanitation.

Target 7.D: By 2020, to have achieved a significant improvement in the lives of at least 100 million slum dwellers.

Goal 8: Develop a global partnership for development

Target 8.A: Develop further an open, rule-based, predictable, non-discriminatory trading and financial system.

Target 8.B: Address the special needs of the least developed countries.

Target 8.C: Address the special needs of landlocked developing countries and small island developing States (through the Programme of Action for the Sustainable Development of Small Island Developing States and the outcome of the twenty-second special session of the General Assembly).

Target 8.D: Deal comprehensively with the debt problems of developing countries through national and international measures in order to make debt sustainable in the long term.

Target 8.E: In cooperation with pharmaceutical companies, provide access to affordable essential drugs in developing countries.

Target 8.F: In cooperation with the private sector, make available the benefits of new technologies, especially information and communications.

Appendix 2
The Johannesburg Statement on the Millennium Development Goals

19 January 2011

GPS/MDG/TF/S/1

We live in an age of unprecedented global connections and recognition of a global responsibility for the conditions of all humans living on our planet. Persisting pockets of debilitating poverty and deep deprivations degrade the lives of hundreds of millions, diminish all, threaten social cohesion, political stability and international order, and are an indictment of governments and international institutions.

The United Nations exists to bring about a safer world and a better life for all. It has unique legitimacy and unmatched convening power, based on universal membership. It is the forum of choice for promoting global norms and setting the global agenda. In 2000 world leaders signed the historic Millennium Declaration from which eight Millennium Development Goals (MDGs) were derived. The leaders accepted individual and collective responsibility to reduce poverty in their own countries and globally.

The MDGs captured the normative consensus on the nature and meaning of development and articulated measurable and timetabled indicators. They corrected the skewed focus on markets and stabilisation, redirecting attention and efforts towards the reduction of poverty and the promotion of human development. They served as a powerful tool for mobilising governments, the UN system and civil society.

Substantial progress has been recorded in many places. This includes primary education and greater gender equality in education in Africa, investment in social sectors, a renewed commitment to aid, gains in life expectancy, reduced income poverty in two-thirds of the countries of the world and a decline in conflicts.

However, gains have been uneven and performance to date has fallen short of the ambitious targets. Inequality has widened within and among countries. HIV prevalence remains critically high in southern Africa, threatening the achievement of many MDGs. Chronic hunger, child malnutrition, and maternal and infant mortality rates are distressingly and unacceptably high. Unemployment, especially among the young, is stubbornly persistent.

The goals did not include reference to macro-economic development. While social infrastructure grew, in many countries this was at the cost of economic infrastructure. Aid did not reach pledged commitments nor always conform with the national priorities of recipient countries. There was insufficient progress towards national adaptation of the goals. As a result "local ownership" has been little more than a slogan. The eighth goal—on building an international partnership for development—lacked accompanying tight indicators to measure progress.

New issues and concerns have emerged in the decade since 2000. Of overwhelming importance is climate change and the accompanying desertification and rising incidence of natural disasters, from which the poor suffer most. Associated issues of water scarcity, food availability and affordability present looming problems. The global financial crisis shook the foundations of the former neoliberal consensus. The dramatic rise of new powers as southern engines of growth has provided alternative models of growth, development and South–South co-operation and changed the discourse on the best terms of engagement with the international economy.

The experience since 2000 has shown the value of the goals, particularly a global commitment to worldwide poverty reduction in the medium term and the aim of achieving poverty eradication in the long term. The deadline is close but there remains some time to improve MDG performance through accelerated efforts. Review of performance since 2000 suggests two immediate priorities: (i) reducing maternal mortality which cuts many lives tragically short and debilitates families; and (ii) calling on governments, in rich and poor countries, and international institutions to take responsibility for failures.

We need also to initiate a new process leading to the formulation of global goals in 2015 and international commitment to them. The world needs to start a new process of consultation and discussions urgently, leading to the formulation of a new set of goals to be adopted in 2015. These would: (i) build on the MDGs; (ii) modify the goals chosen; (iii) reflect the new problems; and (iv) address pressing new global concerns. This process will need to include the participation of the poorest and most excluded, civil society and governments. Ultimately it must be the United Nations that agrees on the chosen goals and is responsible for convening representatives of the nations of the world to that end. The UN should take responsibility for initiating worldwide consultations so that the goals are formulated by the governments which will commit themselves to fulfilling them, and by the people most affected by them.

To consolidate and build on the undoubted successes of the MDGs, it is important that development advocates, agencies and partners begin a conversation immediately on a new policy framework for national development and global poverty reduction beyond 2015.

Accordingly, we urge the United Nations to begin preparations now for convening a summit in 2015 to adopt a new set of Global Development Goals (GDGs), with particular emphasis on gender parity and voice for the poorest and the marginalised. We recommend that, in the process of the consultations, a new set of goals be articulated, comprising measurable targets and indicators, while confronting the shortfalls and gaps in MDG achievements.

Particular considerations that could be included in these consultations are:

- Promoting **national ownership** by: (i) adapting the goals to national circumstances and priorities; (ii) creating mechanisms whereby external aid conforms to priority needs identified in national development plans prepared by the countries themselves; and (iii) putting in place financial aid and technical assistance to strengthen the analytical, policy development and programme delivery capacity of target countries.
- Ensuring **equitable economic growth**.
- **Resetting the balance** between the productive sectors of the economy and the social sectors of the nation.
- Incorporating **climate change** and the need for mitigation and adaptation.
- Paying special attention to **food availability and affordability**.
- Including the need to **reduce inequalities** between individuals and groups within and among countries.
- Reformulating specific goals to **reflect progress**, such as a shift in priority from primary education to the attainment of universal literacy through completed secondary education qualifications.

- Ensuring that the **rights** of all vulnerable and minority groups are enacted in legislation and enforced.
- Establishing conditions to enable women to lead lives **free from the threat of violence** and with equal opportunities for realising their wellbeing.
- Adopting a more rigorous set of **reporting, monitoring and accountability** mechanisms for developing country efforts and results, donor pledges and the performance of international institutions.

The Johannesburg Global Poverty Summit
Johannesburg 17–19 January 2011

Index

Routledge Global Institutions Series

UN Industrial Development Organization (UNIDO)
by Stephen Browne (FUNDS Project)

The Changing Political Map of Global Governance
by Anthony Payne (University of Sheffield) and Stephen Robert Buzdugan (Manchester Metropolitan University)

Coping with Nuclear Weapons
by W. Pal Sidhu

Crisis of Global Sustainability
by Tapio Kanninen

Private Foundations and Development Partnerships
by Michael Moran (Swinburne University of Technology)

Integrating Africa
Decolonization's legacies, sovereignty, and the African Union
by Martin Welz (University of Konstanz)

Feminist Strategies in International Governance
edited by Gülay Caglar (Humboldt University of Berlin), Elisabeth Prügl (Graduate Institute of International and Development Studies, Geneva), Susanne Zwingel (SUNY Potsdam)

The International Politics of Human Rights
edited by Monica Serrano (Colegio de Mexico) and Thomas G. Weiss (The CUNY Graduate Center)

For further information regarding the series, please contact:
Craig Fowlie, Publisher, Politics & International Studies
Taylor & Francis
2 Park Square, Milton Park, Abingdon
Oxford OX14 4RN, UK
+44 (0)207 842 2057 Tel
+44 (0)207 842 2302 Fax
Craig.Fowlie@tandf.co.uk
www.routledge.com